# BARRON'S

# FCAT

## GRADE 10 ASSESSMENT TESTS IN READING AND WRITING

### 2ND EDITION

**Claudine A. Townley, MS.Ed.**
Florida Virtual School
Orlando, Florida

BARRON'S

**About the Author:** Claudine A. Townley earned her BA in education from the State University of New York at Oswego and her MS.Ed. in reading and literacy from Capella University. Claudine taught junior high and high school for over 14 years. She currently resides in Florida with her husband and two young children, where she works in the Global Services department of Florida Virtual School.

© Copyright 2011 by Barron's Educational Series, Inc.
© Copyright 2004 by Barron's Educational Series, Inc., under the title *How to Prepare for the FCAT Grade 10 Florida Comprehensive Assessment Tests in Reading and Writing*.

*All inquiries should be addressed to:*
Barron's Educational Series, Inc.
250 Wireless Boulevard
Hauppauge, New York 11788
**www.barronseduc.com**

*Library of Congress Control No.:* 2010045035

ISBN: 978-0-7641-4199-7

**Library of Congress Cataloging-in-Publication Data**
Townley, Claudine A.
  FCAT : grade 10 Florida comprehensive assessment test in reading and writing / Claudine A. Townley. — 2nd ed.
      p. cm.
  At head of title: Barron's.
  Rev. ed. of: How to prepare for the FCAT, grade 10 Florida Comprehensive Assessment Tests in reading and writing / Claudine A. Townley. c2005.
  Includes index.
  ISBN 978-0-7641-4199-7
  1. Florida Comprehensive Assessment Test—Study guides. 2. Reading (Secondary)—Ability testing—Florida. I. Townley, Claudine A. How to prepare for the FCAT, grade 10 Florida Comprehensive Assessment Tests in reading and writing. II. Title.
  LB3060.33.F54T69 2011
  373.126'2—dc22
                              2010045035

PRINTED IN THE UNITED STATES OF AMERICA

9 8 7 6 5 4 3 2 1

# Contents

# Preface

Welcome to Barron's *FCAT Grade 10 Assessment Tests in Reading and Writing*. This book is designed to help students prepare for the new Florida Comprehensive Assessment Test (FCAT 2.0) in the areas of both reading and writing. Everything in this book has been researched and developed through the use of the Florida State Sunshine Standards. By using the information provided in this book, students should gain a strong knowledge about these tests as well as valuable practice and test-taking strategies. Parents and teachers may also aid their students by reading and using this workbook in the classroom and at home. Good luck to all test takers, and happy reading.

# UNIT ONE

## FCAT READING

# Chapter 1 | **Before You Begin**

## FCAT FACTS

Before taking any kind of test, it is a good idea to know as much as possible about the test itself. So here are some answers to questions that you should know before taking the FCAT test.

## 1. What Does FCAT Stand For?

FCAT stands for Florida Comprehensive Assessment Test. The FCAT tests different areas of knowledge; this book focuses on the areas of reading and writing.

## 2. A Little History, Please . . .

The FCAT test was first administered in 1998. It started as a test to measure students' abilities in only reading and math. The test itself is based on the Sunshine State Standards, which are the framework for what students are expected to learn in the Florida Public School System. The writing test, which has been around since 1992, became part of the FCAT in 1998. Beginning in 2001, students had to pass both the math and reading portions of the FCAT in order to graduate. In 2003, the science portion was added. However, the math and science FCAT exams are now being replaced with end of course exams, and the revised reading FCAT is known as FCAT 2.0. Learn more at *http://fcat.fldoe.org/fcat2*.

## 3. Who Takes the FCAT?

As you may already be aware, the FCAT is given starting with the third grade in elementary school and continuing every year up to the eleventh grade. Passing the tenth-grade administration of the FCAT is required to earn a diploma.

## 4. What Can I Expect to See on the Reading Portion of the FCAT?

On the reading portion of the FCAT, you will be expected to read eight to nine passages and then answer questions based on those passages. The average passage is 1,000 words long, but passages can range anywhere from 300 to 1,500 words. After reading each passage, you will answer multiple-choice questions about what you have read.

## 5. What Kinds of Passages Will I Read on the FCAT Test?

The reading test is divided into two types of passages: literary text (30 percent of test) and informational text (70 percent of test). Literary text is what you read in your English classes—short stories, poems, plays, and so on. Often you will not get the entire play or story but, instead, just an excerpt (small portion pulled out) of the piece of literature. Informational text, on the other hand, is similar to what you see in many of your textbooks, for example your social studies or science book. Other types of informational text include articles from newspapers and magazines, famous speeches and other historical writings, biographies, and so on. Informational text can also come in the form of graphs, tables, charts, pictures, and drawings.

## 6. Is This a Timed Test?

All levels of the FCAT are timed. At the tenth-grade level, the reading test is divided into two 70-minute sessions. The good news is that anyone taking the test after their tenth-grade year no longer has to worry about the timing of the test. Those students may have as long as one school day, if they need it, to complete the exam.

## 7. What Score Do I Need to Pass?

Currently, you must earn a scale score of at least 300 out of a possible 500 points in order to pass the reading portion of the FCAT. However, you should consult your teacher or guidance counselor for an answer to this question in case the passing score has changed. The state has upped the passing score over the years, from 287 points in the year 2001 to 300 points currently. The highest scale score you can achieve is 500.

## 8. Do I Have to Pass the Test on the First Try?

Hopefully you will pass the test on the first try. However, if you do not, you are in luck. The major administration of the test is in the spring (usually March), but there are other administrations throughout the year. So you can continue to retake the test until you score high enough to pass. (This is true until you are 20 years old. At that time you can no longer earn a high school diploma—you must get a GED.) Again, check with your teacher or guidance counselor for testing dates or consult the Florida Department of Education's web site. Finally, students who cannot pass the FCAT can still graduate by earning a concordant score on the ACT or SAT. There are specific requirements tied to this option, so again, consult your guidance counselor or local school district for more information.

## STONE-COLD STANDARDS

Now we will get more specific about the focus of the FCAT in reading. Basically, you are going to be tested on four major areas, or **categories**. Within each of these categories are particular benchmarks, or skills. These benchmarks are the very specifics of what the FCAT expects you to master. On the next pages, you will find the list of the categories and benchmarks that are tested on the FCAT. Do not worry if they seem a little difficult to understand at this point. In Chapter 3 you will learn what each benchmark means and how to answer FCAT questions on the benchmarks.

| Category 1: Vocabulary | |
|---|---|
| **Benchmarks Tested:** | |
| Context Clues | LA.910.1.6.3: The student will use context clues to determine meanings of unfamiliar words. |
| Words Relationships | LA.910.1.6.8: The student will identify advanced word/phrase relationships and their meanings. |
| Multiple Meanings | LA.910.1.6.9: The student will determine the correct meaning of words with multiple meanings in context. |

| Category 2: Reading Application | |
|---|---|
| **Benchmarks Tested:** | |
| Author's Purpose and Perspective | LA.910.1.7.2: The student will analyze the author's purpose and/or perspective in a variety of text and understand how they affect meaning. |
| Main Idea, Relevant Details, Conclusions/Inferences | LA.910.1.7.3: The student will determine the main idea or essential message in grade-level or higher texts through inferring, paraphrasing, summarizing, and identifying relevant details. |
| Cause and Effect | LA.910.1.7.4: The student will identify cause-and-effect relationships in text. |
| Organizational Patterns | LA.910.1.7.5: The student will analyze a variety of text structures (e.g., comparison/contrast, cause/effect, chronological order, argument/support, lists) and text features (main headings with subheadings) and explain their impact on meaning in text. |
| Compare and Contrast | LA.910.1.7.7: The student will compare and contrast elements in multiple texts. |

| Category 3: Literary Analysis—Fiction/Nonfiction | |
|---|---|
| **Benchmarks Tested:** | |
| Literary Elements | LA.910.2.1.5: The student will analyze and develop an interpretation of a literary work by describing an author's use of literary elements (e.g., theme, point of view, characterization, setting, plot), and explain and analyze different elements of figurative language (e.g., simile, metaphor, personification, hyperbole, symbolism, allusion, imagery). |
| Literary Devices: Descriptive and Figurative Language | LA.910.2.1.7: The student will analyze, interpret, and evaluate an author's use of descriptive language (e.g., tone, irony, mood, imagery, pun, alliteration, onomatopoeia, allusion), figurative language (e.g., symbolism, metaphor, personification, hyperbole), common idioms, and mythological and literary allusions, and explain how they impact meaning in a variety of texts. |
| Text Features—Fiction and Nonfiction | LA.910.2.2.1: The student will analyze and evaluate information from text features (e.g., transitional devices, tables of contents, glossary, index, bold or italicized text, headings, charts and graphs, illustrations, subheadings). |

| Category 4: Informational Text/Research Process | |
|---|---|
| **Benchmarks Tested:** | |
| Text Features—Informational Text | LA.910.6.1.1: The student will explain how text features (e.g., charts, maps, diagrams, subheadings, captions, illustrations, graphs) aid the reader's understanding. |
| Synthesis, Analysis & Evaluation, Validity & Reliability | LA.910.6.2.2: The student will organize, synthesize, analyze, and evaluate the validity and reliability of information from multiple sources (including primary and secondary sources) to draw conclusions using a variety of techniques, and correctly use standardized citations. |

## QUESTIONS QUERY

Any time you take a test, you should try to find out what kind of questions might be asked. Once you know what kinds of questions to expect, you can use this information to prepare for the test better. The FCAT is no exception. Once you learn about the types of questions, you should be able to answer them more successfully.

> *The tenth grade FCAT reading test now has only one type of question: multiple-choice.*

### Multiple-Choice Questions (MC)

You are probably very familiar with multiple-choice questions by now. You have seen them on tests since elementary school. You know what they are and how they work (a question is asked, and four possible choices are given for the answer). On the FCAT, you will answer 50–55 multiple-choice questions. (Retakes have 55–60 MC questions.) You answer multiple-choice questions by bubbling in the correct answer on your answer sheet. Multiple-choice questions are machine scored.

### Performance Tasks

Before 2011, the tenth-grade FCAT in reading included performance task items: short and extended response questions. However, these types of questions have been removed from the FCAT.

> **Tip:** The most important thing to remember when answering questions on the FCAT is that the FCAT is testing you on your ability to read. **Therefore, all of your answers should be supported by the passages that you have read.**

## TEST-TAKING TIPS

Having strategies anytime you try something difficult is important. Here are some tips and strategies to help you pass the FCAT in reading. Some strategies need to be started weeks or even months before taking the test, and some are for during the test itself.

### Weeks Before the Test

1. **Read as Much as Possible:** Since this part of the FCAT is a reading test, the better your reading skills, the better you will do. Anything you read will prepare you for the test, but remember that the test includes both literary and informational text. Therefore, you should definitely try to read both kinds of text. So even if you do not like reading that science book of yours—remember it can help you pass the FCAT (and your science class!).

2. **Practice Reading Informational Text:** As mentioned before, 70 percent of the FCAT in reading is informational text. The way that you read informational text is not the same way that you read for enjoyment (novels, magazines, and so on). You should practice

interacting with the text (discussed in the next chapter), so you know what to expect and how to read informational passages on the FCAT.

3. **Improve Your Vocabulary:** Since difficult words appear on the FCAT, the better your vocabulary, the better you will perform. The more words you know, the better you will understand the passages and the better you will do on vocabulary questions. Another good strategy is to learn Latin and Greek prefixes, suffixes, and root words.

4. **Familiarize Yourself with the Test:** Just knowing how the test is set up and what kinds of questions are on it will allow you to do better on the FCAT. Reading this book should definitely help you feel more comfortable about the test.

5. **Practice FCAT-type Questions:** The more questions you answer that are in the same format as the questions on the FCAT, the better you will do on the test. So when you see multiple-choice questions in your classes, do not complain—be glad! Your teachers are preparing you. Another good place to practice FCAT-type questions is on a free web site called FCAT Explorer. Check it out at *www.FCATexplorer.com*

6. **Get Used to Pressure:** Since the FCAT is a timed test for first-time takers, it would be very beneficial if you got used to working under timed situations. Many people get very nervous during testing. When a timed-situation is involved, some people just freeze up. If you are already used to feeling that pressure of time, on the day of the test, it will be no big deal to you.

## Days Before the Test

1. **Get Rested:** You know that you do not really do anything very well when you are tired. So make sure that you rest up the few days before the test. Get a good eight hours of sleep each night or more!

2. **Eat Well**: Not only does your body need to be rested to perform well, it also needs to be fortified. Eat lots of "good for you food" days before the test, and your body will get those nutrients into your system.

3. **Hydrate Yourself:** Drink lots of water! This is also good for your body and, specifically, your brain. Just do not wait until the night before or the day of the test to do this; you will succeed only in making yourself have to go to the bathroom during the test!

4. **Keep Reading:** Just because the test is getting close does not mean you should stop preparing. Read, read, read!

## The Morning of the Test

1. **Eat a Good Breakfast:** If you are hungry during the test, you will only be distracted by the growling of your stomach. You will also find concentrating on the reading passages to be difficult. Your body will not have the energy it needs.

2. **Do Not Drink Too Much:** Again, if you have to go to the bathroom during the test, you will be distracted from concentrating on what you are doing. Also, you will break your concentration and use up valuable time if you have to get up and leave the room to use the restroom.

3. **Dress in Layers:** This may seem like silly advice, but sometimes testing rooms are very cold or very hot. If you are uncomfortable because of the temperature, you will not concentrate well on what you are doing. If you dress in layers, you can put on or peel off as the temperature lowers or rises, allowing you to stay comfortable!

4. **Be Sure You Have All the Right Supplies:** Do not throw yourself into a tizzy the morning of the test because you do not have the supplies you need. For the FCAT in reading you will need a couple of number 2 pencils with good erasers—that is all.

5. **Know Where and When to Report:** Every school is different, so be sure that you know what time and what room to report to on the day of testing. You do not want to create more stress for yourself by running around at the last minute, not knowing where to go.

6. **Stay Calm:** You will not help yourself at all if you are very nervous. Relax, you have prepared. Just do your best.

## During the Test

1. **Listen to the Directions:** On the FCAT test, a monitor will read the instructions to you. Pay attention, even if you *think* you know what you are doing. Better safe than sorry. Also, do not be afraid to ask questions if you are not sure what to do.

2. **Read and Interact with the Passages:** If you do not read the passages completely, you will find answering all of the questions to be difficult. Do not get bogged down, but read through each passage to get the main idea of what it is about. Underline and circle important items. You should do this *before* attempting to answer the questions.

3. **Read Everything:** This means titles, italics, charts, graphs, maps, and, obviously, the passages. All information provided can help you find the correct answers.

4. **Read the Questions Carefully:** How many times have you gotten a test back and realized that you got an answer wrong just because you did not read the question carefully enough? Be sure you know what the question is really asking before you answer it.

5. **NEVER Leave an Answer Blank:** On the FCAT, a blank answer means an incorrect answer. It is important to at least guess—you have got nothing to lose.

6. **Budget Your Time:** If you are taking the test during a timed session, be sure to watch the clock. Do not get so bogged down on one question that you do not get to the others. If you cannot answer a question, guess and then come back if there is time.

7. **Go Back to the Passage to Find Answers:** Remember that this is a reading test, not a memory test. All of the answers to the questions can be found or inferred from the passages you have read. Even if you think you remember the correct answer, *go back and check*. Some passages are long and confusing, so it is better to be sure.

8. **Write on the Test:** This copy of the test is yours (even though you will never see it again). Write all over it. Underline, circle, cross out items; this should help you concentrate and get the right answers.

9. **Answers Should Be Based Only on What You Have Read:** Since this is a reading test, you should get your answers only from the passages. Do not answer questions based on your own knowledge (they are not testing that). Do not choose answers that have nothing to do with what you have read—even if they sound good. They cannot be correct.

10. **Come Back to Questions You Do Not Know:** You might be surprised if you come back to a question you could not answer before and find that you can now figure out the answer. You mind's subconscious may have been working on it all the time. However, if you still do not have an answer, guess!

11. **Stick With It:** The FCAT in reading may be more difficult than other tests you have taken, and you may have to read more and different kinds of material than you are used to reading. As a result, you may be tempted not to read the passages or just to quit altogether. However, if you just "Christmas tree" the test, you will only have to take it again. Stick with it and try your hardest.

12. **Do Not Panic:** Panicking cannot not help you. Breathe and relax. Concentrate on the test, and do your best.

## Tips for Multiple-Choice Questions

1. **Read All of the Choices:** Even if you are positive that the first answer is correct, you should still read *all* of the choices. Many times FCAT questions will have you choose the *best* answer, so more than one may sound correct.

2. **Practice the Process of Elimination:** When answering multiple-choice questions, you should always cross out the answers that you know are incorrect. This will help you arrive at the correct choice. It is also helpful when you are not sure of an answer and have to guess. You should be able to eliminate at least two of the answers, giving you a 50/50 shot at getting the question right. Those are pretty good odds!

3. **Watch Your Bubbles:** When you answer the multiple-choice questions, you will bubble in your answer with your pencil. Be sure that you bubble the answer you really want and that you fill in the bubble completely. Erase completely if you need to change your answer. Also, always be sure that you are bubbling the correct answer for the right question. This is especially important if you have skipped questions to come back to later.

## After You Finish the Test

- **Check Your Answers:** No one really likes to check their answers, but doing so is very important. It could be the difference between passing and failing the test. Be sure you have not left any blanks. Be careful not to change answers that you are not sure of; usually your first instinct is the correct one.

- **Check Your Time:** If the majority of the time is still left and you have finished the test, then you probably have not done a very good job. This test is not a simple test, and you will need to spend a good chunk of time on it in order to get the answers correct.

## You Are an Expert Now!

At this point, you should have a good idea of how the FCAT in reading is set up and some strategies that you can use to perform better on the test. However, before moving on to the next chapters, try this pretest. How you perform on this test will help you determine where to best spend your time in this book. Although it is a good idea to review all the items in this book, there is a good chance that you are already proficient in one or more of the categories tested on the FCAT.

## PRETEST

## Information about This Pretest

This pretest covers all four categories tested on the FCAT. However, it is not the same length as the actual FCAT. As mentioned earlier, the FCAT will have 50–55 questions (this pretest has only 28) and 8–9 reading passages (this pretest has only four). This pretest is designed to allow you to easily determine your strengths and weaknesses in each of the four FCAT categories. There is one reading passage per category and a set of accompanying questions. You should give yourself 30 minutes to complete the pretest. After you finish, check the answer grid to see where you need to focus your preparation time. If you would like to see how you would perform on a test that is more like the actual FCAT, turn to page 97. There you will find two FCAT sample exams which include answer keys that identify each type of question.

# PRETEST

**Directions**    Read "Barack Obama" before answering questions 1 through 6.

## Barack Obama

Barack H. Obama is the 44th President of the United States.

His story is the American story—values from the heartland, a middle-class upbringing in a strong family, hard work and education as the means of getting ahead, and the conviction that a life so blessed should be lived in service to others.

With a father from Kenya and a mother from Kansas, President Obama was born in Hawaii on August 4, 1961. He was raised with help from his grandfather, who served in Patton's army, and his grandmother, who worked her way up from the secretarial pool to middle management at a bank.

After working his way through college with the help of scholarships and student loans, President Obama moved to Chicago, where he worked with a group of churches to help rebuild communities devastated by the closure of local steel plants.

He went on to attend law school, where he became the first African-American president of the Harvard Law Review. Upon graduation, he returned to Chicago to help lead a voter registration drive, teach constitutional law at the University of Chicago, and remain active in his community.

President Obama's years of public service are based around his unwavering belief in the ability to unite people around a politics of purpose. In the Illinois State Senate, he passed the first major ethics reform in 25 years, cut taxes for working families, and expanded health care for children and their parents. As a United States Senator, he reached across the aisle to pass groundbreaking lobbying reform, lock up the world's most dangerous weapons, and bring transparency to government by putting federal spending online.

He was elected the 44th President of the United States on November 4, 2008, and sworn in on January 20, 2009. He and his wife, Michelle, are the proud parents of two daughters, Malia, 10, and Sasha, 7.

—Source: *http://www.whitehouse.gov/about/ presidents/barackobama*

*Answer questions 1 through 6. Base your answers on the passage "Barack Obama."*

1. Read this sentence from the passage.

   **After working his way through college with the help of scholarships and student loans, President Obama moved to Chicago, where he worked with a group of churches to help rebuild communities devastated by the closure of local steel plants.**

   What does the word *devastated* mean as used in the sentence above?
   A. angered
   B. hidden
   C. overwhelmed
   D. plundered

2. Read this sentence from the passage.

   **As a United States Senator, he reached across the aisle to pass groundbreaking lobbying reform, lock up the world's most dangerous weapons, and bring transparency to government by putting federal spending online.**

   Which sentence best restates the meaning of the sentence above?
   F. As a U.S. Senator, Obama got married before he took office in Washington.
   G. As a U.S. Senator, Obama crossed party lines to accomplish major initiatives.
   H. As a U.S. Senator, Obama allowed people to vote on spending in an online poll.
   I. As a U.S. Senator, Obama lobbied to have all the world's nuclear weapons locked up.

3. Read this sentence from the passage.

   **He was elected the 44th President of the United States on November 4, 2008, and sworn in on January 20, 2009.**

   In which sentence does *sworn* have the same meaning as used in the excerpt above?
   A. Michelle had been sworn to secrecy regarding the breakup.
   B. Janie had sworn in school and got her mouth washed out with soap.
   C. I could have sworn that I saw him leaving the school over an hour ago.
   D. The new student council president was sworn in at the meeting on Tuesday.

4. Read this sentence from the passage.

   **President Obama's years of public service are based around his unwavering belief in the ability to unite people around a politics of purpose.**

   What does the word *unwavering* mean as used in the sentence above?
   F. flickering
   G. scornful
   H. unchangeable
   I. unrealistic

5. Read this sentence from the passage.

   **His story is the American story—values from the heartland, a middle-class upbringing in a strong family, hard work and education as the means of getting ahead, and the conviction that a life so blessed should be lived in service to others.**

   In which sentence does *conviction* have the same meaning as used in the excerpt above?
   A. The large amounts of evidence led to the burglar's conviction.
   B. The jury's conviction was "not guilty" by reason of mental instability.
   C. Sara was in the apartment only a month before she received a letter of conviction.
   D. The room was filled with students with the conviction that education was important.

6. Read this sentence from the passage.

   **He was raised with help from his grandfather, who served in Patton's army, and his grandmother, who worked her way up from the secretarial pool to middle management at a bank.**

   Which sentence best restates the meaning of the sentence above?
   F. Obama learned many of his values from his grandparents' dedication to hard work.
   G. Obama was brought up by his grandparents, who were both hardworking individuals.
   H. Obama grew up traveling around the world because his grandfather was in the army.
   I. Obama's grandmother had many different jobs, from a secretary at the bank to a pool store manager.

**Directions:**     Read "Elinor Smith: Born to Fly" before answering questions 7 through 14.

# Elinor Smith: Born to Fly
by Denise Lineberry

Elinor Smith in Long Island with an early Bellanca Plane that she used to beat the solo flight record.

In 1928, Elinor Smith, then 16, earned national recognition as the youngest pilot to receive a license from the Federal Aviation Administration. Orville Wright signed her license.

Her final cockpit time was spent in April, 2001, when, at 89, she flew a four-passenger plane while visiting NASA's Langley Research Center.

In between, Smith, who died on March 19 at age 98, set records and blazed a trail for women in flight and for aviation in general.

In 1930, Elinor Smith was voted "best female pilot" by her peers, a group that included Amelia Earhart. Smith's aviation records for endurance, altitude and speed in the 1920s and 30s led to worldwide fame.

"I remember so vividly my first time aloft that I can still hear the wind sing in the wires as we glided down," she wrote in her autobiography, *Aviatrix* (Harcourt Brace Jovanovich, 1981). "By the time the pilot touched the wheels gently to earth, I knew my future in airplanes and flying was as inevitable as the freckles on my nose."

She continuously inspired others to reach for the stars.

She visited Langley in 2001 as a guest of the center's General Aviation Programs Office. While there, she flew a highly modified four-passenger aircraft fitted with the latest in smart aircraft technology that evolved from the NASA-led Advanced General Aviation Transportation Experiments (AGATE) program.

She also signed autographs and delivered a lecture entitled, "Flying: Past, Present and Future," a one-hour talk about her flying experiences and her vision for the future of aviation.

Her lecture took place at the Pearl Young Theatre, which was named for the first female professional at Langley—Pearl I. Young.

Elinor Smith, portrait. Credit: *Aviatrix*

"Elinor wowed us all with her energy and joy of life at age 89," said Liz Ward who hosted Smith's visit as the education and outreach lead for Langley's General Aviation Programs. "It's been almost 10 years since she was here, but those who met her would remember. I keep her picture on my office bookshelf to remind me of her example of living life to the fullest."

Smith's visit made a lasting impression on Hank Jarrett, then manager of the AGATE program. He recalls her eagerness at lunch to get to the hangar. "She really wanted to get in the planes and see what we were doing with them," he said.

"She was a beautiful, vital woman and I would never have believed she was 89," said Jarrett. "She deserves to be remembered for all the contributions she made to aeronautics and as a wonderful human being."

Jarrett sent Smith a copy of her book, and she returned it to him with a note in the flyleaf. "I keep the book, her picture and a couple of other special books in the shelf next to my desk," Jarrett said. "I will really miss her, but she is in good company."

Elinor Smith in Oct. 1928. Smith is the first—and only—pilot to fly under all four New York East River bridges. Credit: *cradleofaviation.org*

Her eventful arrival to Langley was followed by an eventful exit when the vehicle in which she was riding in was hit broadside just outside of the gates of Langley. "I honestly think it is one of the reasons we finally got a new intersection and a light out there," said Jarrett.

"Maybe we should dedicate the gate intersection as the Elinor Smith light," he proposed. For the record, Smith wasn't behind the wheel and wasn't injured.

Some of her early accomplishments went overlooked because Smith's family had deliberately kept her out of the limelight to keep her focused on flying. It wasn't until 1928 when her family would welcome publicity.

On a dare that year, she flew a Waco 10 under all four of New York City's East River bridges; according to the Cradle of Aviation Museum, she is the only person ever to do so.

Bellanca and Fairchild Aircraft companies hired her as their first woman test pilot.

An unexpected first for Smith was in 1934, when she became the first woman to appear on a Wheaties cereal box.

Only a few years after her aviation fame had set in, she gave it all up to marry New York lawyer and politician Patrick Sullivan and to concentrate on raising their four children. It was not until the 1960s that Smith returned to flying.

In 2000, she was still breaking records at NASA's Ames Research Center with an all-woman crew. She took on NASA's Space Shuttle vertical motion simulator, and became the oldest pilot to succeed in a simulated shuttle landing.

Other known firsts include her first plane ride at the age of 6. At 10, she took her first flying lessons. At 15, she soloed for the first time. Three months later, she set her first of many records at 11,889 feet in a Waco 9.

"She is a part of history now and will be that beautiful, excited, young 15-year-old forever," said Jarrett. "That is a history we can each hope for."

—Source: *http://www.nasa.gov/topics/people/
features/elinor-smith.html*

*Answer questions 7 through 14. Base your answers on the article "Elinor Smith: Born to Fly."*

7. What is the main idea of the article "Elinor Smith: Born to Fly"?
    A. Smith flew a Waco 10 under all four of New York City's East River bridges.
    B. Smith set records and blazed a trail for women in flight and for aviation in general.
    C. Smith's aviation records for endurance, altitude, and speed in the 1920s and 30s led to worldwide fame.
    D. Smith took on NASA's Space Shuttle vertical motion simulator, and became the oldest pilot to succeed in a simulated shuttle landing.

8. What is the author's purpose in writing this passage?
    F. to describe how it feels to fly
    G. to emphasize the importance of test pilots
    H. to illustrate the relationship of flying and space
    I. to relate the amazing experiences of Smith's life

9. What statement would the author be most likely to make about Elinor Smith?
   A. More women today attend college because of Elinor Smith's success.
   B. Women's aviation would not be the same today without Elinor Smith.
   C. Elinor Smith committed flying feats that were unnecessarily dangerous.
   D. Elinor Smith cannot be compared to Amelia Earhart or Orville Wright.

10. Which of the following is *not* a first for Elinor Smith?
    F. first woman on a Wheaties cereal box
    G. set her first record in a Waco 9 aircraft
    H. first woman test pilot for Bellanca and Fairchild Aircraft
    I. set a record for the most books sold about aviation and women

11. From reading the article, the reader can infer that
    A. Smith's family did not support her desire to become a pilot.
    B. If Smith was born today, she might have become an astronaut.
    C. If Smith had the chance, she would not have ever gotten married.
    D. Smith might have been a great pilot but she was a terrible driver.

12. What was the outcome of Smith's first flight?
    F. It was where she met her husband, Patrick Sullivan.
    G. It helped to solidify her love for flying for the future.
    H. It allowed her to understand the mechanics of airplanes.
    I. It scared her so badly that it took her a great deal of courage to fly again.

13. How does Denise Lineberry organize the article "Elinor Smith: Born to Fly"?
    A. She describes the life of Elinor Smith in chronological order.
    B. She compares Elinor Smith's life to those of many other pilots.
    C. She focuses on the most important accomplishments in Elinor Smith's life.
    D. She persuades the readers to accept that Smith was the best pilot in history.

14. How was Elinor Smith's late life similar to that her youth?
    F. She was sheltered by her family.
    G. She did not set more "firsts" or records.
    H. She continued to fly and have new experiences.
    I. She wrote another book about the joys of flying.

**Directions:** Read "Chapter I—Down the Rabbit-Hole" before answering questions 15 through 22.

## Chapter I—Down the Rabbit-Hole
## from *Alice's Adventures in Wonderland*
by Lewis Carroll

Alice was beginning to get very tired of sitting by her sister on the bank, and of having nothing to do: once or twice she had peeped into the book her sister was reading, but it had no pictures or conversations in it, 'and what is the use of a book,' thought Alice 'without pictures or conversation?'

So she was considering in her own mind (as well as she could, for the hot day made her feel very sleepy and stupid), whether the pleasure of making a daisy-chain would be worth the trouble of getting up and picking the daisies, when suddenly a White Rabbit with pink eyes ran close by her.

There was nothing so VERY remarkable in that; nor did Alice think it so VERY much out of the way to hear the Rabbit say to itself, 'Oh dear! Oh dear! I shall be late!' (when she thought it over afterwards, it occurred to her that she ought to have wondered at this, but at the time it all seemed quite natural); but when the Rabbit actually TOOK A WATCH OUT OF ITS WAISTCOAT-POCKET, and looked at it, and then hurried on, Alice started to her feet, for it flashed across her mind that she had never before seen a rabbit with either a waistcoat-pocket, or a watch to take out of it, and burning with curiosity, she ran across the field after it, and fortunately was just in time to see it pop down a large rabbit-hole under the hedge.

In another moment down went Alice after it, never once considering how in the world she was to get out again.

The rabbit-hole went straight on like a tunnel for some way, and then dipped suddenly down, so suddenly that Alice had not a moment to think about stopping herself before she found herself falling down a very deep well.

Either the well was very deep, or she fell very slowly, for she had plenty of time as she went down to look about her and to wonder what was going to happen next. First, she tried to look down and make out what she was coming to, but it was too dark to see anything; then she looked at the sides of the well, and noticed that they were filled with cupboards and book-shelves; here and there she saw maps and pictures hung upon pegs. She took down a jar from one of the shelves as she passed; it was labeled 'ORANGE MARMALADE', but to her great disappointment it was empty: she did not like to drop the jar for fear of killing somebody, so managed to put it into one of the cupboards as she fell past it.

'Well!' thought Alice to herself, 'after such a fall as this, I shall think nothing of tumbling down stairs! How brave they'll all think me at home! Why, I wouldn't say anything about it, even if I fell off the top of the house!' (Which was very likely true.)

Down, down, down. Would the fall NEVER come to an end! 'I wonder how many miles I've fallen by this time?' she said aloud. 'I must be getting somewhere near the centre of the earth. Let me see: that would be four thousand miles down, I think—' (for, you see, Alice had learnt several things of this sort in her lessons in the schoolroom, and though this was not a VERY good opportunity for showing off her knowledge, as there was no one to listen to her, still it was good practice to say it over) '—yes, that's about the right distance—but then I wonder what Latitude or Longitude I've got to?' (Alice had no idea what Latitude was, or Longitude either, but thought they were nice grand words to say.)

Presently she began again. 'I wonder if I shall fall right THROUGH the earth! How funny it'll seem to come out among the people that walk with their heads downward! The Antipathies, I think—' (she was rather glad there WAS no one listening, this time, as it didn't sound at all the right word) '—but I shall have to ask them what the name of the country is, you know. Please, Ma'am, is this New Zealand or Australia?' (and she tried to curtsey as she spoke—fancy CURTSEYING as you're falling through the air! Do you think you could manage it?) 'And what an ignorant little girl she'll think me for asking! No, it'll never do to ask: perhaps I shall see it written up somewhere.'

Down, down, down. There was nothing else to do, so Alice soon began talking again. 'Dinah'll miss me very much to-night, I should think!' (Dinah was the cat.) 'I hope they'll remember her saucer of milk at tea-time. Dinah my dear! I wish you were down here with me! There are no mice in the air, I'm afraid, but you might catch a bat, and that's very like a mouse, you know. But do cats eat bats, I wonder?' And here Alice began to get rather sleepy, and went on saying to herself, in a dreamy sort of way, 'Do cats eat bats? Do cats eat bats?' and sometimes, 'Do bats eat cats?' for, you see, as she couldn't answer either question, it didn't much matter which way she put it. She felt that she was dozing off, and had just begun to dream that she was walking hand in hand with Dinah, and saying to her very earnestly, 'Now, Dinah, tell me the truth: did you ever eat a bat?' when suddenly, thump! thump! down she came upon a heap of sticks and dry leaves, and the fall was over.

Alice was not a bit hurt, and she jumped up on to her feet in a moment: she looked up, but it was all dark overhead; before her was another long passage, and the White Rabbit was still in sight, hurrying down it. There was not a moment to be lost: away went Alice like the wind, and was just in time to hear it say, as it turned a corner, 'Oh my ears and whiskers, how late it's getting!' She was close behind it when she turned the corner, but the Rabbit was no longer to be seen: she found herself in a long, low hall, which was lit up by a row of lamps hanging from the roof.

There were doors all round the hall, but they were all locked; and when Alice had been all the way down one side and up the other, trying every door, she walked sadly down the middle, wondering how she was ever to get out again.

—From: *Alice's Adventures in Wonderland* by Lewis Carroll, 1865

*Answer questions 15 through 22. Base your answers on "Chapter I—Down the Rabbit-Hole."*

**15.** What conflict is Alice left with at the end of the passage?
  **A.** how to get out of the hall
  **B.** where to find her cat, Dinah
  **C.** how to save herself from falling
  **D.** if she should eat the marmalade

**16.** How does the mood change from the beginning to the end of the passage?
  **F.** It changes from sad to scared.
  **G.** It changes from sleepy to angry.
  **H.** It changes from intense to calm.
  **I.** It changes from pleasant to desperate.

**17.** Read the following sentences.

**'Well!' thought Alice to herself, 'after such a fall as this, I shall think nothing of tumbling down stairs! How brave they'll all think me at home! Why, I wouldn't say anything about it, even if I fell off the top of the house!'**

What do Alice's thoughts reveal about her character?
  **A.** She is very matter-of-fact and does not scare easily.
  **B.** She is annoying and likes to brag about her adventures.
  **C.** She is easily excitable and not able to control her feelings.
  **D.** She is a thrill seeker and likely will want to jump off roofs.

**18.** Read the sentence from the passage.

**There was not a moment to be lost: away went Alice like the wind, and was just in time to hear it say, as it turned a corner, 'Oh my ears and whiskers, how late it's getting!'**

What type of literary device does the author use in the sentence above?
  **F.** irony, because you do not expect Alice to run so fast
  **G.** simile, comparing Alice's speed to the speed of the wind
  **H.** tone, expressing how Alice feels about the White Rabbit
  **I.** alliteration, using repeating sounds at the beginning of words

**19.** Why does the author choose to put some words in all capital letters?
  **A.** to show all the actions of the White Rabbit to the reader
  **B.** to note titles of important characters and terms for the reader
  **C.** to help the reader know that those words should be emphasized
  **D.** to help the reader find a place to break between important ideas

**20.** What is the most likely setting of this chapter?
  **F.** in a kitchen and then into a bat cave
  **G.** in a door-less hallway and into a tunnel
  **H.** in a daisy field and then into to the Antipathies
  **I.** on the bank of a river and then into a rabbit hole

**21.** To make his writing more realistic to the reader, the author filled many of the descriptions in the chapter with
  **A.** personification, giving human qualities to objects that are not human.
  **B.** imagery, helping the reader to imagine all of the things that Alice sees.
  **C.** metaphors, comparing items that are not like one another for a humorous effect.
  **D.** symbolism, allowing the reader to note that some items represent other ideas.

**22.** Read the following sentence from the passage.

**'Now, Dinah, tell me the truth: did you ever eat a bat?' when suddenly, thump! thump! down she came upon a heap of sticks and dry leaves, and the fall was over.**

What type of literary device does the author use in the sentence above?
  **F.** hyperbole, extremely exaggerating the idea of eating a bat
  **G.** irony, creating a feeling of unexpected twists in words and actions
  **H.** pun, using a play on words to show that Alice's long fall is finally over
  **I.** onomatopoeia, using words that look like the sounds they are describing

**Directions:** Read "That Day Ended Isolationism" and "President Franklin Roosevelt's Pearl Harbor Speech" before answering questions 23 through 28.

# That Day Ended Isolationism
Senator Arthur Vandenberg describing the effect of the
Japanese attack on Pearl Harbor,
Hawaii, December 7, 1941

Source: *http://www.archives.gov/exhibits/ treasures_of_congress/Images/page_21/67b.html*

By late 1941 the United States and Japan had clashed over Japanese expansion in China and Indochina for over a decade. When the United States attempted to contain this aggression by imposing embargos on raw materials needed by the Japanese, the diplomatic situation deteriorated, and while negotiations continued, both sides began to prepare for war. The United States reinforced its Pacific bases in the Philippine Islands and at Pearl Harbor, Hawaii. The Japanese military began preparing for an attack on American, British, and Dutch holdings in Asia and the Pacific. When negotiations broke down in late November, these plans went into effect.

War came on Sunday, December 7. Just before 8 a.m., Japanese bombers and torpedo planes attacked the U.S. Pacific Fleet at Pearl Harbor. The surprise was complete, the devastation nearly so. Two waves of planes sank four U.S. battleships, damaged four others, and sank three cruisers and three destroyers. Almost 250 American aircraft were destroyed. There were more than 3,500 American casualties.

The next day President Roosevelt addressed a joint session of Congress. Pronouncing December 7, 1941, "a date which will live in infamy," the President asked that Congress declare war on Japan. Shortly afterward, Congress voted, with only 1 dissent, for a Declaration of War. On December 11 Germany and Italy declared war on the United States.

—Source: *http://www.archives.gov/exhibits/ treasures_of_congress/text/page21_text.html*

## President Franklin Roosevelt's Pearl Harbor Speech
## December 8, 1941, to the Congress of the United States

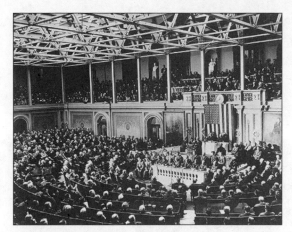

Source: *http://www.archives.gov/ exhibits/treasures_of_congress/Images/ page_21/67a.html*

Yesterday, 7 December 1941—a date which will live in infamy—the United States of America was suddenly and deliberately attacked by naval and air forces of the Empire of Japan.

The United States was at peace with that nation and, at the solicitation of Japan, was still in conversation with its Government and its Emperor looking toward the maintenance of peace in the Pacific. Indeed, one hour after Japanese air squadrons had commenced bombing in Oahu, the Japanese Ambassador to the United States and his colleague delivered to the Secretary of State a formal reply to a recent American message. While this reply stated that it seemed useless to continue the existing diplomatic negotiations, it contained no threat or hint of war or armed attack.

It will be recorded that the distance of Hawaii from Japan makes it obvious that the attack was deliberately planned many days or even weeks ago. During the intervening time the Japanese Government had deliberately sought to deceive the United States by false statements and expressions of hope for continued peace.

The attack yesterday on the Hawaiian Islands has caused severe damage to American naval and military forces. Very many American lives were lost. In addition American ships have been reported torpedoed on the high seas between San Francisco and Honolulu.

Yesterday the Japanese Government also launched an attack against Malaya.

Last night Japanese forces attacked Hong Kong.

Last night Japanese forces attacked Guam.

Last night Japanese forces attacked the Philippine Islands.

Last night Japanese forces attacked Wake Island.

This morning the Japanese attacked Midway Island.

Japan has, therefore, undertaken a surprise offensive extending throughout the Pacific area. The facts of yesterday speak for themselves. The people of the United States have already formed their opinions and well understand the implications to the very life and safety of our nation.

As Commander in Chief of the Army and Navy I have directed that all measures be taken for our defense.

Always will we remember the character of the onslaught against us.

No matter how long it may take us to overcome this premeditated invasion, the American people in their righteous might will win through to absolute victory.

I believe I interpret the will of the Congress and of the people when I assert that we will not only defend ourselves to the uttermost but will make very certain that this form of treachery shall never endanger us again.

Hostilities exist. There is no blinking at the fact that our people, our territory, and our interests are in grave danger.

With confidence in our armed forces—with the unbounded determination of our people—we will gain the inevitable triumph—so help us God.

I ask that the Congress declare that since the unprovoked and dastardly attack by Japan on Sunday, 7 December, a state of war has existed between the United States and the Japanese Empire.

*Answer questions 23 through 28. Base your answers on "That Day Ended Isolationism" and "President Franklin Roosevelt's Pearl Harbor Speech," as well as any pictures included in the passages.*

**23.** Based on the reading passages, which caption would be most appropriate for the picture on page 18?
  **A.** Aggression causes embargos.
  **B.** Japanese bombers attack U.S.
  **C.** Japanese forces attack Hong Kong.
  **D.** Diplomatic negotiations are a success.

**24.** From the two reading passages, you can conclude that
  **F.** the United States had hoped to stay out of the war but now felt they had no choice
  **G.** the United States does not think that it can win against a nation as strong as Japan
  **H.** Japan hoped that the United States would declare war after Japan's attack on Pearl Harbor
  **I.** more people were killed in Malaya, Guam, Hong Kong, and the Philippines than in the U.S. attack

**25.** What makes the passage "That Day Ended Isolationism" most valid?
  **A.** the description of the attack on Pearl Harbor
  **B.** the President of the United States is the speaker
  **C.** the narrator is a senator who lived through the event
  **D.** the United States and Japan had been clashing for over a decade

**26.** Which quote from these passages would be most helpful in writing a research paper on why Japan attacked Pearl Harbor?
  **F.** "The Japanese military began preparing for an attack on American, British, and Dutch holdings in Asia and the Pacific."
  **G.** "By late 1941 the United States and Japan had clashed over Japanese expansion in China and Indochina for over a decade."
  **H.** "With confidence in our armed forces—with the unbounded determination of our people—we will gain the inevitable triumph—so help us God."
  **I.** "It will be recorded that the distance of Hawaii from Japan makes it obvious that the attack was deliberately planned many days or even weeks ago."

27. Which sentence from the passage best explains why Congress agreed with President Roosevelt to go to war?

    **A.** "The surprise was complete, the devastation nearly so."

    **B.** "On December 11 Germany and Italy declared war on the United States."

    **C.** "The United States reinforced its Pacific bases in the Philippine Islands and at Pearl Harbor, Hawaii."

    **D.** "Just before 8 a.m., Japanese bombers and torpedo planes attacked the U.S. Pacific Fleet at Pearl Harbor."

28. Which statement from "President Franklin Roosevelt's Pearl Harbor Speech" is best supported by the diagram on page 19?

    **F.** "The people of the United States have already formed their opinions and well understand the implications to the very life and safety of our nation."

    **G.** "Yesterday, 7 December 1941—a date which will live in infamy—the United States of America was suddenly and deliberately attacked by naval and air forces of the Empire of Japan."

    **H.** "During the intervening time the Japanese Government had deliberately sought to deceive the United States by false statements and expressions of hope for continued peace."

    **I.** "I ask that the Congress declare that since the unprovoked and dastardly attack by Japan on Sunday, 7 December, a state of war has existed between the United States and the Japanese Empire."

## *Check Your Answers*

Use the answer grid below to check your pretest answers. You will also be able to determine in which of the four categories tested by the FCAT you are most proficient and in which area you need the most work.

| Category 1: Vocabulary _____ "Barack Obama" | Category 2: Reading Application _____ "Elinor Smith: Born to Fly" | Category 3: Literary Analysis _____ Chapter I: Down the Rabbit-Hole | Category 4: Informational Text/ Research Process _____ "That Day Ended Isolationism" *and* "President Franklin Roosevelt's Pearl Harbor Speech" |
|---|---|---|---|
| 1. **C** *(context clues)* | 7. **B** *(main idea)* | 15. **A** *(literary elements— conflict/resolution)* | 23. **B** *(text features)* |
| 2. **G** *(word relationships)* | 8. **I** *(author's purpose)* | 16. **I** *(literary devices— descriptive language)* | 24. **F** *(synthesize)* |
| 3. **D** *(multiple meanings)* | 9. **B** *(author's perspective)* | 17. **A** *(literary elements—character)* | 25. **C** *(validity & reliability)* |
| 4. **H** *(context clues)* | 10. **I** *(details)* | 18. **G** *(literary devices —figurative language)* | 26. **G** *(analyze & evaluate)* |
| 5. **D** *(multiple meanings)* | 11. **B** *(conclusions/ inferences)* | 19. **C** *(text features)* | 27. **D** *(validity & reliability)* |
| 6. **G** *(word relationships)* | 12. **G** *(cause and effect)* | 20. **I** *(literary elements —setting)* | 28. **I** *(text features)* |
|  | 13. **C** *(organizational patterns)* | 21. **B** *(literary devices —descriptive language)* |  |
|  | 14. **H** *(compare/ contrast)* | 22. **I** *(literary devices —figurative language)* |  |
| To review topics in the **Vocabulary** category, turn to page 28. | To review topics in the **Reading Application** category, turn to page 34. | To review topics in the **Literary Analysis** category, turn to page 70. | To review topics in the **Informational Text/Research Process** category, turn to page 85. |

Regardless of how well you did on the pretest, it is still a very good idea to read through this entire book, including the section on the Forgotten First Read, in order to ensure that you are as prepared as possible for the FCAT.

# Chapter 2 | **The Forgotten First Read**

## WHY READ?

To many of you, this may seem like a strange question. If this test is the FCAT in reading, then who would not read the test? Well, believe it or not, many students do not actually read the passages that are on the test. Instead, they have a system of just skimming the passages in search of answers. This is a VERY BAD strategy for taking this test.

One reason why it is a bad idea not to read every passage completely is that the questions on the FCAT are primarily based on your higher-level thinking skills—70 to 80 percent of the test, in fact, is made up of moderately to highly complex questions. These types of questions require you to go beyond just reading and searching for answers. They require higher-level thinking skills such as application, analysis, synthesis, and evaluation of the information that you have read.

## This Could Be You—Yikes!

If you take this test without reading the passages, the following could happen:

- You will not get all of the information presented in the passages.
- You may choose the incorrect answers to questions based on what you DID NOT read.
- You might be misled by answers that seem correct because you only skimmed the reading.

## Remember This

Since this is a reading test, there will be answers that seem correct but are not. Details from the passages will also be presented as answers that *do not actually answer the questions*. You need to read the entire passage before moving on to answer the questions to avoid being fooled. Reading the entire passage will also give you the "big picture" of what the passage is really about.

## A Better Strategy

1. Read the directions at the beginning of the new passage(s).
2. Take about one minute to read over the questions, underlining any key words that refer to the standard being tested (for example, main idea, author's purpose).
3. Do a first read of the passage(s) to get the big picture. This includes reading titles, headings, charts, and graphs and also looking at pictures and captions.
4. Interact with the text as you read to stay focused.
5. Reread the questions.
6. Return to the passage(s) to find the answers.
7. Carefully answer the questions, being sure all answers are supported by the passage(s).

> **Reminder:** Do NOT be tempted to go directly to the questions. Read the passage(s) first and *then* move on to the questions.

## INTERACTING WITH THE TEXT

Face it: not everything that you will read on the FCAT is going to be interesting to you. Different people have different interests; it is unlikely that everything on the test will be interesting to *you*. Often, it is difficult to read passages in which you have no interest. You may find your mind wandering and find focusing to be difficult. By interacting with the text as you read, you will stay focused and not waste time. In addition, you may find that some of the passages are quite difficult to read; they may be complex in subject matter and/or vocabulary. If you interact with the text during your first reading of the passage, you can increase your understanding of the passage and will more easily find answers when you are later answering the questions.

## The First Read

Before you attempt to answer any of the questions on the FCAT test, you should do a first read of the passage. What does that mean, though? Basically, during a first read you:

- Read the passage through—from beginning to end—to get a general understanding of what it is saying. This includes looking at titles, headings, charts, graphs, pictures, or anything else that is presented along with the passage.
- Do NOT stop every few seconds to reread.
- Do NOT try to understand every sentence.
- Read to get the big picture.
- Interact with the text during reading.

## Be "One" with the Text

Interacting with the text means going a step beyond reading to think about what you are reading. You might underline, circle, and comment as you read the passage. As you interact with a reading passage you might try some of the following strategies:

- Underline important names and numbers.
- Circle or underline ideas and details that seem important.
- Place question marks near concepts that are unclear.
- Write paragraph topics in the margins.
- Write questions or other comments in the margins.
- Underline a possible main-idea sentence.

All of these strategies will keep you focused and will increase your understanding as you read. They will also help you find the answers to the questions more quickly and competently.

## EXAMPLES AND PRACTICE

Consider the following passage. As you read, underline, circle, and write comments in the margins on anything you consider to be important. There are no right or wrong answers to this exercise, so you do not need to be too apprehensive (worried). One caution, however: do not underline or circle too many things. This will not serve any purpose nor will it indicate what ideas might be important.

## *The Story of My Life*
by Helen Keller

The beginning of my life was simple and much like every other little life. I came, I saw, I conquered, as the first baby in the family always does. There was the usual amount of discussion as to a name for me. The first baby in the family was not to be lightly named, every one was emphatic about that. My father suggested the name of Mildred Campbell, an ancestor whom he highly esteemed, and he declined to take any further part in the discussion. My mother solved the problem by giving it as her wish that I should be called after her mother, whose maiden name was Helen Everett. But in the excitement of carrying me to church my father lost the name on the way, very naturally, since it was one in which he had declined to have a part. When the minister asked him for it, he just remembered that it had been decided to call me after my grandmother, and he gave her name as Helen Adams.

I am told that while I was still in long dresses I showed many signs of an eager, self-asserting disposition. Everything that I saw other people do I insisted upon imitating. At six months I could pipe out "How d'ye," and one day I attracted every one's attention by saying, "Tea, tea, tea" quite plainly. Even after my illness I remembered one of the words I had learned these early months. It was the word "water," and I continued to make some sound for that word after all other speech was lost. I ceased making the sound "wah-wah" only when I learned to spell the word.

They tell me I walked the day I was a year old. My mother had just taken me out of the bath-tub and was holding me in her lap, when I was suddenly attracted by the flickering shadows of leaves that danced in the sunlight on the smooth floor. I slipped from my mother's lap and almost ran toward them. The impulse gone, I fell down and cried for her to take me up in her arms.

These happy days did not last long. One brief spring, musical with the song of robin and mocking-bird, one summer rich in fruit and roses, one autumn of gold and crimson sped by and left their gifts at the feet of an eager, delighted child. Then, in the dreary months of February, came the illness which closed my eyes and ears and plunged me into the unconsciousness of a new-born baby. They called it acute congestion of the stomach and brain. The doctor thought I could not live. Early one morning, however, the fever left me as suddenly and as mysteriously as it had come. There was great rejoicing in the family that morning, but no one, not even the doctor, knew that I should never see or hear again.

I fancy I still have confused recollections of that illness. I especially remember the tenderness with which my mother tried to soothe me in my wailing hours of fret and pain, and the agony and bewilderment with which I awoke after a tossing half sleep, and turned my eyes, so dry and hot, to the wall away from the once-loved light, which came to me dim and yet more dim each day. But, except for these fleeting memories, if, indeed, they be memories, it all seems very unreal, like a nightmare. Gradually I got used to the silence and darkness that surrounded me and forgot that it had ever been different, until she came—my teacher—who was to set my spirit free. But during the first nineteen months of my life I had caught glimpses of broad, green fields, a luminous sky, trees and flowers which the darkness that followed could not wholly blot out. If we have once seen, "the day is ours, and what the day has shown."

—From *The Story of My Life* by Helen Keller, 1902

## Check Your Answers

As mentioned previously, there are no right or wrong answers to this exercise. However, you should still compare what you have underlined, highlighted, or circled and what you have written in the margins to what others have done. That is a good way to see if you are on the right track. Reading for information in this manner takes practice. Take a look at the same passage below; it has been marked up for you as an example.

## *The Story of My Life*
### by Helen Keller

Main idea:

The beginning of my life was simple and much like every other little life. I came, I saw, I conquered, as <u>the first baby</u> in the family always does. There was the usual amount of discussion as to a name for me. The first baby in the family was not to be lightly named, every one was emphatic about that. My <u>father suggested the name of Mildred Campbell</u>, an ancestor whom he highly esteemed, and he declined to take any further part in the discussion. My <u>mother solved the problem</u> by giving it as her wish that <u>I should be called after her mother, whose maiden name was Helen Everett</u>. But in the excitement of carrying me to church my father lost the name on the way, very naturally, since it was one in which he had declined to have a part. When the minister asked him for it, he just remembered that it had been decided to call me after my grandmother, and <u>he gave her name as Helen Adams</u>.

I am told that while I was still in long dresses I showed many signs of an eager, self-asserting disposition. Everything that I saw other people do I insisted upon imitating. At <u>six months I could pipe out "How d'ye,"</u> and one day I attracted every one's attention by saying, <u>"Tea, tea, tea"</u> quite plainly. <u>Even after my illness I remembered one of the words I had learned these early months</u>. It was the word "<u>water</u>," and I continued to make some sound for that word after all other speech was lost. I ceased making the sound "<u>wah-wah</u>" only when I learned to spell the word.

They tell me I <u>walked the day I was a year</u> old. My mother had just taken me out of the bath-tub and was holding me in her lap, when I was suddenly <u>attracted by the flickering shadows of leaves that danced in the sunlight</u> on the smooth floor. I slipped from my mother's lap and almost ran toward them. The impulse gone, I fell down and cried for her to take me up in her arms.

These happy days did not last long. One brief spring, musical with the song of robin and mocking-bird, one summer rich in fruit and roses, one autumn of gold and crimson sped by and left their gifts at the feet of an eager, delighted child. Then, in the dreary months of <u>February</u>, came <u>the illness</u> which closed my eyes and ears and plunged me into the unconsciousness of a new-born baby. They called it <u>acute congestion of the stomach and brain</u>. The <u>doctor thought I could not live</u>. Early one morning, however, the <u>fever left me</u> as suddenly and as mysteriously as it had come. There was great rejoicing in the family that morning, but <u>no one, not even the doctor, knew that I should never see or hear again</u>.

How Helen was named

Baby words and attitude

When she walked

Illness

I fancy I <u>still have confused recollections of that illness</u>. I especially remember the <u>tenderness with which my mother</u> tried to soothe me in my wailing hours of fret and pain, and the agony and bewilderment with which I awoke after a tossing half sleep, and turned <u>my eyes, so dry and hot</u>, to the wall away from the once-loved light, which came to me dim and yet more dim each day. But, except for these fleeting memories, if, indeed, they be memories, it all seems very unreal, <u>like a nightmare</u>. Gradually <u>I got used to the silence and darkness</u> that surrounded me and forgot that it had ever been different, until she came—my <u>teacher—who was to set my spirit free</u>. But during the <u>first nineteen months of my life I had caught glimpses of broad, green fields, a luminous sky, trees and flowers which the darkness that followed could not wholly blot out</u>. If we have once seen, "the day is ours, and what the day has shown."

—From *The Story of My Life* by Helen Keller, 1902

Memories of illness/ teacher set her free

# Chapter 3 | **Practicing with the Standards**

## CATEGORY 1: VOCABULARY

On almost any reading test, you can bet there will be questions about vocabulary, and the FCAT is no exception. However, the good news is that the vocabulary questions on the FCAT are based on understanding the words in the context of the passage.

Vocabulary questions on the FCAT will focus on context clues, word relationships, and multiple meanings of words. There are many good strategies on how to answer vocabulary questions and ways to prepare before you take the test.

## Strategies to Follow

The best way to prepare for any kind of exam that tests vocabulary is to learn as much vocabulary as you can! You can accomplish this in a couple of ways. You can study words, read as much as possible, and learn the meanings of word parts.

- **Study:** This strategy is the most basic. Learn as many vocabulary words as you can. Study using vocabulary books and lists of SAT words. You can also use vocabulary-building sites on the Internet such as *www.freerice.com* or *www.vocabtest.com*. You may also want to try out some vocabulary podcasts or vocabulary applications so that you can take your studying on the go. Just do a search for vocabulary, and you will be surprised at all the free study aids out there for you!
- **Read:** The more that you read, the more words you will encounter and so the larger your vocabulary will be. In addition, the greater the variety of books you read, the more different kinds of words you will be exposed to.
- **Word Parts:** As you probably know, words are often made up of more than one part. There are prefixes (added to beginnings of words), suffixes (added to the endings of words), and roots (the most basic part of a word). By studying and learning what these word parts mean, you can figure out part or all of the meaning of a word, even if you have never seen it before. Becoming aware of the meaning of some common prefixes, suffixes, and root words is a great way to improve your vocabulary. There are many, many prefixes, suffixes, and root words that you can learn. The best thing you can do is to go to the Internet and do a search for Greek and Latin root words. That will give you a very good place to start your studying.

## Context Clues

> **Standard LA.910.1.6.3:** The student will use context clues to determine the meanings of unfamiliar words.

One of the main things that the FCAT will be testing with vocabulary is how well you can figure out words in the context of the rest of the text. So even if you come across a word in the reading that you have never seen before, the FCAT expects that you will be able to figure out the meaning of the word by the context clues around it. ***Context clues* are all of the words that surround the word in question and that can help you figure out the meaning.** Take the following sentence for example:

> Jane was **exuberant** when her soccer team won the state championship after three years of coming in second place.

Even if you have never heard the word **exuberant** before, you should be able to figure out its meaning with the help of the other words in the sentence, or context clues. How would you be feeling if you were on the soccer team and you finally won the state championship after coming in second for all those years? You probably would be pretty happy, right? Well, the meaning of *exuberant* is just that: *extremely happy.*

## EXERCISE

*Now try a couple more on your own. Check your answers with a dictionary or with your teacher to see if you are correct.*

**1.** Rita and the others were so sleepy in the afternoon that they decided to take a **siesta** before going out later that evening.

The meaning of **siesta** is most likely _____.

What context clues lead you to that conclusion? _____

_____

**2.** By the stern looks on the faces of the people in the courtroom, we could see the **gravity** of the situation.

The meaning of **gravity** is most likely _____.

What context clues lead you to that conclusion? _____

_____

## Word Relationships

 **Standard LA.910.1.6.8:** The student will identify advanced word/phrase relationships and their meanings.

The word relationships standard is testing your ability to use context clues and word structure (think word parts!) to determine the meaning of both word and/or phrases in a reading passage. You may be asked to restate or analyze the meaning of phrases or sentences or to choose words or phrases that best describe a picture, scene, character, or situation from the text. Really, they are only asking you to figure out the answer to a question based on your understanding of the relationship between the words (phrases/sentences) in the passage. These types of questions are very similar to context clues questions. However, instead of asking you to figure out the meaning of one word, they are asking you to figure out the meaning of a group of words.

## Multiple Meanings

 **Standard LA.910.1.6.9:** The student will determine the correct meaning of words with multiple meanings in context.

As you are probably aware, there are many words that have more than one meaning. Depending on how a word is used in the context of the sentence, paragraph, or even passage, you can determine what the meaning of that word is. For an example, take a look at the sentence below.

**You can draw the meaning of a word from the context of the sentence.**

What is the meaning of the word "draw" as it is used in this sentence? Clearly, most of us are familiar with the word "draw"—the most common meaning is "to create as in art." However, this is not the meaning of "draw" in this particular sentence. In this case, "draw" mean "to pull out" or "to determine." If you did not look at the context in which the word was used, you could easily choose the wrong meaning of the word.

## Putting It All Together

Now you know how to prepare yourself before the test. You know you should learn as many vocabulary words as possible through your reading and by learning various word parts. In addition, you understand what context clues are and how to use them. You also know that you may be asked to evaluate an entire phrase from a passage and determine its meaning. Finally, you are aware that words may have more than one meaning, so it is always important to look back at the passage to determine the meaning that is being used. So it is now time to look at some actual FCAT-type questions.

Here is a brief list of strategies to help you while answering vocabulary questions on the test.

1. Try to figure out the meaning of the word by its parts: prefix, root, suffix.
2. Look at the context clues, not only from the sentence where the word is found, but also in the sentences preceding (coming before) and succeeding (coming after) the word.
3. Always go back to the passage to see the context in which the word is used. Remember that some words have more than one meaning. You need to locate the meaning of the word as it is used in the passage.
4. Substitute each answer choice into the sentence to see which makes the most sense.
5. Eliminate choices that cannot be correct.

## FCAT PRACTICE QUESTIONS

**Directions:** Read the passage "A Day at the Amusement Park" before answering the questions that follow.

## A Day at the Amusement Park

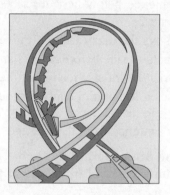

When I go to the amusement park, there is such a plethora of sights, smells, and sounds that I do not know where to turn first. From the inviting aroma of cotton candy to the screams from the roller coaster, my senses are filled to capacity. My first stop, though, has to be the double-loop roller coaster. Although my equilibrium is turned upside down, there is nothing like the thrill of the first 100-foot drop. I then head straight to the hot dog stand where the taste of a foot-long hot dog covered in chili is just delectable. After a few more dizzying rides, I head over to the midway where I try my luck at winning a massive stuffed animal for my little sister. I fail, as usual, but do succeed at attaining a small spotted dog. At the end of the day, I head home, my pockets empty but my senses filled and satisfied from my day of frolicking at the park.

*Answer questions 1–7. Base your answers on the passage "A Day at the Amusement Park."*

1. Which phrase best describes the narrator's feelings toward amusement parks?
   A. He adores them.
   B. He despises them.
   C. He is bored by them.
   D. He is antagonized by them.

**2.** Read this sentence from the passage.

**After a few more dizzying rides, I head over to the midway where I try my luck at winning a massive stuffed animal for my little sister.**

What does *massive* mean?
F. enormous
G. expensive
H. luxurious
I. ornamental

**3.** Read this sentence from the passage.

**When I go to the amusement park, there is such a plethora of sights, smells, and sounds that I do not know where to turn first.**

What does the word *plethora* mean?
A. abundance
B. advantage
C. condition
D. reward

**4.** Which sentence below best describes why the narrator's first stop is the double loop roller coaster?
F. He enjoys the dizzy feeling it gives him.
G. He wants to ride before he eats anything.
H. He loves the intense feeling of the first drop.
I. He uses it to get him ready for the other rides.

**5.** Read this sentence from the passage.

**At the end of the day, I head home, my pockets empty but my senses filled and satisfied from my day of frolicking at the park.**

What does the word *frolicking* mean?
A. eating
B. playing
C. running
D. spending

**6.** Read this excerpt from the passage.

**From the inviting aroma of cotton candy to the screams from the roller coaster, my senses are filled to capacity.**

In which sentence does *inviting* have the same meaning as used in the excerpt above?
F. The giant clown shoes were inviting laughter from all those who saw them.
G. The beautiful music was particularly inviting as we passed the concert hall.
H. The charity was inviting donations from anyone who could spare some change.
I. She was so busy inviting the neighbors into her home that she did see the dog escape.

**7.** Read this excerpt from the passage.

**After a few more dizzying rides, I try my luck at winning a massive stuffed animal for my little sister.**

In which sentence does *winning* have the same meaning as used in the excerpt above?
A. Hannah's winning smile was enough to make anyone like her.
B. Janet's winning from the horse races was two hundred dollars.
C. The basketball team was winning with only 30 seconds left in the game.
D. Mike was winning his way through the thick jungle but not without a struggle.

## Check Your Answers

1. **A** *(Word Relationships)* The narrator clearly adores (or loves) amusement parks through the words he chooses to describe his experience there. He talks about the "inviting smell of the cotton candy," "the thrill of the first 100-foot drop" of the roller coaster, the "delectable" (or delicious) taste of the hot dog, and the satisfaction he gets at the end of the day of "frolicking" at the park. The other choices: despises (hates), bored, and antagonized (irritated) clearly do not fit. Even if you do not know what all of the word choices mean, you should be able to eliminate some by their word parts or by how they fit into the sentence and by all of the context clues in the paragraph.

2. **F** *(Context Clues)* You may have to look beyond the sentence containing the word "massive" in order to figure this one out. The narrator says that he wants to win a massive stuffed animal for his sister. Unfortunately, that does not give you enough information to answer the question. However, the next sentence says that he managed to win only a small dog. That should tell you that what he wanted was a great big prize.

3. **A** *(Context Clues)* The narrator encounters many sights, smells, and sounds at his day at the park. The other context clue in the sentence is that "he does not know where to turn first." That should give you a clue that there are many things to do and see.

4. **H** *(Word Relationships)* You should understand from the rest of the sentence that he really does not like what the ride does to his equilibrium or sense of balance, so he does not necessarily like being dizzy. However, he does enjoy the speed of the first drop.

5. **B** *(Context Clues)* Although the narrator did spend the day eating, running, and spending, what really satisfied him was that he spent the day *playing*.

6. **G** *(Multiple Meanings)* Looking back at the sentence, you can see that the author refers to the aroma, or smell, of the cotton candy as "inviting." It is pleasurable—he likes the smell. It makes him want to eat the candy. The same meaning of inviting is used in Choice G. Although the word "inviting" can also mean "request the presence of" (as in Choice I), that is not its meaning in this case. It also can mean "to request" (Choice H) or "to give occasion for" (Choice F), but none of these meanings are the same as the meaning in the passage.

7. **C** *(Multiple Meanings)* In this sentence, "winning" means success or victory. The only sentence that has that same meaning is Choice C. There are other meanings of "winning," such as "charming" (Choice A), "something that is won" (Choice B), or "to succeed in reaching" (Choice D), but none of them is the correct choice.

> As you continue working through the book, there will be additional vocabulary questions. Practice with these questions, remembering the strategies you have learned.

# CATEGORY 2: READING APPLICATION
## Main Idea, Relevant Details, Conclusions/Inferences

 **Standard LA.910.1.7.3:** The student will determine the main idea or essential message in grade-level or higher texts through inferring, paraphrasing, summarizing, and identifying relevant details.

### MAIN IDEA

If there is one thing you can count on, it is that there will be questions about the main idea on just about every passage that you read in the FCAT. So learning how to answer main idea questions can only work to your advantage.

Before you attempt to find the main idea of a passage, you must understand exactly what main idea is. **The main idea is the central focus of the passage.** It is what ties all the ideas in the passage together. All of the details in the sample must somehow come back to this main idea.

### STATED MAIN IDEA

The main idea can occur in two ways in a passage: stated or implied. A **stated main idea** is just that—a sentence within the passage that actually states the main idea. The work has already been done for you; you just need to find the statement. A stated main idea often comes close to the beginning or to the end of a reading passage, so those are good places to begin looking. However, a stated main idea *can* occur anywhere within the passage. The best rule of thumb is to remember this during your first read of the passage. If you come to a sentence that you believe could be the main idea, underline it. This could be useful to you later when you are answering the questions.

# EXERCISE

*In case you are still unsure about exactly what a stated main idea is, here is a very simple exercise to demonstrate the stated main idea. As you read the paragraph below, look for the stated main idea. Then answer the question that follows.*

## Egypt
### Life in the Villages

    The country-people of Egypt are very poor, and have to work very hard all the year round in their fields. Their houses are built of bricks dried in the sun, plastered together with mud, and the roof is made of plaited palm leaf. Inside there is only one room, which has a big oven made of mud with a flat top on which the father and mother sleep. The work in the fields is very hard, as the ground has to be made fertile by digging canals and ditches all over it to bring the water from the Nile, because, you remember, there is no rain in Egypt. When the Nile begins to fall, the water has to be raised in baskets fastened to a wheel or pole, and thrown to the ground. In order to get enough money, the people plant another kind of seed as soon as one harvest is gathered; first, perhaps, planting wheat, then millet, or cotton, then maize. So the country-people in Egypt are always working hard from sunrise to sunset all the year in their fields, and their little children have to learn to mind the sheep, goats, or cattle, and to help in other ways as soon as they can walk.

—Source: *People of Africa* by Edith A. How, 1921

What is the main idea of the paragraph above?
A. In order to get enough money, the people plant another kind of seed as soon as one harvest is gathered.
B. The country-people of Egypt are very poor, and have to work very hard all year round in their fields.
C. Their houses are built of bricks dried in the sun, plastered together with mud, and the roof is made of plaited palm leaf.
D. Their little children have to learn to mind the sheep, goats, or cattle and to help in other ways as soon as they can walk alone.

## *Check Your Answer*

The correct answer is Choice B. That is the main idea of the paragraph; all of the other ideas in the paragraph fall under the umbrella of that statement. The main idea, in this case, is actually stated in the paragraph.

### IMPLIED MAIN IDEA

The other kind of main idea is implied; this means that nowhere in the passage is the main idea actually written down for you. That does not mean that there is no main idea in the passage; every passage has a main idea. It just means that you should get the idea of what the main idea is through your understanding of what you read. Remember, *to imply* means *to suggest*, so what does the passage suggest to you? An implied main idea can be a little harder to figure out, obviously, because it is not actually written in the passage. You will just need to use your higher-level thinking skills!

# EXERCISE

*Here is another simple exercise to show you the difference between a stated main idea and an implied main idea. Read the paragraph below, and, as you read, try to figure out the main idea of the paragraph.*

## Egypt
### The Country and its River

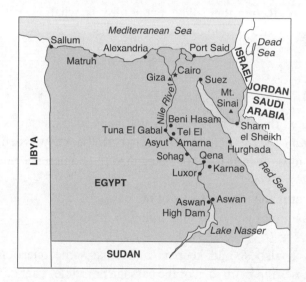

Egypt is a country in the north of Africa. It has sea to the north and sea to the east. On the north it is called the Mediterranean Sea, and on the east, the Red Sea. On the west is the great sandy desert called the Sahara, and to the south are great forests and mountains. Egypt itself is the land of the great River Nile. There is very seldom any rain there, and everyone has to get water from the great river. So all the people live near the Nile or the canals which lead out of it. A "canal" is a waterway, the channel of which has been dug by men. The big towns are where the river flows out in to the sea, or where a canal meets the main stream, because the people bring their merchandise to market in boats. All over the land are little villages, where many people live and work in the fields to grow food. Year by year where there is heavy rain in the mountains far away south, the River Nile rises and floods the fields. Then the people plant their seed quickly and get a good harvest.

—Source: *People of Africa* by Edith A. How, 1921

What is the main idea of this passage?

**A.** Egypt is a country with a sea on both sides and very little rain.

**B.** Egypt is a country north of Africa with big towns and little villages and many sources of water.

**C.** Canals, the channels dug by men, are important to the country of Egypt for traveling and for the trading of merchandise.

**D.** It is not difficult to understand why the Egyptians love their great river, which gives them water for their fields and carries them in their boats from place to place.

*Check Your Answer*

Although the main idea is not stated in the passage, you should be able to figure out that the main idea implied by the paragraph is Choice D.

The bottom line is that whether the main idea is stated or implied, every passage has a main idea. The only way actually to figure out the main idea is to have read the passage.

 **Remember:** The main idea is what every sentence in the passage relates back to—in one way or another.

## The Questions

The next thing to remember is that main idea questions are not always phrased as *What is the main idea?* Therefore, it is important to know when the question is asking you for the main idea, even if it is not stated directly. Sometimes you might be asked:

- What is the central focus of the passage?
- What point is the passage trying to make?

You also should keep in mind that some questions will ask what statement BEST expresses the main idea of the passage or article. That means that more than one answer may *sound* correct, but only one answer will be the right one. Remember this as you look at the answers and refer back to the passage.

## Main Idea Strategy for Multiple-Choice Questions

 Again, you should have a strategy when answering FCAT questions. Here is a strategy to help you answer main idea questions.

1. **Ask Yourself What the Main Idea Is:** When you come to a main idea question, ask yourself what the main idea might be, before you even read any of the answers!
2. **Read the Answers:** If there is an answer similar to your own thought, you have probably found the correct answer.
3. **Go Back to the Passage:** Do not be afraid to go back and check your answer. Go back to the passage and make sure everything in the passage fits under the umbrella statement that you have chosen as the main idea.
4. **Watch Out for Distracters:** Remember that this is a reading test. Some of the answers are designed to throw you off; they are called distracters. Often, there will be an answer that is actually a statement from the passage but is *not* the main idea. However, some students will recognize the statement from their reading and automatically assume that it is the correct answer.
5. **Look for a Broad Statement:** Keep in mind that the main idea will be a broad type of statement that sums up the point of the passage. It is NOT a specific statement that refers to only one point or detail from the passage. Do not let these types of answers trick you!

# FCAT PRACTICE QUESTIONS

*Read the passage "The Birth of the Telephone" before answering the questions that follow.*

**Remember:** Don't forget to interact with the passage as you read!!

## The Birth of the Telephone
by Herbert N. Casson

In that somewhat distant year of 1875, when the telegraph and the Atlantic cable were the wonderful things in the world, a tall young professor of elocution was desperately busy in a noisy machine-shop that stood in one of the narrow streets of Boston, not far from Scollay Square. It was a very hot afternoon in June, but the young professor had forgotten the heat and the grime of the workshop. He was wholly absorbed in the making of a nondescript machine, a sort of crude harmonica with a clock-spring reed, a magnet, and a wire. It was a most absurd toy in appearance. It was unlike any other thing that had ever been made in any country. The young professor had been toiling over it for three years and it had constantly baffled him, until, on this hot afternoon in June, 1875, he heard an almost inaudible sound—a faint TWANG—come from the machine itself.

For an instant he was stunned. He had been expecting such a sound for several months, but it came so suddenly as to give him the sensation of surprise. His eyes blazed with delight, and he sprang in a passion of eagerness to an adjoining room in which stood a young mechanic who was assisting him.

"Snap that reed again, Watson," cried the apparently irrational young professor. There was one of the odd-looking machines in each room, so it appears, and the two were connected by an electric wire. Watson had snapped the reed on one of the machines and the professor had heard from the other machine exactly the same sound. It was no more than the gentle TWANG of a clock-spring; but it was the first time in the history of the world that a complete sound had been carried along a wire, reproduced perfectly at the other end, and heard by an expert in acoustics.

That twang of the clock-spring was the first tiny cry of the newborn telephone, uttered in the clanging din of a machine-shop and happily heard by a man whose ear had been trained to recognize the strange voice of the little newcomer. There, amidst flying belts and jarring wheels, the baby telephone was born, as feeble and helpless as any other baby, and "with no language but a cry."

—From *The History of the Telephone* by Herbert N. Casson

On the lines below, indicate what you think the main idea is:

_____

_____

_____

_____

> **TIP:** Don't forget to use the *title* (if there is one) for clues to the main idea!

*Now circle the answer you feel is correct for the multiple-choice question below. Be sure to consult your own idea from above and to go back to the passage to review the information if necessary.*

The main idea of the passage is
A. Watson, the young mechanic, assisted the professor in the inventing of the telephone.
B. the telephone's first sound was a TWANG created by the snapping of a reed on a clock-spring.
C. the professor was a hard-working, eager man dedicated to the discovery of new inventions.
D. the first telephone was a simple instrument that was developed through years of work by a dedicated man.

## Check Your Answer

Hopefully you chose Choice D as the correct answer. Although there is no stated main idea in the passage, you should recognize that all of the other ideas from the passage relate directly back to Choice D. Choices A and B are both factual details from the passage, but neither reflects the main idea. Choice C is an opinion that seems to be supported by the passage, but it is not the ***main*** idea. The passage is only about the invention of the telephone; no other inventions are mentioned. Remember, the main idea is supported by all of the other details in the passage, not just a few. *So even if a choice is true, it is not necessarily the main idea.*

### RELEVANT DETAILS

Everything you read has hundreds of details. Details are what authors add to their writing to support the main idea. They add clarity and make the passages more interesting. For example, think of a stalk of broccoli. Imagine the stalk as the main idea and all of the florets as the details. The stalk connects them all and is important, but without the florets, you would not have much of a vegetable!

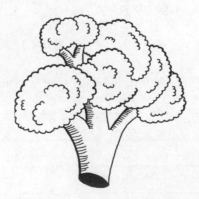

Another analogy (in case you are not big on veggies) is a bouquet of balloons. All of the balloons are different colors, styles, and shapes and make the bouquet beautiful and unique. Without the weight that connects all the strings of balloons together, though, they would all just float away. That weight is the main idea; the balloons are the details.

Luckily, there are always detail questions asked on the FCAT, and they are probably the easiest kinds of questions to answer. If you **go back and read** to find the answer, you should not miss detail questions. It is when students do not go back to check their answers or do not read the question carefully that they miss detail questions.

**Remember:** This is a READING test. The state wants to see how well you can read. You *must read* the questions to make sure you know what is being asked, and you *must read* the passages to be sure you get the answers correct.

## CONCLUSIONS AND INFERENCES

An inference or a conclusion is the answer you come to by using your thinking and reasoning skills. Think about it: every day you make inferences and draw conclusions based on what your senses take in (what you see, hear, smell, touch, and taste). If you hear thunder in the distance and see the sky is getting darker, then you might infer that it is going to rain soon. Using all the details you took in from your senses, you made a logical inference.

When you read FCAT passages, you will be asked to make inferences and draw conclusions based on the information in the text. What is really being tested here is how well you understand what you read. When answering these types of questions, you should ask yourself, "What is a logical answer based on everything I have read? Which answer is supported by the text?" Take a look at the sample question below to test your understanding:

**Jenny wakes up early. She is so excited about the day ahead! She puts on her favorite dress and has her mother help curl her hair. She wraps the gift in the fancy blue paper they purchased yesterday. Finally, it is time to go! Jenny can't wait to see all her friends.**

From the passage above, you can infer that Jenny is most likely
A. going to a pool party
B. going to a birthday party
C. going to the airport to pick up her relatives
D. going to school for the annual class field trip

If you chose answer B, you are correct! All of the details in the passage lead you to the conclusion that the girl is attending a birthday party: she is excited, puts on a nice dress, does her hair, and wraps a present. She is obviously happy about the place she is going, and she wants to look good. She also will see her friends there. Choice A cannot be correct because there is nothing in the paragraph about swimming or a bathing suit; Choice C cannot be correct because there is nothing in the paragraph about her relatives, just her friends. Finally, Choice D is not correct since you would not normally bring a gift to a class field trip. The best conclusion you can draw from what you have read is that the girl is going to a birthday party—Choice A.

Let's think a little more about conclusion and inference questions as some students find them a bit difficult.

## CALLING ALL DETECTIVES!

Drawing a conclusion or making an inference is definitely a higher-level thinking skill. It requires you to take in information, process it, and then come out with a logical end result. What is hard about drawing a conclusion is that the answer is not provided for you. Instead, you get clues as to what the answer is, and then you need to process the clues in order to get the answer. It is really like solving a mystery. The reading passage will provide you with clues. As the detective, you need to figure out the meaning of the clues to come to a logical answer to the mystery. So instead of getting frustrated or afraid of this type of question, think of it as a challenge. You just need to analyze the evidence in order to solve the mystery. It really can be quite elementary.

## EXERCISE

*You draw conclusions every day without ever really thinking about it. In addition, you use multiple sources to draw those conclusions. Read the following paragraph, and answer the short-response question that follows.*

A woman is standing in line at the register of the local grocery store. An annoyed look crosses her face as she repeatedly looks at her watch. She rolls her eyes and begins sighing loudly. The young man standing behind her begins to shift his weight back and forth and looks at the ceiling. Another person in line, a young lady with a small baby, moves her cart out of line and relocates to a register nearby.

What logical conclusion can you draw about the situation described above? Be sure to support your answer with details and information from the passage.

_____

_____

_____

_____

_____

_____

_____

### Check Your Answer

The most obvious and logical conclusion that you could come to is that the cashier at the register is very slow. You should support this answer with such things as the annoyed woman looking at her watch and sighing, the young man tapping his foot, and the young lady who left the line.

# FCAT PRACTICE QUESTIONS

*The following passage is an excerpt from the autobiography* Night *by Elie Wiesel, about his experiences in a Nazi concentration camp.*

| **Directions:** | *Read the excerpt from* Night *before answering questions 1–5.* |
| --- | --- |

## from *Night*
by Elie Wiesel

The SS gave us a fine New Year's gift.

We had just come back from work. As soon as we had passed through the door of the camp, we sensed something different in the air. Roll call did not take so long as usual. The evening soup was given out with great speed and swallowed down at once in anguish.

I was no longer in the same block as my father. I had been transferred to another unit, the building one, where, twelve hours a day, I had to drag heavy blocks of stone about. The head of my new block was a German Jew, small of stature, with piercing eyes. He told us that evening that no one would be allowed to go out after the evening soup. And soon a terrible word was circulating—selection.

We knew what that meant. An SS man would examine us. Whenever he found a weak one, a *musulman* as we called them, he would write his number down: good for the crematory.

After soup, we gathered together between the beds. The veterans said:

"You're lucky to have been brought here so late. This camp is paradise today, compared with what it was like two years ago. Buna was a real hell then. There was no water, no blankets, less soup and bread. At night we slept almost naked, and it was below thirty degrees. The corpses were collected in hundreds every day. The work was hard. Today, this is a little paradise. The Kapos had orders to kill a certain number of prisoners every day. And every week—selection. A merciless selection. . . . yes, you're lucky."

"Stop it! Be quiet!" I begged. "You can tell your stories tomorrow or on some other day."

They burst out laughing. They were not veterans for nothing.

"Are you scared? So were we scared. And there was plenty to be scared of in those days."

The old men stayed in their corner, dumb, motionless, haunted. Some were praying.

An hour's delay. In an hour, we should know the verdict—death or a reprieve.

And my father? Suddenly I remembered him. How would he pass the selection? He had aged so much . . .

The head of our block had never been outside concentration camps since 1933. He had already been through all the slaughterhouses, all the factories of death. At about nine o'clock, he took up his position in our midst:

"Achtung!"

There was instant silence.

"Listen carefully to what I am going to say." (For the first time, I heard his voice quiver.) "In a few moments the selection will begin. You must get completely undressed. Then one by one you go before the SS doctors. I hope you will all succeed in getting through. But you must help your own chances. Before you go into the next room, move about in some way so that you give yourselves more color. Don't walk slowly, run! Run as if the devil were after you! Don't look at the SS. Run, straight in front of you!"

He broke off for a moment, then added:

"And, the essential thing, don't be afraid!"

Here was a piece of advice we should have liked very much to be able to follow.

—From *Night* by Elie Wiesel, translated by Stella Rodway.
Copyright ©1960 by MacGibbon & Kee. Copyright renewed ©1988
by The Collins Publishing Group. Reprinted by permission of
Hill and Wang, div. of Farrar, Straus and Giroux, LLC.

*Answer questions 1–5. Base your answers on the selection from* Night.

1. What advice does the head of the cell block give to the prisoners on how they can avoid being chosen in the selections?
   A. They should yell out, "Achtung!"
   B. They should run as fast as they can.
   C. They should get completely undressed.
   D. They should look directly at the SS doctors.

2. What did it mean if the SS man wrote down a prisoner's number during selection?
   F. The prisoner would lose his rations.
   G. The prisoner would be sent to hard labor.
   H. The prisoner would be sent to the furnace.
   I. The prisoner would be sent to the infirmary.

3. From reading the excerpt from *Night*, the reader can infer that the "fine New Year's gift" is
   A. not really a gift at all but a form of punishment
   B. a chance for the narrator to see his father again
   C. likely to be more soup and bread than the prisoners normally receive
   D. the time that the prisoners get to sit around and tell stories about paradise

4. Which statement best expresses the main idea of the passage?
   F. The concentration camps had improved from what they were two years before.
   G. The head of the block was an unpleasant man who worked directly for the Nazis.
   H. The Nazis were expected to do a great deal of hard labor during their time at the camps.
   I. Selection was a particularly horrifying time for the prisoners of the concentration camps.

5. Read the sentence below from the passage:

   **The old men stayed in their corner, dumb, motionless, haunted.**

   In the sentence, what does the word *dumb* reveal about the old men?
   A. They have been beaten until they have become senseless.
   B. They are so scared that they have lost their ability to think.
   C. They have been scared speechless by the ghosts of the dead.
   D. They no longer talk due to the trauma they have been through.

*Check Your Answers*

1. **B** *(Details)* The prisoners should run. This is the advice the head of the block gives so the prisoners can help their own chances. He does tell them to get completely undressed (C), but that is not advice to help them succeed in the selection. Choice D is incorrect since he tells the prisoners NOT to look at the SS doctors. Choice A is obviously wrong as well since it has nothing to do with the question being asked, although it is a detail in the passage.

2. **H** *(Details)* The answer is directly stated in the passage—if the prisoner's number was written down, he was "good for the crematory." If you do not know what a "crematory" is, you may have had a problem with this question. You could use the process of elimination: none of the other answers are supported by the text. (Cross out the answers as you figure out that they are incorrect.) Alternatively, you could look carefully at the word "crematory" and see that it looks a great deal like the word "cremation," which may help you figure out the meaning.

3. **A** *(Inference)* From the information in the passage, you can tell that the author is primarily describing the experience of selection—a time when the weakest men would be pulled from the camp and put to death. Based on this knowledge, you can see that the author is being sarcastic and the New Year's gift is actually not a gift at all, but a form of punishment (Choice A). All of the rest of the answers are incorrect inferences: although the author mentions his father, there is no indication he will actually see him (Choice B). And he does talk about food, but nothing in the passage suggests they will get more food (Choice C). Finally, the men are telling stories but their stories are about the concentration camps, and even though they say it is a paradise compared to what it used to be, they are not telling stories about paradise (Choice D).

4. **I** *(Main Idea)* The main idea of the passage centers around the horrible experience of selection. The rest of the choices are details in the passage, but not the main idea. They are not central to the overall meaning of the text.

5. **D** *(Multiple Meanings)* You probably know that the word "dumb" has two basic meanings: "stupid" or "unable to speak." If you look back at how the word "dumb" is used in the context of the sentence and the passage, you can see that in this case the prisoners are not stupid or senseless. They are sitting motionless and quiet. Ask yourself why would they be sitting in complete silence? From the passage you know that these prisoners have been through horrible experiences, so D is the correct answer. They are not silent because they are afraid of ghosts—they are haunted by their past experiences and by what may happen to them.

# Text Structures/Organizational Patterns

**Standard LA.910.1.7.5:** The student will analyze a variety of text structures (e.g., comparison/contrast, cause/effect, chronological order, argument/support, lists) and text features (main headings with subheadings) and explain their impact on meaning in text.

Organizational patterns and text structures: you might be asking yourself, "What does this mean?" The good news and first thing you need to know is that even though this section is called "Text Structures/Organizational Patterns," **you will only be tested on organizational patterns under this benchmark.** Text structures will actually be evaluated in the other categories: Literary Analysis for literary text (stories, poems, biographies, and so on) and Informational Text/Research Process for informational types of text. We will look at text features for each of these types of texts later in the book. However, sometimes the text structures of a passage (for example, the headings and subheadings) can give you a clue as to what the organizational pattern might be, and that is why it is included in this benchmark. So be sure to use those structures whenever you can!

So let's focus on organizational patterns. What are they? Simply put, organizational patterns are a way of identifying how the passage you are reading is organized.

What does this mean? Well, think about something you might write yourself. Once you have a topic in mind, how you go about the writing depends on the topic and the point you are trying to get across. For example, if your teacher asks you to write a persuasive essay, you would probably use the method of argument and support to express your point, stating your specific argument and supporting your ideas with details, facts, and statistics. However, if you were writing a letter to your friend about the happenings at the big dance last weekend, you might use chronological order (telling the events in the order of time in which they occurred). Or you might use order of importance, telling the things that were most important first and gradually getting to the least important items.

Looking at organizational patterns in an FCAT article or passage is no different. Once you have read the article, think about the author's purpose (more on this later!) and how he or she got across the main idea. Some of the most common patterns are outlined below:

- **Problem/Solution:** Author presents a particular problem and then one or more solutions to that problem
- **Compare/Contrast:** Author compares (tells how things are similar) and contrasts (tells how things are different) information
- **Chronological Order:** Author presents information in order of time, how the events actually occurred
- **Order of Importance:** Author presents most important information first then goes on until he/she presents least important information at the end of the passage
- **Argument and Support**: Author presents an argument and then goes on to support the argument with facts, statistics, examples, anecdotes, and so on, often seen in persuasive writing
- **Main Idea and Supporting Details:** Author presents main idea at beginning of passage and then supports that idea with details throughout remainder of passage
- **Circular:** Author begins with a particular idea and ends with the same idea, bringing the passage full circle
- **Flashback:** Story flashes back to a time prior to the present to show events that occurred earlier
- **Foreshadowing:** Author gives clues to the outcome or resolution of the story
- **Cause/Effect:** Author gives cause(s) and/or effect(s) of particular situations

Let's try a matching exercise so you can practice identifying organizational patterns. For practice purposes, these pieces of texts will be short, but even with longer passages, you use the same method of thinking and the same kinds of patterns.

# EXERCISE

*Read each short paragraph. Choose the correct organizational pattern from the list below that best corresponds to the organizational pattern used by the author.*

| | | |
|---|---|---|
| Problem/Solutions | Compare/Contrast | Chronological Order |
| Order of Importance | Argument and Support | Main Idea and Supporting Details |
| Circular | Flashback | Cause/Effect |

_____ 1. The first thing I do when I get up is to brush my teeth. Next I wash my face and get dressed. After I eat breakfast, I head out the door for school.

_____ 2. Although apples and oranges are both fruit, both have outer skins and seeds, and both are relatively sweet, that is where their similarities end. Apples are red and you can eat the skin. Oranges, on the other hand, are orange, and eating the skin is not recommended! In fact, it could make you sick.

_____ 3. The causes of the war were more than obvious: a failing economy and a government desperate to bring its people together against a common enemy—a way to re-energize the nation. The outcomes were not anticipated, though: mass poverty and a country divided against itself on the verge of a civil war.

_____ 4. Clearly we must do something to stop the spread of pollution. There are so many possibilities: the development of cleaner burning fuel, recycling, and use of natural elements, such as wind and sun, to power our everyday utilities.

_____ 5. I am sitting at the table, eating my breakfast in the sunny nook in our kitchen. As I munch on my cereal, I am reminded of my childhood, days spent without much food at all, let alone a simple breakfast of cereal. I was only six when my parents died of the Great Sickness . . .

## Check Your Answers

1. Chronological Order: The author listed what she does in the morning in the order of time. (Clues like "first," "second," "then," "next" can help you identify this pattern.)
2. Compare/Contrast: The author presented the similarities (compare) and differences (contrast) between apples and oranges.
3. Cause/Effect: The author told some of the causes of the war and then provided some of the outcomes or effects.
4. Problem/Solution: The author presented a problem (pollution) and then several solutions to that problem.
5. Flashback: The author started telling his story in the present time, but then slipped back to a time in the past, the time of his childhood.

Hopefully, you felt this practice exercise was pretty simple. Although the texts you will read on the FCAT will be more difficult, the patterns are the same. Learning what the patterns are is the first step. Once you know that the patterns exist, you should have a much easier time identifying them. See how you do on the next set of FCAT practice questions – there will be an organizational patterns question there.

# FCAT PRACTICE QUESTIONS

*Now try a sample passage. There will be questions on vocabulary, main idea, details, conclusions/inferences, and, of course, organizational patterns. Do not forget to interact with the passage during your first read in order to get maximum understanding of the passage.*

**Directions:**    *Read the passage "Hercules" before answering questions 1–5.*

## Hercules
Edited by Hamilton Wright Mabie

Many, many years ago in the far-off land of Hellas, which we call Greece, lived a happy young couple whose names were Alcmene and Amphitryon. Now Amphitryon, the husband, owned many herds of cattle. So also the father of Alcmene, who was King of Mycenae, owned many.

All these cattle grazing together and watering at the same springs became united in one herd. And this was the cause of much trouble, for Amphitryon fell to quarreling with the father of his wife about his portion of the herd. At last he slew his father-in-law, and from that day he fled his home at Mycenae.

Alcmene went with her husband and the young couple settled at Thebes, where were born to them two boys—twins—which were later named Hercules and Iphicles.

From the child's very birth Zeus, the King of all heaven that is the air and clouds, and the father of gods and me—from the boy's very birth Zeus loved Hercules. But when Hera, wife of Zeus, who shared his honors, saw this love she was angry. Especially she was angry because Zeus foretold that Hercules should become the greatest of men.

Therefore one night, when the two babies were but eight months old, Hera sent two huge serpents to destroy them. The children were asleep in the great shield of brass which Amphitryon carried in battle for defence [sic]. It was a good bed, for it was round and curved toward the centre, and filled with soft blankets which Alcmene and the maids of the house had woven at their looms. Forward toward this shield the huge snakes were creeping, and just as they lifted their open mouths above the rim, and were making ready to seize them, the twins opened their eyes. Iphicles screamed with fright. His cries wakened their mother, Alcmene, who called in a loud voice for help. But before Amphitryon and the men of the household could draw their swords and rush to the rescue, the baby Hercules, sitting up in the shield unterrified and seizing a serpent in each hand, had choked and strangled them till they died.

From his early years Hercules was instructed in the learning of his time. Castor, the most experienced charioteer of his day, taught him, Eurytus also, how to shoot with a bow and arrows; Linus how to play upon the lyre; and Eumolpus, grandson of the North Wind, drilled him in singing. Thus time passed to his eighteenth year when, so great already had become his strength and knowledge, he killed a fierce lion which had preyed upon the flocks of Amphitryon while they were grazing on

Mount Cithaeron, and which had in fact laid waste many a fat farm of the surrounding country.

But the anger of Hera still followed Hercules, and the goddess sent upon him a madness. In this craze the hero did many unhappy deeds. For punishment and in expiation he condemned himself to exile, and at last he went to the great shrine of the god Apollo at Delphi to ask whither he should go and where settle. The Pythia, or priestess in the temple, desired him to settle at Tiryns, to serve as bondman to Eurystheus, who ruled at Mycenae as King, and to perform the great labours which Eurystheus should impose upon him. When these tasks were all accomplished, the inspired priestess added, Hercules should be numbered among the immortal gods.

—From *Tales for Young People of the World's Heroes in All Ages*, edited by Hamilton Wright Mabie

*Answer questions 1–5. Base your answers on the passage "Hercules."*

1. The main idea of the passage can best be expressed as
   A. although Zeus loved Hercules, Hera hated him.
   B. Hercules became famous when he killed two serpents.
   C. Hercules faced many trials on his road to becoming a god.
   D. Hercules became great through the instruction of many experienced men.

2. Read this sentence from the passage.

   **For punishment and in expiation he condemned himself to exile, and at last he went to the great shrine of the god Apollo at Delphi to ask whither he should go and where settle.**

   What does *expiation* mean?
   F. atonement
   G. expectation
   H. pleasure
   I. sadness

3. What method of development does the author use to present the information in the passage?
   A. a list
   B. cause and effect
   C. chronological order
   D. main idea/supporting details

4. Where did Hercules need to go in order to fulfill Zeus's prophecy?
   F. Delphi
   G. Hellas
   H. Mount Cithaeron
   I. Tiryns

5. What can you infer about the god Zeus from this passage?
   A. Zeus wanted Hercules to suffer.
   B. Zeus liked to anger his wife, Hera.
   C. Zeus had no power to protect Hercules.
   D. Zeus made prophecies that became truth.

## *Check Your Answers*

1. **C** *(Main Idea)* Remember that the main idea needs to be a broad statement that can serve as an umbrella for the entire text. In this case, Choice C is the best answer since the passage deals with the story of Hercules and what problems faced him in his life. Choices A and D are both correct details from the passage but are not main ideas. Choice B is not correct; although Hercules did kill the serpents, there is nothing in the passage to indicate that this made him famous.

2. **F** *(Word Relationships) Expiation* means *atonement*, so the correct answer is F. This may have been especially difficult for you if you did not know the meaning of *atonement*. (*Atonement* means to do something to make up for what has been done wrong.) The best way to attempt to answer the question would be to substitute each of the choices into the sentence and see which one would fit best. You should easily see that neither answer G (*expectation*) nor H (*pleasure*) would work since being in exile would not bring either of these things. (Do not fall into the trap of picking *expectation* for the answer just because it starts with the same letters as the word in question.) The next best answer is I (*sadness*) since being in exile might bring sadness. However, *atonement* is the best answer since Hercules went into exile to punish himself. If he was punishing himself, it would be logical that he was trying to atone (make up for) his wrongdoings.

3. **C** *(Organizational Patterns)* Chronological order (the order of time) is the only answer that makes sense for this question. The narrator begins to tell the story before Hercules is even born and then progresses into his adulthood, discussing some of the problems he had along the way.

4. **I** *(Details)* This is a straight details question and is easiest to answer if you go back to the passage and look for the correct information. Although all of the answers are places mentioned in the passage, only one of them, Choice I–Tiryns—is the place where Hercules was told to go by the priestess. There he would perform tasks that would make him an immortal god, "the greatest of men," as Zeus had predicted.

5. **D** *(Conclusions/Inferences)* The correct choice to this question is D. In the beginning of the story, Zeus made a prophecy about Hercules, and it did become true. There is no indication anywhere in the passage that Zeus wanted Hercules to suffer (Choice A)—Hercules was Zeus's favorite, so he would not want him to suffer! Choice B might be tempting, but there is nothing in the passage that shows that Zeus enjoyed making Hera angry. The fact is that Hera was angry, but we do not know if Zeus liked that or angered her on purpose, so we cannot draw that conclusion. Finally, we cannot tell if Zeus could protect Hercules or not. We might assume that Zeus could protect him since Zeus was such a powerful god, but he does not protect him in the story, and so we cannot make that inference (Choice C).

# Author's Purpose and Author's Perspective

**Standard LA.910.1.7.2:** The student will analyze the author's purpose and/or perspective in a variety of texts and understand how they affect meaning.

As you read, it is important to keep in mind that the words on the page did not just magically appear there. A person who had real feelings wrote those words, and that person wrote for a reason. That is the real premise behind this next section, author's purpose and point of view.

- The author's purpose is why he or she wrote the text.
- The author's perspective is the author's feelings about that piece of text.

## AUTHOR'S PURPOSE

Most of us do not take the author into consideration when we are reading something. When an author writes, he or she does so with a specific purpose in mind. Authors have choices, and they choose their topics and their words very carefully in order to convey a particular purpose. Sometimes authors will come right out and state their purpose. More often, though, the purpose will be implied, and so you will need to use your reading skills to figure out the purpose.

Think about the last time you wrote something. It might have been an essay for your social studies class, a research paper for science, or a descriptive passage for English. Maybe it was a poem you wrote on your own or lyrics to a song. All of those pieces of writing were written for a purpose—to explain, to inform, to describe, to express feelings, to entertain.

There are many different reasons why authors write, as touched on above. Here are *some* of the reasons:

1. To inform, tell, explain
2. To persuade, convince
3. To express an opinion
4. To entertain
5. To express a mood, feeling, or tone

The author's purpose question can be found on the FCAT. When you see a question like this, you should ask yourself one question: WHY did the author write this piece of literature? What was he or she trying to convey to the audience? Look at the language the author chose; it should give you clues as to the purpose of the passage. Remember that the answer choices will most likely not be simple phrases or general categories such as "to inform" or "to persuade." The answers will be written so that you will have to use your reading skills to decipher the purpose. However, if you begin by asking yourself what you think the author's purpose is, you will be off to a good start.

**A Good Strategy to Use**

Try this strategy and the exercise that follows to see how you do.

1. **Ask Why:** Ask yourself WHY the author wrote this piece of writing. What was he or she trying to convey to the audience?
2. **Cover Up "To + A Verb" Endings:** If the answers come in the form of "to + a verb" (to entertain . . ., to warn . . ., to inform . . .), then try covering up the endings of the multiple-choice answers. If you cover up the endings of the answers, the correct choice may become clearer to you, or you may be able to eliminate answers that are obviously incorrect. If the answers are not in the "to + a verb" format, skip to the next step.
3. **Read the Entire Answer:** Read the entire answer for each choice. Make sure the one you have chosen (if you previously decided upon an answer) is the *best* answer and is supported by the text.

# EXERCISE

*Read the poem by Emily Dickinson below, and see if you can follow the previous strategy to figure out the correct answers to the questions below.*

> How happy is the little stone
> That rambles in the road alone,
> And doesn't care about careers,
> And exigencies never fears;
> Whose coat of elemental brown
> A passing universe put on;
> And independent as the sun,
> Associates or glows alone,
> Fulfilling absolute decree
> In casual simplicity.

What was the author's main purpose in writing this poem?

**A.** to describe the outward appearance of a stone
**B.** to express her feelings on the simplicity of a stone's life
**C.** to persuade the reader that the stone's life is better than hers
**D.** to entertain the reader with humorous anecdotes about stones

- **Step One:** What do YOU think the author's purpose is? Why did she write the poem?

  Write the answer here. _____

  _____

- **Step Two:** The answers come in the form of "to + verb," so cover up the answers so you only see the following:

  **A.** to describe
  **B.** to express
  **C.** to persuade
  **D.** to entertain

Does one of those fit with your idea or does one answer stand out and seem correct?

Which one(s)? _____

Can any answers be eliminated?

Which one(s)? _____

- **Step Three:** Read the complete answers for each choice and make sure the one you chose still seems correct, fits with your original idea, and is supported by the text.

Your Answer: _____

Why? _____

_____

## Check Your Answer

**The correct answer is B:** To express her feelings about the simplicity of a stone's life. You should have been able to eliminate Choice C right off the bat; the author is not trying to persuade someone of anything. There is not any persuasive language to support this choice. As you read each answer completely, you should have also been able to eliminate Choice D—there really is not anything humorous (or funny) in the poem. She does describe the outward appearance of the stone (A), but she does not focus on that. The best answer is Choice B – she is expressing how simple (and seemingly wonderful) the stone's life is.

### AUTHOR'S PERSPECTIVE

Just as every author has a purpose to writing, every author has a perspective (or opinion) toward the topic about which he or she is writing. Just like the author's purpose, the author's perspective may be stated or implied in the text.

On the FCAT, you will have to figure out what the author's perspective really is about the topic. Remember to look carefully at the words that the author has chosen to give you clues about what the perspective is. Author's perspective questions may be phrased in ways other than, "What is the author's perspective regarding . . . ?" For example,

- What is the author's opinion about . . . ?
- What does the author think of (or about) . . . ?
- How does the author feel about . . . ?
- What is the author's point of view about . . . ?

 **Note:** You may be asked to analyze author's purpose or author's perspective within one piece of text or across multiple pieces of texts. However, the strategy is the same, so do not panic!

As you answer author's purpose and author's perspective questions, think about how the author tries to get the reader to understand, identify with, or even go along with his or her purpose or perspective. These are particularly important in persuasive writing when the author wants the reader to side with his perspective. What does the author use in his writing to convince his audience? Some examples of possible methods of appeal include:

1. Specific examples
2. Facts and statistics
3. Opinions from influential people and/or experts
4. Emotional pleas or influences
5. Descriptive language and/or details
6. Use of humor
7. Logical reasoning

 **Note:** Looking at these methods of appeal may give you better insight into the author's purpose and/or perspective!

## FCAT PRACTICE QUESTIONS

**Directions:** *Read the passage "Against Gun Control" before answering questions 1–6.*

### Against Gun Control
by Norman L. Lunger

Gun-rights supporters have their own vision of the way society should work. In that vision, guns play an important part in bolstering individual freedoms and protecting private citizens from both crime and governmental tyranny. Their position is that guns both save lives and reduce crime. Beyond that, gun-rights supporters argue that gun control is just plain unworkable.

**Saving Lives and Property With Guns.** One of the most popular features in the NRA-produced *American Rifleman* magazine relates the experiences of gun owners who have used their weapons in self-defense. There's the woman in Washington State who grabbed a handgun and chased a burglar from her bedroom. And the convenience store clerk in Florida who shot a robber in the chest. And the couple in Arkansas who were accosted by two would-be robbers outside their home and exchanged shots with them, killing one. And the group of neighbors in New Mexico who responded to a woman's summons and helped corner a burglar, with one neighbor holding the suspect at gunpoint until the police arrived. Gun-rights supporters see such stories as proof of the effectiveness of guns in saving lives and property.

Even gun owners who have never used their guns for self-defense find solace in the fact that the gun is there if needed. As NRA research director Paul Blackman told ABC news: "There is potent psychological benefit in having a gun—like [having] iron bars or an alarm system."

There are also stories about what happens when people don't have guns when they need them. In October 1991, an angry man crashed his pickup into a cafeteria in Killeen, Texas, jumped out of the truck, and opened fire with two semiautomatic pistols. He killed twenty-two people and wounded twenty in the worst gun massacre in U.S. history. Suzanna Gratia managed to crawl to safety but lost both her parents in the massacre. She was heart-broken that she had not been carrying her gun in her purse that day. If someone in the cafeteria had had a gun, she told a TV reporter, the massacre might have been stopped. (Some years later, Ms. Gratia—now Dr. Gratia-Hupp—was elected to the Texas state legislature as a strong advocate of gun rights.)

From the gun-control side, such stories seem less than convincing. Supporters of gun control cite other stories about guns intended for self-defense—stories about assailants grabbing guns from gun owners' hands and using them against the owner, or about gun owners who awake in the night and shoot a family member they mistake for a burglar. Supporters of gun control also argue that gun owners themselves contribute unwittingly to the flow of guns to criminals. In one recent year, more than 600,000 guns were reported stolen from some 250,000 U.S. households. That's 600,000 more guns in the hands of bad guys.

Interpreting statistics about the success of using guns in self-defense is not always easy. Serious researchers sometimes disagree about the meaning of a particular set of data. According to Gary Kleck, a professor of criminology at Florida State University, there are about as many defensive uses of guns by citizens each year as there are criminal uses of guns. But another researcher, David Hemenway, calls Kleck's figures for defensive gun use "extreme overestimates."

Contrary to common opinion, Kleck argues, people who wield guns in self-defense against robberies and assaults are less likely to be injured than are victims who do not resist. They are also less likely to lose their money or their valuables. Citing interviews with people in prison, Kleck says that criminals who think a potential victim has a gun will often pick another victim instead, meaning that gun possession can serve as a protection against crime. "Guns," summarizes Kleck, "are a source of both social order and disorder, depending on who uses them . . . ."

Supporters of gun rights argue that the best way to attack crime is to establish stiff laws against the use of guns in crime and to strictly enforce those laws. "I think we've got enough laws on the books [about guns]," says John Ashcroft, U.S. attorney general in the administration of President George W. Bush. "I think what we need is tougher enforcement." A related thought is expressed by a bumper sticker: "GUN CONTROL ISN'T CRIME CONTROL."

—From *Big Bang: The Loud Debate over Gun Control*
by Norman L. Lunger. © 2002. Used by permission of
The Millbrook Press, Inc. All rights reserved.

*Answer questions 1–6. Base your answers on the reading passage "Against Gun Control."*

1. Read this sentence from the passage:

   **In that vision, guns play an important part in bolstering individual freedoms and protecting private citizens from both crime and governmental tyranny.**

   What does *bolstering* mean?
   A. altering
   B. ending
   C. improving
   D. saving

2. What is the author's main purpose in writing the passage?
   F. to persuade people to buy guns to protect themselves
   G. to entertain people with interesting gun-control facts
   H. to convince people that gun-control is, for the most part, unnecessary
   I. to warn people who own guns that they may injure a family member

3. What is the author's perspective on gun control?
   A. Gun control is unnecessary in today's overly violent society.
   B. Gun control is necessary in order to prevent more gun-related crimes.
   C. Gun control is necessary because guns bring about more crimes than they prevent.
   D. Gun control is unnecessary since guns protect people physically and psychologically.

4. What is the main idea of the passage?
   F. Gun control is just plain unworkable.
   G. Guns both save lives and reduce crime.
   H. Gun owners use their weapons in self-defense.
   I. Gun owners contribute unwittingly to the flow of guns to criminals.

5. How does the author organize the passage "Against Gun Control"?
   A. He writes mainly about his own personal experiences with firearms.
   B. He presents the most important information first and then moves on to less relevant details.
   C. He presents an argument, then supports it with anecdotal stories, statistics, and other evidence.
   D. He states the problem of too much gun control and then gives multiple solutions to the problem.

6. What is the U.S. attorney general's opinion on the subject of gun control?
   F. He wants fewer people to break the law.
   G. He feels that there should be stricter gun control laws.
   H. He asserts that more gun control will equal less violence.
   I. He agrees with the author that there are enough gun control laws.

## *Check Your Answers*

1. **C** *(Word Relationships)* In order to figure out the correct answer to this question, you should go back to the passage and read what comes before the sentence in the question since the sentence makes reference to a specific "vision." If you look back at the passage, you will see that it says, "Gun-rights supporters have their own vision of the way society should work." Now you know that the vision is that of the gun-rights supporters. That is a very important context clue. Once you know that, you should be able to figure out that gun-rights supporters would think that guns *improve* individual freedoms more than anything else.

2. **H** *(Author's Purpose)* After reading the passage in its entirety, hopefully you will conclude that the author is primarily against gun control. The passage is definitely persuasive in nature. However, it is not so persuasive that it is encouraging people to go out and buy guns as in Choice A. Although there are many facts presented about guns and gun control, the purpose of the article is clearly not just to entertain us with gun facts (Choice G). Finally, even though there is a reference to family members causing unnecessary deaths by having guns, that reference is only a detail in the passage and is not the author's main purpose (Choice I).

3. **D** *(Author's Perspective)* You should start out by eliminating two of the choices. The author's perspective is that gun control is either necessary or unnecessary. By reading the article, you should conclude that since the majority of what was presented was in favor of less gun control and was about the benefits of having a gun, the author's point of view is that gun control is unnecessary. Therefore, you can eliminate both Choices B and C, even though both were either stated or alluded to in the passage. *Again, just because you can find an answer in the reading does NOT mean that it is the correct answer!* Now you should be able to look at the two remaining answers and see that Choice A is not a good choice since in the passage there was very little, if any, allusions to society being *overly* violent.

4. **G** *(Main Idea)* Choice G is the best answer in this case. Choice F is a little too vague to be the main idea. Although Choices H and I are both details presented in the passage, neither is the main idea.

5. **C** *(Organizational Patterns)* Reading through each of the choices is the best way to determine which organizational pattern is used by the author. Choice A cannot be correct since the author does not relay any of his own experiences. Choice B may look tempting, but the facts presented all are equally important in the passage; in fact, the author actually ends with a quote from the attorney general—pretty important! Choice C is the correct answer. The author does give many stories, statistics, examples, and other evidence to back up his argument. Finally, Choice D cannot be correct as the author does not present any real solutions to this problem.

6. **I** *(Details)* The correct answer to this details question can be found in the last paragraph of the passage. If you read carefully, you will see that the attorney general is in agreement with the author. He thinks there are enough gun control laws. Be careful not to be tricked by Choice H; the attorney general does say he wants greater enforcement of laws that already exist, but that does not mean that there will be fewer criminals, and that does not explain what his opinion on gun control really is.

# Compare and Contrast

 **Standard LA.910.1.7.7:** The student will compare and contrast elements in multiple texts.

Compare and contrast questions on the FCAT will ask you how particular items within the reading are similar or different. Compare and contrast questions may be asked of literary or informational text, and often these questions will ask you to analyze information from more than one passage.

## THE DEFINITIONS

Everytime you make a decision, you compare and contrast items. So you are already familiar with the reasoning behind this skill, whether you realize it or not. However, you still need to know the terminology used by this type of question. If you do not know what it means to compare or to contrast items, answering the questions correctly will be impossible.

**Compare:** To tell how items are similar or the same
**Contrast:** To tell how items are different

## DEVICES

When comparing and contrasting items, it is often best to use some sort of organizer to sort out the details, especially when comparing or contrasting two or more different passages. For example, if an FCAT question asks you to compare and contrast two characters from a story, or from two different stories, it would be best if you had a quick and easy way to organize this information. There are a few good ways to do this.

- **Three-Column List:** This organizer has you simply make three columns. In the first column, you list items that are individual to the first character. In the center column, you list similarities between the two characters. In the third column, you list items that are individual to the second character. An example of a three-column list comparing apples and oranges would look like this:

| Apple | Similarities | Orange |
|---|---|---|
| Red | Round | Orange |
| Has smooth skin | Has skin | Has bumpy skin |
| Has a stem | Has seeds | No stem |
| No sections | Fruit | Has sections |

- **Venn Diagram:** This organizer is similar to the three-column list but uses circles instead of columns. Where the two circles overlap, you write similarities between the two characters. In the spaces of the circles on either side, you fill in differences. A Venn diagram comparing apples and oranges would look something like this:

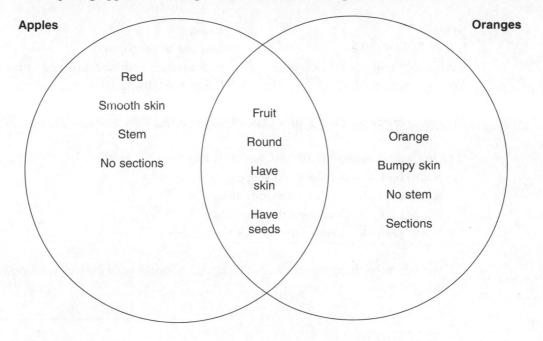

**Apples**                                                                 **Oranges**

Red

Smooth skin                    Fruit

Stem                           Round              Orange

No sections                    Have               Bumpy skin
                               skin
                                                  No stem
                               Have
                               seeds              Sections

 **Note:** These organizational devices are also useful in writing essays.

## LITERARY PASSAGES

Within literary passages, you may be asked to compare and/or contrast some of the following things:

- Characters
- Conflict
- Theme
- Organizational patterns
- Setting
- Tone
- Descriptions and imagery (language that appeals to the senses)

# EXERCISE

*Compare and contrast the two haiku below. Use a Venn diagram or a three-column list as a graphic organizer.*

**Snow**
Silent, falling flakes
Each a diff'rent pattern, shape
Lovely, quiet, cold

**Leaves**
Drifting to the ground
Red, orange, yellow, flame and fire
Crisp, crunchy, fall

*Now answer the following questions on these two haiku.*

1. One way these two haiku are similar is that they
   A. are both about colors and shapes.
   B. are both about things that are falling.
   C. are both about seasons that are cold.
   D. are both about times that are lovely and quiet.

2. Explain how these two haiku are different. Support your answer with details and information from the poems.

   _____

   _____

   _____

   _____

   _____

   _____

   _____

   _____

## Check Your Answers

1. **B**  Both poems are about things that are falling: leaves and snow. All of the other answer choices are partially correct, but none can be applied to both poems.

2. A good response would include at least two to three examples (and more if space allowed) of how the poems are different. Some possible items that might be included in the response include the following:

   • One poem is about fall, and the other is about winter.
   • One poem is about leaves falling, and the other is about snow falling.
   • One poem focuses on patterns and shapes, and the other focuses on colors and fire.
   • One poem is about quiet and cold, and the other is about crunchy and crispy.

**INFORMATIONAL TEXT**

Within informational text, you may be asked to compare and contrast some of the following items:

- Author's purpose
- Author's perspective
- Main idea
- Description or imagery
- Organizational patterns
- Causes and/or effects
- Subjects
- Topics

**A SIMPLE STRATEGY**

When you encounter multiple-choice questions on the FCAT that ask you to compare and contrast ideas, you can use a simple strategy in order to answer the questions correctly. You must first go back to the passage and find the items being compared and/or contrasted. Then look at the choices of answers. As you find each in the passage, underline it. Use this strategy to eliminate answers that cannot be correct. Also, you may be able to use information from other questions to help you find correct answers. This is true of all of the standards tested, not just compare and contrast.

## FCAT READING PRACTICE

**Directions:** *Read both "The Boy That Is Good Does Mind His Book Well" and "School the American Way" before answering questions 1–7.*

### The Boy That Is Good Does Mind His Book Well
by Ruth Tenzer Feldman

The typical colonial school day followed a well-established routine. The citizens of Flatbush, New York, instructed their schoolmaster to ring a bell to start school, a practice that was probably widespread. The school day usually lasted for a few hours in the morning, then a few more hours after lunch. School rules in New Haven, Connecticut, required the schoolmaster to take the roll twice a day and to mark down absences and tardiness. New England boys were expected to bow when they entered and left school and to stay in their assigned seats. Everywhere in the colonies, school days usually began and ended with prayer.

When it was time for orthography—spelling—the whole class bellowed out each word in syllables, then the proper spelling. If words were misspelled, the guilty classmate would be identified, or the whole class would have to spell the word again. When reading aloud, students were instructed to read fast, to mind the "stops and marks"—punctuation—and to speak up.

Schools made do with what was available. Often students wrote with sticks on a dirt floor. Some students wrote with soft stone on boards that had been blackened with a mixture of egg mixture and the carbon of charred potato. Other students used charcoal to write on thin pieces of wood. Since penmanship—good handwriting with fancy flourishes—was sometimes more important than correct spelling, students spent hours practicing handwriting. They copied passages into books of rag paper, using ink pens made of goose quills. Primers—reading books—explained how to make the ink, and students learned that brandy and salt would keep it from freezing or getting moldy.

Used in both church and school, primers were originally prayer books with an alphabet added. The most popular primer throughout the colonies was *The New England Primer*, which first appeared in about 1690. It included rhymed alphabets, religious essays and poems, and instructive questions and answers. Most homes had a copy of this primer; adults read it, too. Students had to buy their own primers, and they often wrote warnings like this one on the inside front page:

Isaac Greenwood is my name,
Steal not this book for fear of shame.
And if this book should chance to roam,
Just box its ears and send it home.

Latin grammar books were called accidences. The most popular one was written by Ezekiel Cheever, master of Boston Latin School from 1670 until his death in 1708. Cheever's *Accidence, a Short Introduction to the Latin Tongue* was the only schoolbook of completely American origin before the Revolutionary War.

Although all students learned to read and write, fewer students could cipher—do arithmetic. Arithmetic textbooks were rare. Instead, students learned rules and studied problems from "sum books," hand-printed by teachers. Most students did not progress beyond the "single rule of three," which is essentially basic algebra, as shown in this problem from a sum book: "If 13 yards of Cloth cost 39 dollars, how many yards of the same may be bought for 156 dollars?"

Teachers also used the Bible to teach reading, penmanship, spelling, and even arithmetic. They were expected to catechize their students—ask questions about religion for which answers were to be memorized—and were sometimes required to attend church services where students repeated the catechism.

Most towns permitted schoolmasters to give "due correccions" in moderation, even for bad behavior out of school. Students who were simply unprepared for class were often punished as well. Boys might be hit with a birch rod, a whip, or a flat piece of wood called a ferule. Girls might have to stand in the corner or sit on a one-legged stool called a uniped. Children who misbehaved in dame school were sometimes tapped on the head with a thimble; pinned to the dame's apron; or made to wear dunce caps, huge leather spectacles, or large labels that said, "Idle Boy." Those in Dutch schools were rapped on the palm with a piece of wood. A common punishment for a boy was to have to sit with the girls.

# School the American Way
by Ruth Tenzer Feldman

The typical American school of the early nineteenth century was not much different from the typical colonial school. Students recited their lessons out loud, and teachers did not hesitate to administer punishment. At Daniel Drake's "blab school" in the Ohio River valley, "the fashion was for the whole school to learn & say their lessons aloud." Daniel's teacher used a wooden switch to prod, gently or otherwise, students who were silent. (Abraham Lincoln and his sister, Sarah, attended a blab school in Indiana.)

The fictitious schoolmaster Ichabod Crane, in Washington Irving's short story "The Legend of Sleepy Hollow" (1819–1820), "swayed a ferrule, that sceptre of despotic power." The real school Irving had attended in New York City had been taught by a Revolutionary War veteran who, like Crane, did not "spare the rod." (Since Irving hated to watch this punishment, which the teacher inflicted on boys after the girls were dismissed, he was allowed to leave when the girls did.)

Schoolwork, too, was much the same as it had been in colonial times, although early nineteenth-century students learned about the geography of the new United States. Using familiar tunes like "Yankee Doodle" and "Go Tell Aunt Rhody," children sang geographical facts about the nation. Songs usually included the name of a state, its capital, and the river that ran through the capital.

In the 1830's, William McGuffey created a set of reading books with different levels of difficulty. Although there were other readers, McGuffey's *Eclectic Readers* (1836, 1837) were among the most popular. Selections such as the story of George Washington and the cherry tree and descriptions of Washington as "the Moses of the United States" were designed to create an American identity. McGuffey was a Presbyterian minister, and his books, like most textbooks then, had a Protestant bias. They included moral lessons, such as "Respect for Sabbath Rewarded," and instructed poor students to be satisfied with their station in life.

Students studied orthography, often consulting Noah Webster's dictionary and his spelling guide nicknamed the Blue-Backed Speller. First published in the late 1700's, this speller was used well into the twentieth century. Spell-downs (spelling contests) were common, with students vying for prizes—usually maps or pictures. Some students learned to spell words by memorizing a sentence, such as "**A rat in the house may eat the ice cream.**" Sometimes, entire communities had contests to see if a local celebrity could "spell down" the teacher. Modern spelling bees harken back to this activity.

Established in 1821, Boston's English Classical School was the first place we would call a high school. Offering instruction to older children, the school was supported by taxes and controlled by public authorities. By the 1850's, high schools were operating in about eighty American cities. The schools usually offered a classical program, emphasizing Greek and Latin in preparation for college; an English program that included literature, writing, and about sixteen other subjects (such as astronomy, history, and logic); and a two-year "normal" program to train students to become teachers. Because parents often needed teenage children to help support the family with paying jobs or to work on the family farm, few students attended high schools. Fewer graduated.

*Answer questions 1–7. Base your answers on both "The Boy That Is Good Does Mind His Book Well" and "School the American Way."*

1. What was one way in which the subject matter of schools in the nineteenth century was different from the subject matter of colonial schools?
   A. It included arithmetic.
   B. It included geography.
   C. It included orthography.
   D. It included religious instruction.

2. Punishment for students in both colonial and nineteenth-century America included
   F. spelling words out loud.
   G. being hit with a switch.
   H. memorizing catechism.
   I. writing with a stick on the dirt floor.

3. Orthography changed from the colonial times to the nineteenth century in that in the nineteenth century,
   A. students used McGuffey's *Eclectic Readers*.
   B. students went on to study orthography in high school.
   C. students sang songs to help them remember correct spelling.
   D. students used Webster's dictionary and the Blue-Backed Speller.

4. What happened when a student misspelled a word during spelling lessons?
   F. The guilty student had to be identified.
   G. The student was hit with a wooden switch.
   H. The student had to write a warning inside of his primer.
   I. The whole class had to use sticks to write their lessons on the dirt floor.

5. Read the following sentence from "School the American Way."

   **Daniel's teacher used a wooden switch to prod, gently or otherwise, students who were silent.**

   What does *prod* mean?
   A. to reward
   B. to make fun of
   C. to urge to action
   D. to hit as punishment

6. Colonial schools were similar to schools of the nineteenth century in that
   F. both used McGuffey's set of reading books.
   G. both learned about the geography of the United States.
   H. both had children attending elementary and high school.
   I. both used the method of reciting lessons aloud to learn material.

7. How are the public schools of today different from both colonial and nineteenth-century schools?
   A. In today's public schools we no longer teach orthography.
   B. In today's public schools we do not regularly use textbooks.
   C. In today's public schools we do punish students by whipping them.
   D. In today's public schools we do not teach subjects such as arithmetic or geography.

## Check Your Answers

1. **B** *(Compare and Contrast)* To answer this question correctly, you need to refer back to the passages. If you marked up the passages as you read, you should be able to find the answer more quickly and easily. Specifically in the third paragraph of "School the American Way," it says that schools of the nineteenth century taught geography, which is different from colonial schools.

2. **G** *(Compare and Contrast)* In both the colonial period and the nineteenth century, American school teachers hit students with a switch as punishment. That fact is mentioned in both passages. If you go back to the passages and try to find each of the answer choices, you will see that the only one mentioned in BOTH passages is Choice G.

3. **D** *(Compare and Contrast)* To answer this question, you first need to understand from the reading that *orthography* is simply *spelling*. Then, once again, if you go back to the passages, you will see that in the nineteenth century, the students used Webster's dictionary and the Blue-Backed Speller (Choice D). Although students did use McGuffey's *Eclectic Reader* in the nineteenth century (Choice A), they did not use them for spelling. Choices B and C contain only partially correct information.

4. **F** *(Details)* If you read carefully in the first passage, you will see that a student who misspelled a word during orthography had to be identified or the whole class had to spell the word again. All of the other answer choices were items mentioned in the reading passage but do not correctly answer the question.

5. **C** *(Context Clues)* If you go back to the first paragraph of "School the American Way," you will see that *prod* is being used in reference to punishment. You should be able to eliminate Choice A—*to reward*—once you note this. You will also be able to eliminate Choice B since it does not really make sense *to make fun of* someone using a wooden switch. You may be tempted to choose Choice D as the correct answer, but *to prod* does not mean *to hit*. The key context clue is the word *gently*. This should help you to choose the correct answer, Choice C—*to urge into action*. The other context clue should be that the switch was prodding those "who were silent" to get them to speak out loud.

6. **I** *(Compare and Contrast)* If you read back through the two passages, you will find that everything mentioned in the answer choices come from schools of the nineteenth century, except for Choice I. In both colonial and nineteenth-century schools, students recited their lessons aloud in order to learn the material.

7. **C** *(Compare and Contrast)* This question requires you to take the information that you read from both passages and compare it to the schools of today. Reading through the answer choices you should realize that in today's schools we do still teach orthography or spelling (Choice A); we do still use textbooks (Choice B); and we do teach both math and geography (Choice D). The correct answer is Choice C; we no longer hit or whip students in public schools.

# Cause and Effect

**Standard LA.910.1.7.4:** The student will identify cause-and-effect relationships in text.

Cause and effect questions on the FCAT may be asked for both kinds of reading: literary and informational. Additionally, you may be asked to identify cause and effect relationships within a passage or across multiple passages.

## A SIMPLE EXPLANATION

Most everyone realizes that cause and effect relationships exist in every aspect of life. For example, a lost pacifier might *cause* a baby to cry, while an *effect* of not brushing your teeth might be cavities. Look for these types of relationships in your reading to help figure out cause and effect questions.

A **cause** is the reason why something happens. An **effect** is the end result.

## THE "WHY" FACTOR

The best way to identify a cause and effect question is that it contains the word "why." If a questions asks you "why" about anything in the text, you can bet that it will be a cause and effect question. If you come across this type of question, you should try to find the "because" answer in the passage.

• **Strategy:** If you find yourself with a "why" MC question, you should search for the "because" answer in the passage. For example, you might be asked a question like the following:

According to the author, why do poachers hunt elephants?

You should immediately return to the passage, and, hopefully by using what you marked up during your first read, find the answer quickly. Phrase the answer in your own words:

Because the poachers want to obtain their tusks.

Then see if you can match your answer to the answers provided. (You should be able to do this, even without the reading passage.)

A. Poachers need the elephant meat to survive.
B. Poachers want to move the elephants to national parks.
C. Poachers sell the ivory tusks for a great deal of money.
D. Poachers use the money from elephants to support their families.

You should be able to match your answer to one of the choices (C) even though the word "because" is not there. Be sure that the answer that you choose is supported by the reading. Choice D may sound like a correct answer and may even be true, but if it is not in the passage, then it cannot be a correct answer.

## THE OTHER SIDE

Although some cause and effect questions may be asked with the word "why," there are other types of cause and effect questions. Consider some of the following:

- What is the *reason* . . . ?
- What were the *effects* of . . . ?
- What are the *causes* of . . . ?
- What was the *outcome* . . . ?
- What *result* . . . ?

Just remember this: everything has a cause and/or an effect. When you encounter a cause/effect question, go back to the passage and look for the causes or the effects. They may be stated directly, or they may be implied (which means that there will be clues but you must figure out the answers).

**Remember:** No matter what, make sure the answer that you choose is supported logically by the reading.

# FCAT PRACTICE QUESTIONS

Read the following passages, "Marine Iguana Adaptations" and "The Galapagos Tortoise" before answering questions 1–7.

## Marine Iguana Adaptations
### by James Barter

The Galapagos marine iguana has evolved more adaptations for survival than any other species on the islands. The majority of its adaptations allow it to survive in the marine environment. Because of their adaptation to the ocean, they have survived better than any other Galapagos land animal, with a population throughout all of the islands of between two and three hundred thousand.

Marine iguanas have vertically flat tails that they use in a whipping motion to propel them through the water, and all four of their feet are partially webbed for the same purpose. Although they warm themselves on the rocks, they feed exclusively on seaweed in cold, shallow waters. Capable of holding their breath for up to one hour, they have been seen as deep as fifty-five feet.

Modern biologists who have performed detailed analyses of the marine iguana have discovered additional survival techniques of the species. It is the only known air-breathing animal capable of drinking saltwater as a normal part of its diet. The marine iguana possesses a salt filtration system that removes the salt from its blood, depositing it in sacks behind the eyes. When the salt sacks are full, the iguana excretes the salt through its nostrils in a sneezing action. When threatened, they will sneeze salt to ward off aggressive predators.

Iguanas are cold-blooded animals whose body temperatures are determined by their immediate surroundings. Their temperature must be kept high to remain active, and when they plunge into the cold ocean, their temperature plummets quickly. To avoid dropping to dangerously low temperatures, they have adapted the ability to survive for long periods in the cold water by shunting blood away from their body surface to conserve heat and by drastically reducing their heart rates to conserve oxygen on deep dives.

Marine iguanas have also developed longer claws than the land species to help them cling to rocks while feeding and avoid being dislodged by violent waves. When exiting the water on to volcanic rock, their long claws also assist them in gripping and scrambling up the rocks where they rest and warm their bodies in the sun.

## The Galapagos Tortoise
### by James Barter

Although diversity makes each tortoise sub-species unique, the species as a whole has a great deal in common that has sustained its existence. One of the survival techniques, which has enabled the Galapagos tortoise to persevere in the desert environment, is a remarkably slow metabolism. Metabolism is the chemical conversion of food into energy. Some species, such as the hummingbird, have a remarkably high rate of metabolism, necessitating constant eating to remain alive. The survival advantage of having such a slow metabolism is that tortoises have been known to survive for up to one year without eating or drinking. Their slow metabolism also explains their long life expectancy. One tortoise that was presented to the queen of Tonga by English explorer Captain James Cook during the 1770s lived until 1966.

Regardless of their ability to adapt to many habitats, Galapagos tortoises are the most endangered species on the islands. Three tortoises are the most endangered species on the islands. Three tortoise species are known to have become extinct during the 1900s, and a fourth has a population of one and will become extinct when that lone survivor dies. There are a number of reasons for the unfortunate plight of these reptiles. One reason why several species of tortoises remain in danger of extinction is because females lay only two to sixteen eggs per year. This is a low rate compared to a sea turtle, which may lay six hundred eggs annually. A second reason relates to their longevity. Although they may live for two hundred years, this longevity means that they do not reach sexual maturity until they are quite old, and many die before they are able to reproduce.

—From *The Galapagos Islands.* © 2002 Gale, a part of Cengage Learning, Inc. Reproduced by permission. *www.cengage.com/permissions*

*Answer questions 1–7. Base your answers on both "Marine Iguana Adaptations" and "The Galapagos Tortoise."*

1. What effect does the Galapagos tortoise's slow metabolism have on its ability to survive in a desert environment?
   A. It can more easily survive because it is cold-blooded.
   B. It can more easily survive because it can live for 200 years.
   C. It can more easily survive because it needs to eat constantly to stay alive.
   D. It can more easily survive because the tortoise does not need to eat very often.

2. Why has the marine iguana been able to survive better than any other Galapagos creature?
   F. because it can drink saltwater as part of its everyday diet
   G. because it has been able to adapt to the ocean in many ways
   H. because it can survive for long periods of time in the cold ocean
   I. because of its vertically flat tail that it uses to propel itself through the water

3. What causes the marine iguana to sneeze salt out of its nostrils?
   A. full salt sacs behind its eyes
   B. a long period of holding its breath
   C. a drastic reduction in its heart rate
   D. as an invitation to aggressive predators

4. What is the main idea of the passage "Marine Iguana Adaptations"?
   F. The iguana has many adaptations that allow it to ward off predators.
   G. The iguana has developed many adaptations that have allowed it to survive in a marine habitat.
   H. The iguana has developed an extremely low metabolism that allows it to live for long periods without eating or drinking.
   I. The iguana has the ability to survive for long periods in cold water by shunting blood from the body surface to conserve heat.

5. Read the following sentence from the passage "The Galapagos Tortoise."

   **There are a number of reasons for the unfortunate plight of these reptiles.**

   What is the meaning of *plight* as it is used in this sentence?
   A. bad condition
   B. interesting existence
   C. place
   D. platitude

6. What has caused the Galapagos tortoise to become endangered?
   F. Galapagos tortoises are endangered because they live to very old ages.
   G. Galapagos tortoises are endangered due to a lack of a salt filtration system.
   H. Galapagos tortoises are endangered because only 2–16 of their 600 eggs ever hatch.
   I. Galapagos tortoises are endangered due to their extremely high rate of metabolism.

7. How is the marine iguana similar to the Galapagos tortoise?
   A. Each animal is on the endangered species list.
   B. Each animal has adapted to its specific environment.
   C. Each animal is able to swim in dangerously cold water.
   D. Each animal can control its metabolism and body temperature.

## Check Your Answers

1. **D** *(Cause and Effect)* The tortoise's slow metabolism allows it to have an easier existence in the desert because it does not have to eat or drink very often. The passage says the tortoise can survive by eating and drinking only once a year. All of the other choices are incorrect because they present incorrect information or do not answer the question.

2. **G**  *(Cause and Effect)* The marine iguana has been successful because, although it is a land animal, it has been able to adapt to life in the ocean. All of the other answers provide a particular adaptation that has helped the iguana. However, the adaptations as a whole have allowed for the iguana's success.

3. **A**  *(Cause and Effect)* The marine iguana sneezes for two reasons: because its salt sacs are full and because it is trying to ward off an aggressive predator (not invite predators as is indicated in Choice D). Choices B and C are details mentioned in the passage but not correct answers for this question.

4. **G**  *(Main Idea)* The main idea of the passage is how the marine iguana's adaptations have allowed it to become a successful ocean creature. The other answers are either incorrect information from the passage (such as Choice H) or just details from the passage that do not reflect the main idea.

5. **A**  *(Context Clues) Plight* means "bad condition." You must read more than just the sentence in order to get all the context clues for this word. Placing each word choice into the sentence should also help eliminate incorrect choices.

6. **F**  *(Cause and Effect)* The last paragraph of the passage on Galapagos tortoises gives two reasons why the tortoises are endangered. The first, Choice F, has to do with how long the tortoise lives (many die before they have a chance to reproduce)—this is the correct answer. You may be tempted by Choice H, but if you read carefully, you will see that the Galapagos tortoises lay only 2–16 eggs every year; it is the sea turtle that lays 600 eggs. Finally, Choice G about salt filtration actually refers to the marine iguana, and Choice I is completely incorrect: the Galapagos tortoise has a very low metabolism.

7. **B**  *(Compare and Contrast)* Each of these animals has been able to adapt to very specific environments, which is what makes them similar (Choice B). Choice A is incorrect because the marine iguana is not on the endangered species list. Choice C is incorrect as well: the marine iguana can swim in dangerously cold water but the Galapagos tortoise lives in the desert and there is nothing in the passage about its being able to swim in cold water. Choice D is also incorrect; neither animal can control its metabolism, and only the marine iguana can control its body temperature.

## CATEGORY 3: LITERARY ANALYSIS: FICTION AND NONFICTION

The questions on the FCAT that deal with literary analysis are the kinds of questions that you would probably expect to see in your English classes. These kinds of questions are generally asked on literary passages, such as poems, excerpts from short stories, autobiographies, and so on.

## Literary Elements

**Standard LA.910.2.1.5:** The student will analyze and develop an interpretation of a literary work by describing an author's use of literary elements (e.g., theme, point of view, characterization, setting, plot), and explain and analyze different elements of figurative language (e.g. simile, metaphor, personification, hyperbole, symbolism, allusion, imagery).

Note that although the standard mentions figurative language, figurative language will be assessed in the next standard. This section will just focus on literary elements. So let's take a look at some of those literary elements to be sure you understand each of them.

## PLOT

Every piece of literature has a plot. **Plot is simply the sequence of events,** or how things happen in a story. Through the development of plot, the other literary elements are developed and/or revealed, such as the setting, theme, characters, conflict, and tone. Plot includes rising action (or all the events leading up to the high point or turning point in the story, also called the climax), the **climax**, the falling action (the events that occur after the climax), and the **resolution** (how the story is wrapped up or how the problem is solved). Because plot is the sequence of events in the story, it also includes **flashback** (when the story flashes to a time prior to the present to show events that occurred earlier) and **foreshadowing** (when the author gives hints of what is going to happen later in the story).

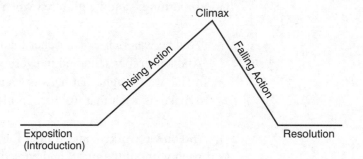

On the FCAT, plot questions will generally be questions about what happened in the passage. The questions will try to figure out if you understand the events of the story. Included in plot questions can be questions on setting and theme.

 **Setting:** The setting of a piece of literature is the time and place of the action.

Setting can be very specific or very general. For example, time can be as specific as the day of the week, the month, the season, or the year; or it might be as general as the past, present, or future. The same goes for the place. A place might be a specific town, city, country, or just someone's house in a small town. As you complete your first read of the passage, you should look for clues about the setting and underline them as you find them.

 **Theme:** The theme of a piece of literature is the message that the author is trying to convey to the reader.

The theme is very much like the purpose in a piece of informational text. What is tricky about theme is that very rarely does the author come right out and tell you the message of what he or she is writing. Instead, you need to interpret the theme through your reading and understanding of the plot, characters, conflict, and tone.

# EXERCISE

*Read the following poem, "Richard Cory," by Edwin Arlington Robinson, and answer the questions on **plot** that follow.*

## "Richard Cory"
by Edwin Arlington Robinson, from *Children of the Night,* 1897

Whenever Richard Cory went down town,
We people on the pavement looked at him:
He was a gentleman from sole to crown,
Clean favored, and imperially slim.

And he was always quietly arrayed,
And he was always human when he talked;
But still he fluttered pulses when he said,
"Good-morning," and he glittered when he walked.

And he was rich—yes, richer than a king—
And admirably schooled in every grace;
In fine we thought that he was everything
To make us wish that we were in his place.

So on we worked, and waited for the light,
And went without the meat, and cursed the bread;
And Richard Cory, one calm summer night,
Went home and put a bullet through his head.

1. Why did the townspeople "curse the bread"?
   A. because that is all they had to eat
   B. because they did not have any bread
   C. because they were waiting for the light
   D. because they wanted Richard to bring them bread

2. What is the theme of the poem "Richard Cory"?
   F. Greedy people are very bad people.
   G. Money does not equal happiness.
   H. The poor sometimes murder the rich.
   I. Money causes people to commit suicide

3. What is the setting of the poem "Richard Cory"?
   A. a castle
   B. a hospital
   C. a school
   D. a town

## Check Your Answers

1. **A** *(Literary Elements—Plot)* The townspeople "cursed the bread" because that was all that they had to eat. Bread was for the poor and meat was for the rich; they had no meat. They were poor—unlike Richard Cory.

2. **G** *(Literary Elements—Theme)* The theme of the poem is that money does not equal happiness; Richard Cory shot himself even though he had a great deal of money. Obviously, his money did not make him happy, as the townspeople thought that it did.

3. **D** *(Literary Elements—Setting)* The setting of the poem (the place in this case) is in the town. The only other answer that could possibly be considered is a castle, since Richard Cory is described as a king, but if you read the poem carefully, you will realize that he is not a king at all.

## CHARACTERS

Characters and character development are very important to a piece of literature. The characters in a piece of literature are the people in the story, but keep in mind that characters can also include animals (like in *Charlotte's Web*), fantasy creatures (like in *Harry Potter* books), or machines/robots (like in the *Terminator* movies). How the characters interact with each other is often what makes the story interesting and creates conflicts or problems. Characters sometimes also change within a story. Just like people in real life, characters can develop. Look for this development as you read. There may be questions about how the characters have changed and/or grown. Look for clues about characters, including:

1. How the characters dress or look
2. What the characters say—or what other characters say about them
3. How the characters act and interact

Additionally, it is important to consider a character's point of view. What is the character's opinion about particular events, ideas, or even other characters? All of these points are important to plot development.

## CONFLICT

Conflict is a very important literary element. Conflict is what, in many cases, creates the interest and excitement in a piece of literature. Conflict involves two things that are, in some way, fighting against each other. There are different types of conflict; below are the main four types.

> **Conflict is a struggle between opposing forces.**

- **Person vs. Person:** Two people in conflict, can be physical, emotional, verbal
- **Person vs. Society:** A person in conflict with some element that is valued by society (i.e., money, fame, morals)
- **Person vs. Nature:** A person in conflict with some element of nature, could be an animal, weather, fire, and so on
- **Person vs. Him/Herself:** A person in conflict or struggling with some inner element, some element of himself or herself, perhaps a decision or an emotion

Of course, there are other conflicts (such as person vs. machine and person vs. science). However, these are the main four. On the FCAT, you will probably encounter questions about conflict. They may ask you what the conflict in the story is, who it is between, or how it is resolved. The resolution of a conflict is simply the way the conflict (or problem) is resolved (or solved). When answering these types of questions, ask yourself what things are struggling against one another and how the struggle is finally ended.

# EXERCISE

*Read the following situations, and on the lines below, identify the conflict. Then decide on a resolution of your own. (Share if you are working on this with others.)*

1. The tornado was bearing down on the little Central Florida town. In the Brown household, all of the family members were peacefully sleeping, completely oblivious to the fact that an F5 tornado, the strongest tornado known, sometimes referred to as "the finger of God," was headed straight for their quaint little house.

   Conflict: _____ vs. _____

   Possible Resolution: _____

   _____

2. Michael had lied to his parents about going to the party last night. Because he knew that they would not approve, he had told them that he would be going to the movies with his buddy, Ron, and then spending the night at Ron's house. The problem was that while he was at the party (which was on the opposite side of town from the theater), his parents' car, which he had been driving, was rear-ended and rendered not drivable.

   Conflict: _____ vs. _____

   Possible Resolution: _____

   _____

3. Jennie and Mark were no longer speaking. Jennie had called Mark a "pig-headed rat," and, in turn, Mark called Jennie a "foolish Daddy's girl." The two had been friends and neighbors since they were three and had had arguments before. This time, though, it looked as if neither was willing even to consider speaking to the other.

   Conflict: _____ vs. _____

   Possible Resolution: _____

   _____

# EXERCISE

*Use the poem "Richard Cory" to answer the following questions on **character** and **conflict**.*

1. What did the townspeople think of Richard Cory?
   A. They thought that he was just an ordinary guy.
   B. They wished that they could be in his place.
   C. They thought he should share his money with them.
   D. They wondered if he should check into a mental hospital.

2. Who is the narrator of the poem?
   F. a king
   G. the author
   H. Richard Cory
   I. the townspeople

3. What words would the "people on the pavement" use to describe Richard Cory?
   A. They would describe Richard as crazy and scary.
   B. They would describe Richard as rich and unhappy.
   C. They would describe Richard as kinglike and stuck up.
   D. They would describe Richard as friendly and personable.

4. How is the conflict of this poem resolved?
   F. The townspeople commit Richard to an insane asylum.
   G. Richard commits suicide due to his extreme unhappiness.
   H. Richard shares his money with the townspeople to make more friends.
   I. The townspeople continued their hard work and waited for a better life.

## Check Your Answers

1. **B** *(Literary Elements—Character)* The townspeople wanted to be like Richard Cory. They greatly admired him and his money. They wished they were in his shoes; they thought money would bring them happiness. None had any idea of how unhappy Richard really was.

2. **I** *(Literary Elements—Character)* The "narrator" is the person who is telling the story. In this case, that person is the townspeople, "We people on the pavement."

3. **D** *(Literary Elements—Character)* The townspeople think that Richard is friendly: he said good morning and was "human when he talked." In other words, he was very down to earth, friendly, and normal. Although Richard was rich as a king, he was not stuck up (Choice C). There is nothing to make you think that the townspeople thought Richard was scary or crazy (Choice A), and although Richard was rich and unhappy (Choice D), the townspeople had no idea he was so unhappy.

4. **G** *(Literary Elements—Conflict)* The conflict of the poem is resolved when Richard kills himself. He is very unhappy and, sadly, that is how he resolves the issue within himself. Choices F and H cannot be correct because they are not events in the poem. Choice I might be tempting because the townspeople do continue to work hard and wait for a better life, but that does not resolve the conflict in the poem.

# Descriptive and Figurative Language (Literary Devices)

> **Standard LA.910.2.1.7:** The student will analyze, interpret, and evaluate an author's use of descriptive language (e.g., tone, irony, mood, imagery, pun, alliteration, onomatopoeia, allusion), figurative language (e.g., symbolism, metaphor, personification, hyperbole), common idioms, and mythological and literary allusions, and explain how they affect meaning in a variety of texts.

This standard covers many different types of descriptive and figurative language. Let's define some of these terms to ensure you understand questions that might be asked on the test.

- **Descriptive Language:** language that helps the author describe what he or she is trying to relate to the reader. There are many ways the author can do this; some are very obvious, and some take a little more work to understand. Here are some common types of descriptive language.
  - **Alliteration**—repetition of initial consonant sounds
    - Example: The **b**ig **b**rown **b**ear **b**linked his **b**eautiful **b**rown eyes.
  - **Allusion**—reference to a person, place, event (real or fictitious)
    - Example: "Chocolate is my Achilles heel." This means that chocolate is my weakness. The allusion is to Greek mythology and the warrior Achilles who could only be harmed if he was shot in the heel.
  - **Irony—can have different meanings:**
    - **Verbal:** when words are used to convey the opposite of what you really mean (as in sarcasm)
    - **Situational:** when the opposite of what is expected happens
      - Example of situational irony: Superman wins a contest and the prize is an airplane. (Ironic because Superman can already fly; he does not need a plane.)
    - **Dramatic:** when the reader or audience knows more than the characters in the story
  - **Imagery:** language that appeals to the senses
    - Example: The warm smell of chocolate cookies wafted through the bright sunny kitchen.
  - **Mood:** the feeling that a text conveys to a reader
    - Example: The detective story created a mysterious mood. Other examples of mood might be sarcastic, sadness, joy, anger, love, etc.
  - **Onomatopoeia:** words that sound like their meaning
    - Example: bang, sizzle, snap, splash, crack
  - **Pun:** a play on words
    - Example: An apple and orange make a great pair. (plays on the word "pair" because "pear" is also a fruit)
  - **Tone:** writer's attitude or feeling about his or her subject
    - Example: John's tone toward his teacher was angry and critical.
- **Figurative Language:** language that is not meant to be taken literally (does not mean what it actually says) For example, if someone says it is raining cats and dogs, that does not mean that cats and dogs are literally falling from the sky. It is a way for the author to get the reader to understand just how hard it is raining.
  - **Hyperbole:** extreme exaggeration for effect
    - Example: It was so hot you could fry an egg on the sidewalk.

- **Metaphor:** compares two unlike things
  - Example: Life is a journey of routes and destinations. (compares "life" to a "journey")
- **Personification:** giving human qualities to nonhuman entities
  - Example: The wind blew its cold breath down my neck as a walked home on a winter day. (Wind is given the human quality of having breath.)
- **Simile:** compares two unlike things using the words "like" or "as" or "than"
  - Example: That boy eats like a pig. (compares "boy" to a "pig")
- **Symbolism:** word or object that stands for/represents something else
  - Example: The eagle is a symbol for freedom and bravery.

# EXERCISE

*Try the following fill-in-the-blank exercise to test your knowledge of **descriptive** and **figurative language**. See if you can identify the correct literary device in each example below.*

_____ 1. She shook him until his very eyeballs rattled in his skull.

_____ 2. Bob can run as fast as a horse.

_____ 3. The high pitched scream of the kettle frightened me.

_____ 4. Six slippery snakes slithered down the slide.

_____ 5. The fog and full moon created a feeling of suspense.

_____ 6. He tried to run from the ghost, but his legs were rubber.

_____ 7. The red bars on the Canadian flag stand for the Atlantic and Pacific Oceans.

_____ 8. I used to be a carpenter, but then I got bored.

_____ 9. The brilliant sun caused the sand to glimmer and shine against the salty blue ocean.

_____10. The young man is considered a real Romeo when it comes to his girlfriend; he is always bringing her flowers, chocolates, and other gifts.

## Check Your Answers

1. Hyperbole (extreme exaggeration—you cannot literally make someone's eyeballs rattle)
2. Simile (comparison between two unlike things using words "like," "as," or "than"—Bob and horse)
3. Personification (tea kettle is given the human quality of being able to scream)
4. Alliteration (repetition of initial consonant sounds—all the "s's")
5. Mood (feeling conveyed by the text)
6. Metaphor (comparison between two unlike things—legs and rubber)
7. Symbol (something that stands for something else—the bars on the flag stand for or represent the oceans)
8. Pun (plays on the word "bored," which also sounds like "board," something a carpenter uses)
9. Imagery (descriptive words that appeal to any of the five senses—most of these words appeal to your sense of sight and taste: brilliant, glimmer, shine, salty, blue)
10. Allusion (refers to Romeo of the famous Shakespeare play *Romeo and Juliet,* refers to someone who is very romantic)

 You do not need to know the definition of these different literary devices—often the definitions will be provided in the answer choices—however, you do need to know how to correctly identify them within a piece of text.

# EXERCISE

*Use the poem "Richard Cory" to answer the following questions on **literary devices**, as well as a practice question on **context clues**.*

1.  What is the overall mood of the poem?
    A.  sad
    B.  dreary
    C.  humorous
    D.  matter-of-fact

2.  The first stanza of the poem states,

    **He was a gentleman from sole to crown,**
    **Clean favored, and imperially slim.**

    What does the word "imperially" mean in this sentence?
    F.  kingly
    G.  happily
    H.  extremely
    I.  impressively

3.  Read this line from the poem.

    **And he was rich—yes, richer than a king—**

    What literary device does the writer use in the line above?
    A.  simile, comparing Richard Cory to a king
    B.  hyperbole, exaggerating how rich Richard is
    C.  metaphor, comparing Richard Cory to royalty
    D.  personification, portraying Richard as a king

4.  Read these lines from the poem.

    **And he was always quietly arrayed,**
    **And he was always human when he talked;**

    What literary device does the writer use in the lines above?
    F.  metaphor, comparing Richard Cory to a quiet human being
    G.  irony, due to the fact that Richard was actually very snobby
    H.  imagery, creating a vivid picture of what Richard looked like
    I.  allusion, making a reference to what it is like to be a human being

### Check Your Answers

1. **D** *(Literary Devices—Figurative Language)* Although the subject matter of this poem is quite sad, the tone in which it is expressed is very much matter-of-fact, without much emotion put forth at all.

2. **F** *(Context Clues)* The word "imperially" means "kingly." The reference to "crown" should help you figure this out.

3. **A** *(Literary Devices—Figurative Language)* The first clue to your answer here should be that Richard is being compared to something (a king). That should tell you that the answer is either simile (Choice A) or metaphor (Choice C). Your second clue is that the comparison uses the word "than," which should tell you the literary device is a simile. Choice B is not correct because the author is not exaggerating how rich Richard Cory is. Choice D is not correct either as personification is giving human qualities to nonhuman things; Richard *is* a human!

4. **H** *(Literary Devices—Descriptive Language)* These lines are descriptions that are appealing to your senses, so the correct answer is Choice H, imagery. Choice F cannot be correct because a metaphor compares two unlike items and Richard actually is a quiet human being. Choice G cannot be correct either because there is nothing in the poem to indicate that Richard is snobby. Finally, Choice I cannot be correct since the author is not making a reference to what it is like to be human. Again, Richard is human, so it would not make sense to make a reference to that.

## Text Features

**Standard LA.910.2.2.1:** The student will analyze and evaluate information from text features (e.g., transitional devices, table of contents, glossary, index, bold or italicized text, headings, charts and graphs, illustrations, subheadings).

You will be evaluated on text features on the FCAT. That is why it is very important to look at everything that is presented in the passage. You need to look at the titles, pictures, captions, headings, bold text, author's notes, charts, graphs . . . everything! Anything that is included within the text is fair game for a question. Often questions on text features are not difficult; it is just that students forget to read these parts of the text.

In this particular standard, you are being evaluated on text features that are found in literary texts. Later, there will be a standard that evaluates text features in informational text. Let's practice with some of these types of questions.

# EXERCISE

*Read the following short passage "Summer Solitude," and answer the question on text features that follows.*

## Summer Solitude

Amid all the hustle and bustle of summer, sometimes I need to just take a break. One of my favorite things to do is to walk down the beach as the sun sets. I take off my shoes, roll up my pants, and just meander in and out of the warm surf. The water on my toes and the sun on my back are just the right recipe to strip away any stress from the day. The soothing smells of salty air and the cries of the seagulls above add to my feelings of peace. By the time I return from my walk, I feel like a brand new person.

Source: *www.freeimages.co.uk*

Based on the passage "Summer Solitude," which caption would be most appropriate for the picture?

    **A.** sunset on the beach
    **B.** footsteps in the sand
    **C.** the ocean draws near
    **D.** a peaceful day's ending

## Check Your Answer

Hopefully you chose Choice D as the correct answer. Although Choices B and C do describe what you see in the picture, they do not capture what is in the passage, and Choice A describes more of what is in the passage than what is in the picture. Choice D is the best answer as it matches both the image and the text.

# FCAT PRACTICE QUESTIONS

*The following is a literary passage as you might see on the FCAT. It may seem very lengthy, but keep in mind that FCAT passages can be as long as 1,500 words. Keep focused during your first read by interacting with the text. The questions that follow will be literary element questions as well as questions from the other benchmarks you have studied so far.*

**Remember:** As this is a literary piece, be looking for such things as setting, characters and character development, plot, conflict, and conflict resolution, as well as descriptive and figurative language.

*Read "Chapter One" from* My Antonia *before answering questions 1–7.*

## Chapter One
from *My Antonia* by Willa Cather

I first heard of Antonia on what seemed to me an interminable journey across the great midland plain of North America. I was ten years old then; I had lost both my father and mother within a year, and my Virginia relatives were sending me out to my grandparents, who lived in Nebraska. I traveled in the care of a mountain boy, Jake Marpole, one of the "hands" on my father's old farm under the Blue Ridge, who was now going West to work for my grandfather. Jake's experience of the world was not much wider than mine. He had never been in a railway train until the morning when we set out together to try our fortunes in a new world.

We went all the way in day-coaches, becoming more sticky and grimy with each stage of the journey. Jake bought everything the newsboys offered him: candy, oranges, brass collar buttons, a watch-charm, and for me a "Life of Jesse James," which I remember as one of the most satisfactory books I have ever read. Beyond Chicago we were under the protection of a friendly passenger conductor, who knew all about the country to which we were going and gave us a great deal of advice in exchange for our confidence. He seemed to us an experienced and worldly man who had been almost everywhere; in his conversation he threw out lightly the names of distant states and cities. He wore the rings and pins and badges of different fraternal orders to which he belonged. Even his cuff-buttons were engraved with hieroglyphics, and he was more inscribed than an Egyptian obelisk. Once when he sat down to chat, he told us that in the immigrant car ahead there was a family from "across the water" whose destination was the same as ours.

"They can't any of them speak English, except one little girl, and all she can say is 'We go Black Hawk, Nebraska.' She's not much older than you, twelve or thirteen, maybe, and she's as bright as a new dollar. Don't you want to go ahead and see her, Jimmy? She's got the pretty brown eyes, too!"

The last remark made me bashful, and I shook my head and settled down to "Jesse James." Jake nodded at me approvingly and said you were likely to get diseases from foreigners.

I do not remember crossing the Missouri River, or anything about the long day's journey through Nebraska. Probably by that time I had crossed so many rivers that I was dull to them. The only thing very noticeable about Nebraska was that it was still, all day long, still Nebraska.

I had been sleeping, curled up in a red plush seat, for a long while when we reached Black Hawk. Jake roused me and took me by the hand. We stumbled down from the train to a wooden siding, where men were running about with lanterns. I couldn't see any town, or even distant lights; we were surrounded by utter darkness. The engine was panting heavily after its long run. In the red glow from the fire-box, a group of people stood huddled together on the platform, encumbered by bundles and boxes. I knew this must be the immigrant family the conductor had told us about. The woman wore a fringed shawl tied over her head, and she carried a little tin trunk in her arms, hugging it as if it were a baby. There was an old man, tall and stooped. Two half-grown boys and a girl stood holding oil-cloth bundles, and a little girl clung to her mother's skirts. Presently a man with a lantern approached them and began to talk, shouting and exclaiming. I pricked up my ears, for it was positively the first time I had ever heard a foreign tongue.

Another lantern came along. A bantering voice called out: "Hello, are you Mr. Burden's folks? If you are, it's me you're looking for. I'm Otto Fuchs. I'm Mr. Burden's hired man, and I'm to drive you out. Hello, Jimmy, ain't you scared to come so far west?"

I looked up with interest at the new face in the lantern light. He might have stepped out of the pages of "Jesse James." He wore a sombrero hat, with a wide leather band and a bright buckle, and the ends of his moustache were twisted up stiffly, like little horns. He looked lively and ferocious, I thought, and as if he had a history. A long scar ran cross one cheek and drew the corner of his mouth up in a sinister curl. The top of his left ear was gone, and his skin was brown as an Indian's. Surely this was the face of a desperado. As he walked about the platform in his high-heeled boots, looking for our trunks, I saw that he was a rather slight man, quick and wiry, and light on his feet. He told us we had a long night drive ahead of us, and had better be on the hike. He led us to a hitching-bar where two farm wagons were tied, and I saw the foreign family crowding into one of them. The other was for us. Jake got on the front seat with Otto Fuchs, and I rode on the straw in the bottom of the wagon-box, covered up with a buffalo hide. The immigrants rumbled off into the empty darkness, and we followed them.

I tried to go to sleep, but the jolting made me bite my tongue, and I soon began to ache all over. When the straw settled down I had a hard bed. Cautiously I slipped from under the buffalo hide, got up on my knees and peered over the side of the wagon. There seemed to be nothing to see; no fences, no creeks or trees, no hills or fields. If there was a road, I could not make it out in the faint starlight. There was nothing but land—slightly undulating, I knew, because often our wheels ground against the brake as we went down into a hollow and lurched up again on the other side. I had the feeling that the world was left behind, that we had got over the edge of it, and were outside man's jurisdiction. I had never before looked up at the sky when there was not a familiar mountain ridge against it. But this was the complete dome of heaven, all there was of it. I did not believe that my dead father and mother were watching me from up there; they would still be looking for me at the sheepfold down by the creek, or along the white road that led to the mountain pastures. I had left even their spirits behind me. The wagon jolted on, carrying me I knew not whither. I don't think I was homesick. If we never arrived anywhere, it did not matter. Between that earth and that sky I felt erased, blotted out. I did not say my prayers that night: here, I felt, what would be would be.

—From *My Antonia* by Willa Cather, 1918

*Answer questions 1–7. Base your answers on "Chapter One" from* My Antonia.

1. What is the tone of the last paragraph of "Chapter One"?
   A. happy
   B. empty
   C. curious
   D. depressed

2. Read the following sentence from the passage.

   **A long scar ran cross one cheek and drew the corner of his mouth up in a sinister curl.**

   What is the meaning of *sinister*?
   F. evil
   G. hopeful
   H. kind
   I. smug

3. The conductor's remark about the little girl with the pretty brown eyes makes Jimmy feel bashful. What does this reveal about his character?
   A. He misses his mother's brown eyes.
   B. He dislikes the conductor of the train.
   C. He most likely has never had a girlfriend.
   D. He does not speak any languages but English.

4. What writing strategy does Willa Cather use to express the setting to the reader?
   F. use of an upbeat tone
   G. use of a believable theme
   H. use of complex characters
   I. use of descriptive language

5. Why was Jimmy moving to Nebraska?
   A. He wanted to live with his grandparents.
   B. He was hoping to meet Jesse James and Otto Fuchs.
   C. His best friend, Jake, was going out there to work for his grandfather.
   D. Both of his parents had died, and he needed someone to take care of him.

6. Read the sentence from the passage.

   **The engine was panting heavily after its long run.**

   What type of literary device does the author use in the sentence above?
   F. simile, comparing the engine to a running person
   G. allusion, referencing a particular person, idea, or event
   H. onomatopoeia, using a word that sounds like its meaning
   I. personification, giving the engine human-like characteristics

7. How do you know that this passage occurs at the beginning of the story?
   A. The passage is marked "Chapter One."
   B. The table of contents shows that information.
   C. By the tone that the author uses throughout the passage.
   D. By the author using the word "first" in the first paragraph.

## *Check Your Answers*

1. **B**   *(Literary Elements—Tone)* As soon as this question asks you about the last paragraph, you should go back to the text and reread or skim the paragraph to try to get a feel for the tone (of voice). Try to catch the feeling of the writing. As you read, you should begin to sense the emptiness that Jimmy is feeling. He does not even bother to pray because the emptiness is so strong. The next best answer would be *depressed* (Choice D). However, he is not really depressed; he does not have any feelings at all. You should be able to eliminate both Choices A and C. Jimmy is neither happy nor curious at this point.

2. **F**   *(Context Clues)* It is important to go back to the paragraph and read the other sentences describing Otto to use the context clues fully to figure out the meaning of the word *sinister*. If you plug in each word, you should be able to eliminate at least Choices G and H, *hopeful* and *kind*. You may have chosen smug as your answer, especially if you are not sure what *smug* means (self-satisfied), but the best answer is *evil*. Hopefully you got that idea from all of the surrounding details, specifically his long scar.

3. **C**   *(Literary Elements—Character Development)* Since Jimmy feels bashful (or shy) about the conductor's comment, he probably has never had a girlfriend. Being shy does not have anything to do with any of the other choices. Although Jimmy probably does miss his mother and he does not speak any other languages (Choices A and D), they do not have anything to do with why he feels bashful. Finally, nothing in the reading indicates that Jimmy dislikes the conductor (Choice B), even after he makes the comment.

4. **I**   *(Literary Elements—Setting)* Cather is very descriptive as she expresses the setting to the reader. She uses many details and a great deal of imagery. Although there are complex characters in the story (Choice H), they do not express the setting. The other choices (tone—Choice F and theme—Choice G) also have nothing to do with how the setting is relayed to the reader.

5. **D**   *(Details)* This is a straightforward details question. You need only to reread the first paragraph of the chapter to find this answer. Although some of the other choices include some correct information from the story, only Choice D is fully correct.

6. **I**   *(Literary Devices—Figurative Language)* In this sentence, you can see that the train engine is described as "panting heavily." This is a characteristic of a person, so the literary device being used is personification (Choice I). Although Choice F seems likely because in some ways the author is comparing the engine to a running person, there is no "like" or "as" in the comparison. Neither Choice G nor H can be correct as there is no onomatopoeia or allusion in the sentence.

7. **A**   *(Text Features)* If you are a careful reader, you will have noticed that this passage is actually marked "Chapter One," which tells you that this passage is at the beginning of the story (Choice A). You would be surprised, however, to know that many readers do not pay attention to text features such as headings. If you noticed the chapter heading, then the other answers should easily appear incorrect. There is no table of contents (Choice B); although the table of contents could give you that information. The tone does not give you the answer (Choice C); and just because the author uses the word "first" in the first paragraph (Choice D), that does not necessarily mean that the passage is at the beginning of the story.

# CATEGORY 4: INFORMATIONAL TEXT/RESEARCH PROCESS
## Research Process

 **Standard LA.910.6.2.2:** The student will organize, synthesize, analyze, and evaluate the validity and reliability of information from multiple sources (including primary and secondary sources) to draw conclusions using a variety of techniques, and correctly use standardized citations.

Wow! This standard is really complex! Let's analyze each part separately to see if we can figure out what kinds of questions you will be expected to answer.

To begin, note that this standard focuses on the following three items:

- Synthesizing information within or across texts
- Analyzing and evaluating information within or across texts
- Determining the validity and reliability of information within or across texts

Let's see if we can break things down a bit further to really get an understanding of what you will be expected to do.

This first part of the standard allows the FCAT to ask you a very wide variety of questions. Basically, you may be asked to do any of the following:

- **Organize:** to give structure to
- **Synthesize:** to bring together
- **Analyze:** to study the parts of a whole
- **Evaluate:** to determine the worth

### MULTIPLE SOURCES

Notice that each bullet point repeats the idea of "within or across texts." That means that you may be asked to use one piece of text or multiple pieces of text to answer your questions. For example, you may be asked to use more than one article or passage as well as graphics, including charts, maps, or photos, in order to come up with the correct answer. Or, you may be asked to identify a particular idea by using a photo and an article OR two different articles OR two articles and a graph. There really is no end to the combinations. However, all the text you deal with in the standard will be informational text and not literary.

### PRIMARY AND SECONDARY SOURCES

A *primary source* is a source used by a writer to provide first-hand information, experiences, and facts to the reader. For example, if you were writing a research paper on the career of a police officer and you needed a primary source in your paper, you might interview a police officer to get firsthand information for your paper. Sometimes the reader himself may be the primary source. If you were reading an article about horse training and the author himself had been training horses for the past ten years, then the experiences and information that he shared with you, the reader, would be primary source information. Other primary sources include:

- An autobiography
- A scientist's notes and observations
- A diary or journal entry
- Other eyewitness accounts (letters, historical documents, and so on)

A *secondary source* is a document that presents information that was originally presented somewhere else. In other words, it is not the firsthand account of the information. Most of the information text that you read is probably secondary source information. Some examples of secondary sources are newspapers, magazine articles, books, and encyclopedias.

## RELIABILITY AND VALIDITY

So what does it mean for a primary source to be reliable and valid? To answer those questions, you first need to look at these words one at a time.

**Reliable:** A reliable primary source is a source of information that is dependable; you can count on that source giving true and real information every time.
**Valid:** A primary source that is valid is a source of information that is correct. A valid source will not give you false information; you can count on that information being right or correct, NOT wrong or incorrect.

## MAKING THE DECISION

The FCAT will include questions that ask you to examine both the reliability and validity of primary source information. The good news is that more than likely the primary source will *be* both valid and reliable, and it will be your job to tell how you know. You may have to identify how an author is qualified to give information or how an author's experiences make that person a valid or reliable source. Those answers will always be in the information provided in the text. Your job is to identify this and perhaps understand.

Some words that indicate that a question is asking you about the reliability or validity of a source include:

- Evidence
- Qualifications
- Experience
- Expert
- Education

# EXERCISE

*Read the following beginning of a passage on feline behavior, and answer the two questions that follow. This should give you an idea what a question on primary source validity and reliability looks like.*

## Feline Behavior

Many people keep cats as pets, but few really consider what a cat's behavior really means. Scientist Cody Wells, a graduate of Columbia University, has been studying feline behavior at Cornell University for the past ten years. In that time, he has identified many different feline characteristics as well as what these characteristics indicate. In addition, Wells has charted the behavior of several different cats over their lifetimes and compared this behavior with the behavior of big cats in the wild.

1. The scientist mentioned in the passage seems qualified to offer reliable and valid information on felines because he
   A. has lived with big cats in the wild.
   B. is a graduate of Columbia University.
   C. owns several felines himself and has studied their behavior.
   D. has studied feline behavior for ten years at a renowned university.

2. What information from the passage leads you to believe that scientist Cody Wells is a reliable source of information about feline behavior?

   _____

   _____

   _____

   _____

   _____

   _____

   _____

   _____

## *Check Your Answers*

1. **D**  Choice D is the correct answer because *experience* in studying felines is what would make him both a reliable and valid source of information. In addition, the fact that his experience comes from studying at a renowned university like Cornell makes him an even more qualified source. Choice A is not correct since there is no mention in the article about Wells living with big cats in the wild (although he did study big cats). Choice C is incorrect for the same reason: nothing in the article supports the fact that Wells owns any cats himself. Finally, Choice B is not correct either. Admittedly, Columbia is a reputable university. However, just because Wells studied there does not mean he is an expert on feline behavior.

2.    A correct response to this question would have to include as much proof as possible from the passage that scientist Cody Wells is a reliable source of information concerning feline behavior. The following are examples of some information that could be included in your answer.

- Wells has been studying feline behavior for ten years.
- He has been studying this behavior at Cornell University.
- He has identified many different feline characteristics and what those characteristics indicate.
- He has charted the behavior of several cats over their lifetimes.
- He has compared domestic cat behavior with the behavior of big cats in the wild.

## IT IS REALLY RESEARCH

These kinds of questions are really evaluating (checking and deciding) if you can do the kinds of things you are supposed to do when you write a research paper. For example, imagine you are writing a paper on pollution and you come across information from an encyclopedia, the Internet, a book, and a magazine. The information includes both graphics (such as charts, graphs, photos, and so on) as well as text. How will you evaluate what information you will use in your paper? You have to be able to *recognize* that the information is applicable to your topic; *identify* what is appropriate and valuable; *analyze* it in order to weed out what is good, bad, or irrelevant information; *synthesize* the information into one paper; and *evaluate* every piece of information as well as your paper as a whole when you are finished. A part of this process includes determining the reliability and validity of information from both primary and secondary sources. So as you answer research process questions, imagine what you might do if you were writing an actual research paper. This may help you to better answer these types of questions.

# FCAT PRACTICE QUESTIONS

*Read the passage "A Ball of Fire" and the chart "Other Airship Disasters" before answering questions 1–7.*

## A Ball of Fire
by Victoria Sherrow

Hundreds of spectators waited on the airfield below the *Hindenburg*. Verna Thomas was among them. She recalled the weather that day. "It was raining very badly, an electrical storm," Thomas said.

Some spectators waved. Flashbulbs popped as they photographed the famous airship and its smiling passengers. Newsreel photographers aimed their movie cameras at the *Hindenburg*. Reporters wrote in their notebooks. Radio announcer Herbert Morrison called the airship "a great floating palace." He told his listeners, "The sun is striking the windows . . . and sparkling like glittering jewels against a background of black velvet." Morrison continued his report: "It's coming down out of the sky pointed directly at us."

The *Hindenburg* was about two hundred feet above the ground. Suddenly the ship began to shake. Passengers heard a loud noise. People on the ground gasped. They stared at the airship in horror. Flames were shooting from the *Hindenburg*. Pieces of the ship fell to the ground in flames. Spectators ran away, screaming.

Passengers later recalled feeling a jolt. Crew member Eugen Bentele said, "My first thought was that the landing crew has pulled too hard and something had broken. But that wasn't it. When I looked out, I saw flames shooting forward from the rear of the *Hindenburg* toward my engine car." Then Bentele passed out for a few seconds.

On the ground, Herbert Morrison was still broadcasting over the radio. Now he sounded greatly distressed. He said, "It's burst into flames . . . . Get out of the way, please, oh my, this is terrible, oh my, get out of the way, please! It is burning, bursting into flames and is falling . . . . Oh! This is one of the worst catastrophes in the world! . . . Oh, the humanity and all of the passengers!" Then Morrison said, "I can't talk, ladies and gentlemen, I'm sorry. I must step inside where I can't see it."

Inside the airship, people saw a bright flash of light. They lost their balance as the floor slanted. Furniture and other objects bounced around. Flames shot through the plane. They burned up the carpeting and everything else they touched. Smoke poured through the rooms. Passengers could barely see as they tried to escape the intense heat that surrounded them.

Some crew in the extra control station escaped. They dashed out as the lower tail fin touched ground. Other people jumped as they came closer to the ground. They landed amid flaming wreckage. People covered in soot and burns ran or crawled away from the fire. Some people's clothing had burned off.

John Iannaccone was part of the Navy ground crew. He watched a man trying to escape. Iannaccone said, "He walked out of the ship after the nose of the ship was on the ground. He didn't have a stitch of clothes on. And everything was burned . . . the only thing he had on him was his shoes." This man died soon afterward.

Alfred Grozinger was a cook on the *Hindenburg*. He recalled, "I thought my end had come. But suddenly there was the ground. Luckily it was sandy and soft and I had more or less fallen on my feet. Immediately I picked myself up and ran away."

People watched the scene in horror. Verna Thomas recalled hearing other spectators say, "Oh God, oh God." She said, "There was nothing you could do. All I could do was just look . . . and cry."

Captain Ernst Lehmann staggered out of the burning ship. He was badly burned. Someone heard him say, "I couldn't understand it."

American naval officers tried to help people coming out of the airship. Sirens screamed as ambulances sped to the scene. They carried the injured and the dead into the zeppelin's empty hangar. Some victims cried in pain. Others were too stunned to speak.

People who heard the radio broadcast were shocked and horrified. Newspapers carried the story. A headline in *The New York Times* compared the *Hindenburg* to "a giant torch."

The airship burned up within minutes. The ground fires went on for hours. When it ended, the remains of the airship lay on the ground. Bits of blackened cloth were all that remained of the silver covering. Smoke blew around the crumpled metal frame. Metal objects, including some coins and eating utensils, were scattered on the ground. A horrible smell filled the air.

People felt sad and confused. What could have gone wrong? Mechanic John Iannaccone would later say, "You couldn't fathom how something like that could happen."

**Other Airship Disasters**

| Date | Place | Disaster |
| --- | --- | --- |
| June 14, 1887 | Germany | Karl Wolfert and his mechanic, Hans Knabe, became the first men to die in an airship when the ship's carburetor sets off the hydrogen-filled envelope. |
| August 24, 1921 | Kingston-on-Hull, England | The *R38* crashes due to structural failure. Forty-four die; five survive. |
| February 21, 1922 | Langley Field, Virginia | The *Roma*, a semirigid dirigible, crashes due to a possible elevator problem. Thirty-four die; eleven survive. |
| December 21, 1923 | Pantallaria, south of Sicily | The *Dixmude* goes down. Fifty-two fatalities; no survivors. |
| September 2, 1925 | Ava, Ohio | The helium-buoyed *Shenandoah* crashes as a result of bad weather conditions. Fourteen die; twenty-eight survive. |
| May 24, 1928 | The North Pole | Climatic conditions cause the *Italia*, a semirigid dirigible, to crash. Seven die; nine survive. |
| October 4, 1930 | Beauvais, France | The *R101* goes down as a result of pilot error. Forty-eight people die; six survive. |
| April 14, 1933 | Barnegat, New Jersey | The helium ship the *Akron* crashes due to poor weather. Seventy-three die; only three survive. |

—From *The Hindenburg Disaster: Doomed Airship* by Victoria Sherrow. Copyright © 2002 by Enslow Publishers, Inc. Published by Enslow Publishers, Inc. Berkeley Heights, NJ. All rights reserved.

*Answer questions 1–7. Base your answers on both the passage "A Ball of Fire" and the chart "Other Airship Disasters."*

1. What makes Eugen Bentele a reliable source to relay the events that occurred on the *Hindenburg* on the day it crashed?
   A. He was a passenger on the *Hindenburg* for that flight.
   B. He was a member of the *Hindenburg* crew for that flight.
   C. He was a spectator watching the *Hindenburg* from the ground on that day.
   D. He was a radio announcer relaying the events to the public as they occurred.

2. Which airship disaster claimed the lives of the most people?
   F. the *Akron*
   G. the *Hindenburg*
   H. the *R101*
   I. the *Shenandoah*

3. What makes the passage "A Ball of Fire" the most valid?
   A. the description of the burning airship
   B. the quote from mechanic Iannaccone
   C. the words of the captain of the ship
   D. the numerous eyewitness accounts

4. When and where did the *Dixmude* crash?
   F. Ava, Ohio in 1928
   G. The North Pole in 1928
   H. Beauvais, France in 1923
   I. Pantallaria, south of Sicily in 1923

5. What is the author's purpose in writing the article "A Ball of Fire"?
   A. to entertain readers with the exciting account of the crash of the *Hindenburg*
   B. to persuade readers not to ride in airships due to the large number of disasters
   C. to inform readers about the *Hindenburg* disaster, using first-hand accounts and witnesses for validity
   D. to explain how and why the *Hindenburg* crashed in order to prevent this type of disaster from happening again

6. From reading both the passage and the chart, what conclusion can you draw about why airships crash?
   F. The most common reason for airship crashes stems from structural design errors.
   G. The least likely reason for an airship to crash would be possible elevator problems.
   H. There are a variety of reasons why airships crash, but weather seems to be the most common cause of crashes.
   I. Fire is the most likely and horrible cause of airship crashes, as demonstrated by the *Hindenburg* tragedy and the large number of deaths.

7. The crash of the *Hindenburg* can be most closely compared to the crash of what airship?
   A. The *Akron*
   B. The *Dixmude*
   C. The *R38*
   D. The *R101*

## *Check Your Answers*

1. **B** *(Research Process—Validity/Reliability)* Reviewing the reading passage should result in your remembering that Bentele was a member of the *Hindenburg* crew. Although there were accounts by passengers, spectators, and radio announcers, none were called Eugen Bentele.

2. **F** *(Research Process—Analyze/Evaluate)* In order to find the answer to this question, you need to look at the "Other Airship Disasters" chart. From that you should see that the *Akron* crash claimed the most lives at 73. There is no indication from the reading passage or the chart how many people died in the *Hindenburg* crash (Choice G). Both the *R101* and the *Shenandoah* crashes (Choices H and I) claimed only 48 and 14 lives, respectively.

3. **D** *(Research Process—Validity/Reliability)* Validity is a measure of how truthful something is. Therefore, all of the eyewitness accounts mentioned in the article make the passage the most valid. All other answer choices are specific information from the eyewitness accounts.

4. **I** *(Research Process—Analyze/Evaluate)* Again, review the "Other Airship Disasters" chart carefully. This should lead you to Choice I—Pantallaria in 1923. All other answer choices are places and dates of other disasters, not the Dixmude.

5. **C** *(Author's Purpose)* The main purpose of this passage was to retell what happened during the *Hindenburg's* crash, primarily by using the first-hand accounts of witnesses. Choices B and D are definitely incorrect, and you should be able to rule them out. The author is not trying to persuade the reader of anything, nor is she recounting the story in order to prevent a similar disaster. Choice A may be tempting since the crash was an exciting event, but the primary purpose of the passage is not to entertain.

6. **H** *(Research Process—Synthesize)* Choice H is the correct choice. If you read carefully you will see that the weather was bad the day that the *Hindenburg* crashed. There is no other indication of why it may have crashed. Looking at the chart will also show you that three other ships crashed as a result of weather. Choices F and G cannot be correct. Although both of these reasons are stated in the chart, there is no mention of either in the passage. Choice H may look inviting, but there are no other ships that caught fire that we can tell from looking at the chart.

7. **A** *(Compare/Contrast)* The crash of the *Akron* (Choice A) can most closely be compared to the crash of the *Hindenburg* since both were related to weather. All other answer choices are from the chart but do not have anything in common with the crash of the *Hindenburg*.

## DRAWING CONCLUSIONS

Earlier in the book we discussed how to draw conclusions. This standard also focuses on drawing conclusions. What can be difficult about answering this type of question on the FCAT is that sometimes you will need to use more than one source of information. You will notice that these FCAT questions may ask you to use more than one reading passage, and sometimes some form of graphic, in order to come up with a correct conclusion. Sometimes when students realize that they need to go back to the reading and look in more than one place in order to find and/or support their answer, they just quit. Do not do this! These questions are not always as difficult as they first may appear. You just need to use your reading and deductive skills. You must go back to the reading passages and do some rereading to figure out the answer.

## Informational Text—Text Features

> **Standard LA.910.6.1.1:** The student will explain how text features (e.g., charts, maps, diagrams, subheadings, captions, illustrations, graphs) aid the reader's understanding.

You should recognize this standard on text features as we have already discussed it. This time we arc just applying the same standard to informational text. Make sure that you do not just read the passage itself; you also need to focus on any graphs, charts, and pictures that are included, as well as any picture captions or headings. Everything that is included in the passage is fair game and may have a question written about it.

## FCAT PRACTICE QUESTIONS

*Read the passages "Columbus and the Bermuda Triangle" and "The Sea of Lost Ships" before answering questions 1–8.*

### Columbus and the Bermuda Triangle
by Nathan Aaseng

Although there is some evidence that others may have risked journeys far into the Atlantic before him, Christopher Columbus led the first documented voyage across the mid-Atlantic and into the region now known as the Bermuda Triangle. Columbus kept a detailed captain's log in which he describes two curious events—the first indications that something strange was going on in this area of the world.

The first took place on September 13, 1492, when Columbus observed that his ship's compass needle had shifted. Instead of pointing directly to the north star, it now pointed six degrees to the northwest. Columbus worried about the effect this information would have on his crew. They were already nervous about sailing into the unknown. How would they react to evidence that they had reached a place where the laws of nature no longer applied? Columbus tried to keep this discovery a secret, but his crew included veteran sailors who discovered the compass shift on their own. When confronted, Columbus explained the shift by saying that apparently a compass needle did not point to the north star as previously thought, but pointed to something else. This turned out to be an astute guess (as scientists learned much later) and it apparently satisfied his men enough to continue the journey.

The second event occurred at 10 P.M. on October 11, when Columbus reported seeing a "remarkable ball of fire" on the western horizon. It looked something like a lighted candle, and the crew at first thought they must be approaching some inhabited land. They soon found that this was not the case. Whether the fireball was a meteor or some unexplained phenomenon, it did not appear to upset the crew, which went on to find land shortly after.

### The Sea of Lost Ships
by Nathan Aaseng

Ironically, the most frightening element of nature that Columbus and his crew encountered in the Atlantic was not howling winds, violent storms, and towering waves but just the opposite. They sailed into a large area of the middle Atlantic—about the size of the United

States—that was deathly calm. This region, whose western boundaries overlap the Bermuda Triangle, was so filled with floating seaweed that Columbus's crew at first thought they must be near land or at least in very shallow water. But they found no land, and their soundings showed the water was deeper than they could measure.

They had sailed into what eventually became known as the Sargasso Sea, named after the type of seaweed that dominated the waters. Its stillness is due to the fact that the major ocean currents, the Gulf Stream, the North Atlantic Current, and the Equatorial Drift converge on it from different directions. These currents revolve around the Sargasso Sea in a clockwise direction, leaving it as calm as the eye of a hurricane, with little current, wind, clouds, or rain. The area was so frightening to Columbus and his crew because their ability to travel depended entirely on winds and currents. The Sargasso Sea had very little of either, and sailors feared they would get stuck in it until they died of thirst or starvation.

Over the years, ships sailing through the stagnant Sargasso Sea encountered the debris from many ships. Sailors took this as evidence that these ships met their doom in this sea. They dreaded the area and their fears spawned legends and folktales. Sailors warned of sea monsters and of slimy tendrils growing up around ships, holding them prisoner forever. The air was so still, said the sailors, that the crew could not breathe it, and died of suffocation.

Much of this talk was undeniably the result of overactive imaginations, triggered by fear and ignorance. Marine experts note that the ocean currents carry many things, including seaweed and ship debris, into the Sargasso Sea. These get caught in the unmoving stillness of the sea and remain there virtually forever. Bermuda Triangle researchers, however, note that for centuries the Sargasso Sea has been known to sailors as the Sea of Lost Ships.

## Map of the Sargasso Sea

—From Nathan Aaseng. *The Bermuda Triangle* © 2001, a part of Cengage Learning, Inc. Reproduced by permission. *www.cengage.com/permissions*

*Answer questions 1–8. Use both the passages as well as the map of the Sargasso Sea.*

1. According to the reading passages, some of the strange items encountered by Columbus and his sailors were
   A. deadly calm water and a ball of fire in the sky.
   B. large amounts of seaweed and sea monsters.
   C. a shift in the compass needle and very shallow water.
   D. a great deal of debris and slimy tendrils holding down the ship.

2. Where are the Bermuda Triangle and the Sargasso Sea located?
   F. mid-Atlantic, north of the Gulf Stream
   G. eastern Atlantic, south of the Gulf Stream
   H. mid-Atlantic, north of the Straits of Florida
   I. eastern Atlantic, north of the Straits of Florida

3. According to these passages, what was the main reason that Columbus and his men were alarmed by the Bermuda Triangle?
   A. They encountered an unexplained fireball.
   B. The water in the area of the Sargasso Sea was calm and still.
   C. They sailed into howling winds, violent storms, and towering waves.
   D. They thought that sea monsters would grab their ship with their slimy tendrils.

4. What was the author's purpose in writing these passages?
   F. to educate readers about the currents of the Sargasso Sea
   G. to entertain readers with exciting tales of the Bermuda Triangle
   H. to relate the first documented voyage to the area of the Bermuda Triangle
   I. to frighten readers about the horrors of the Bermuda Triangle and its surrounding areas

5. Which statement is most likely an opinion supported by the author?
   A. The air around the Sargasso Sea caused sailors to die of suffocation.
   B. The Sargasso Sea was named after the stillness that dominated its waters.
   C. On October 11, Columbus and his men saw a ball of fire on the western horizon.
   D. Columbus was a brave sea captain, and sailors respected and trusted his leadership.

6. The water surrounding the Sargasso Sea flows
   F. clockwise through the Gulf Stream and Greenland.
   G. clockwise through the Gulf of Mexico and Caribbean Sea.
   H. counterclockwise through the Gulf of Mexico and the Gulf Stream.
   I. counterclockwise through the Straits of Florida and the Caribbean Sea.

7. The use of arrows in the map of the Sargasso Sea helps the readers to
   A. see the path of Columbus and his crew
   B. determine different types of water currents
   C. identify the countries near the Sargasso Sea
   D. understand the function of the Gulf of Mexico

8. The solid color gray in the map of the Sargasso Sea identifies
   F. water
   G. land masses
   H. warm currents
   I. cold currents

## Check Your Answers

1. **A** *(Research Process—Synthesize)* A review of both passages should lead you to Choice A—deadly calm water and a ball of fire in the sky. All of the other answer choices were mentioned in the passages, but not all of them were actually encountered by the sailors.

2. **H** *(Research Process—Synthesize)* For this question, you need to use both the article "The Sea of Lost Ships" and the map of the Sargasso Sea. The passage will tell you that the Sargasso Sea is in the middle Atlantic. Then, if you go to the map, you can see that the Sargasso Sea is north of the Straits of Florida.

3. **B** *(Research Process—Synthesize)* The thing that most frightened Columbus and his men was that the water was calm and still. The sailors depended on the winds for movement, so calm water could be deadly to them. Although the men did see a ball of fire (Choice A), this was not the most frightening. The other two answer choices were details mentioned in the passages, but they were not actual things encountered by the sailors.

4. **H** *(Author's Purpose)* You should be able to get the correct answer to this question fairly easily. Choice I can be eliminated right away since clearly *to frighten* is not the author's purpose. You should also be able to eliminate Choice F since the main purpose of the passages is not to educate about the currents of the Sargasso Sea (although it is mentioned). Choice G is also no good since the passages are not a bunch of entertaining stories about the Bermuda Triangle. Clearly, the correct choice and the only answer remaining is Choice H.

5. **D** *(Author's Perspective)* Your first clue that Choice D is the correct answer is that it contains opinion words such as "brave," "respected," and "trusted." All of the other choices, whether they are true or not, are facts, not opinions.

6. **G** *(Research Process—Synthesize)* The map and "The Sea of Lost Ships" both tell you that the water surrounding the Sargasso Sea flows clockwise. Therefore, you can eliminate Choices H and I. When looking at the map, you should see that the water flows through both the Caribbean Sea and the Gulf of Mexico.

7. **B** *(Text Features)* By looking at the key in the map of the Sargasso Sea, you should see that the arrows (both dotted and solid) refer to water currents (Choice B). Although there are countries on the map, the arrows do not identify them (Choice C). The arrows definitely do not have anything to do with the function of the Gulf of Mexico (Choice D); that is not even mentioned in the map at all. You may have been tempted to choose Choice A, but there is nothing on the map to indicate the arrows have anything to do with Columbus's journey, and they do not. The arrows represent the Gulf Stream, warm water currents, and cold water currents.

8. **G** *(Text Features)* Look closely at the map and you can see that where there is a solid color, there is a land mass (Choice G). You can see that the land masses are North America, South America, Greenland, Europe, and Africa. Water is represented by the white color (Choice F). Both the currents (Choices H and I) are represented by different types of arrows.

# Chapter 4 | **Practice Makes Perfect: Two Sample Exams**

At this point in the book, you should be familiar with the following elements of the FCAT in reading:

- Background about the test
- Test-taking strategies
- Sunshine State Standards tested as well as particulars about each standard

Now you are ready to take an FCAT practice test in its entirety. Following are two complete practice tests. Remove the answer sheet that appears before each test, and use it to answer the questions. Fill in the appropriate circle completely. Be sure to answer all the questions and time yourself as you take each test (60 minutes per test). That way you will get a true feeling for how well you can perform on the actual FCAT.

# ANSWER SHEET: PRACTICE TEST 1

1. Ⓐ Ⓑ Ⓒ Ⓓ     21. Ⓐ Ⓑ Ⓒ Ⓓ     41. Ⓐ Ⓑ Ⓒ Ⓓ
2. Ⓕ Ⓖ Ⓗ Ⓘ     22. Ⓕ Ⓖ Ⓗ Ⓘ     42. Ⓕ Ⓖ Ⓗ Ⓘ
3. Ⓐ Ⓑ Ⓒ Ⓓ     23. Ⓐ Ⓑ Ⓒ Ⓓ     43. Ⓐ Ⓑ Ⓒ Ⓓ
4. Ⓕ Ⓖ Ⓗ Ⓘ     24. Ⓕ Ⓖ Ⓗ Ⓘ     44. Ⓕ Ⓖ Ⓗ Ⓘ
5. Ⓐ Ⓑ Ⓒ Ⓓ     25. Ⓐ Ⓑ Ⓒ Ⓓ     45. Ⓐ Ⓑ Ⓒ Ⓓ
6. Ⓕ Ⓖ Ⓗ Ⓘ     26. Ⓕ Ⓖ Ⓗ Ⓘ     46. Ⓕ Ⓖ Ⓗ Ⓘ
7. Ⓐ Ⓑ Ⓒ Ⓓ     27. Ⓐ Ⓑ Ⓒ Ⓓ     47. Ⓐ Ⓑ Ⓒ Ⓓ
8. Ⓕ Ⓖ Ⓗ Ⓘ     28. Ⓕ Ⓖ Ⓗ Ⓘ     48. Ⓕ Ⓖ Ⓗ Ⓘ
9. Ⓐ Ⓑ Ⓒ Ⓓ     29. Ⓐ Ⓑ Ⓒ Ⓓ     49. Ⓐ Ⓑ Ⓒ Ⓓ
10. Ⓕ Ⓖ Ⓗ Ⓘ     30. Ⓕ Ⓖ Ⓗ Ⓘ     50. Ⓕ Ⓖ Ⓗ Ⓘ
11. Ⓐ Ⓑ Ⓒ Ⓓ     31. Ⓐ Ⓑ Ⓒ Ⓓ     51. Ⓐ Ⓑ Ⓒ Ⓓ
12. Ⓕ Ⓖ Ⓗ Ⓘ     32. Ⓕ Ⓖ Ⓗ Ⓘ     52. Ⓕ Ⓖ Ⓗ Ⓘ
13. Ⓐ Ⓑ Ⓒ Ⓓ     33. Ⓐ Ⓑ Ⓒ Ⓓ     53. Ⓐ Ⓑ Ⓒ Ⓓ
14. Ⓕ Ⓖ Ⓗ Ⓘ     34. Ⓕ Ⓖ Ⓗ Ⓘ     54. Ⓕ Ⓖ Ⓗ Ⓘ
15. Ⓐ Ⓑ Ⓒ Ⓓ     35. Ⓐ Ⓑ Ⓒ Ⓓ     55. Ⓐ Ⓑ Ⓒ Ⓓ
16. Ⓕ Ⓖ Ⓗ Ⓘ     36. Ⓕ Ⓖ Ⓗ Ⓘ     56. Ⓕ Ⓖ Ⓗ Ⓘ
17. Ⓐ Ⓑ Ⓒ Ⓓ     37. Ⓐ Ⓑ Ⓒ Ⓓ     57. Ⓐ Ⓑ Ⓒ Ⓓ
18. Ⓕ Ⓖ Ⓗ Ⓘ     38. Ⓕ Ⓖ Ⓗ Ⓘ     58. Ⓕ Ⓖ Ⓗ Ⓘ
19. Ⓐ Ⓑ Ⓒ Ⓓ     39. Ⓐ Ⓑ Ⓒ Ⓓ     59. Ⓐ Ⓑ Ⓒ Ⓓ
20. Ⓕ Ⓖ Ⓗ Ⓘ     40. Ⓕ Ⓖ Ⓗ Ⓘ

Cut along dotted line.

# PRACTICE FCAT READING TEST #1

**Directions:** Read "The Battle of Shiloh" ("The First Day" and "The Second Day") as well as "The Battle of Shiloh Battle Map" before answering questions 1 through 15 on the answer sheet.

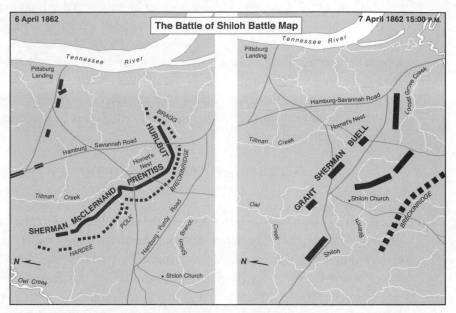

Source: "The Historical Times Encyclopedia of the Civil War" edited by Patricia L. Faust

## The Battle of Shiloh
by James M. McPherson

## The First Day
April 6, 1862

With the loss of Forts Henry and Donelson in February, General Johnston withdrew his disheartened Confederate forces into west Tennessee, northern Mississippi and Alabama to reorganize. In early March, General Halleck responded by ordering General Grant to advance his Union Army of West Tennessee on an invasion up the Tennessee River.

Occupying Pittsburg Landing, Grant entertained no thought of a Confederate attack. Halleck's instructions were that following the arrival of General Buell's Army of the Ohio from Nashville, Grant would advance south in a joint offensive to seize the Memphis & Charleston Railroad, the Confederacy's only east-west all weather supply route that linked the lower Mississippi Valley to cities on the Confederacy's east coast.

Assisted by his second-in-command, General Beauregard, Johnston shifted his scattered forces and concentrated almost 55,000 men around Corinth. Strategically located where the Memphis & Charleston crossed the Mobile & Ohio Railroad, Corinth was the western Confederacy's most important rail junction.

On April 3, realizing Buell would soon reinforce Grant, Johnston launched an offensive with his newly christened Army of the Mississippi. Advancing upon Pittsburg Landing with 43,938 men, Johnston planned to surprise Grant, cut his army off from retreat to the Tennessee River, and drive the Federals west into the swamps of Owl Creek.

In the gray light of dawn, April 6, a small Federal reconnaissance discovered Johnston's army deployed for battle astride the Corinth road, just a mile beyond the forward Federal camps. Storming forward, the Confederates found the Federal position unfortified. Johnston had achieved almost total surprise. By mid-morning, the Confederates seemed within easy reach of victory, overrunning one frontline Union division and capturing its camp. However, stiff resistance on the Federal right entangled Johnston's brigades in a savage fight around Shiloh Church. Throughout the day, Johnston's army hammered the Federal right, which gave ground but did not break. Casualties upon this brutal killing ground were immense.

Meanwhile, Johnston's flanking attack stalled in front of Sarah Bell's peach orchard and the dense oak thicket labeled the "hornet's nest" by the Confederates. Grant's left flank withstood Confederate assaults for seven crucial hours before being forced to yield ground in the late afternoon. Despite inflicting heavy casualties and seizing ground, the Confederates only drove Grant towards the river, instead of away from it. The Federal survivors established a solid front before Pittsburg Landing and repulsed the last Confederate charge as dusk ended the first day of fighting.

## The Second Day
April 7, 1862

Shiloh's first day of slaughter also witnessed the death of the Confederate leader, General Johnston, who fell at mid-afternoon, struck down by a stray bullet while directing the action on the Confederate right. At dusk, the advance division of General Buell's Federal Army of the Ohio reached Pittsburg Landing, and crossed the river to file into line on the Union left during the night. Buell's arrival, plus the timely appearance of a reserve division from Grant's army, led by Major General Lewis Wallace, fed over 22,500 reinforcements into the Union lines. On April 7, Grant renewed the fighting with an aggressive counterattack.

Taken by surprise, General Beauregard managed to rally 30,000 of his badly disorganized Confederates, and mounted a tenacious defense. Inflicting heavy casualties on the Federals, Beauregard's troops temporarily halted the determined Union advance. However, strength in numbers provided Grant with a decisive advantage. By midafternoon, as waves of fresh Federal troops swept forward, pressing the exhausted Confederates back to Shiloh Church, Beauregard realized his armies' peril and ordered a retreat. During the night, the Confederates withdrew, greatly disorganized, to their fortified stronghold at Corinth. Possession of the grisly battlefield passed to the victorious Federals, who were satisfied to simply reclaim Grant's camps and make an exhausted bivouac among the dead.

General Johnston's massive and rapid concentration at Corinth, and surprise attack on Grant at Pittsburg Landing, had presented the Confederacy with an opportunity to reverse the course of the war. The aftermath, however, left the invading Union forces still poised to carry out the capture of the Corinth rail junction. Shiloh's awesome toll of 23,746 men killed, wounded, or missing brought a shocking realization to both sides that the war would not end quickly.

—From *Atlas of the Civil War* by Stephen E. Woodworth and
Kenneth J. Winkle (2004) 699w from Chp. "The Battle of Shiloh."
by permission of Oxford University Press, Inc.

*Answer questions 1 through 15. Base your answers on the passage "The Battle of Shiloh" and the accompanying map.*

1. What is the main idea of the articles?
   A. There were heavy casualties at the Battle of Shiloh.
   B. A Confederate leader, General Johnston, died at the Battle of Shiloh.
   C. The Confederate army planned a surprise attack at Pittsburg Landing.
   D. In a tough battle, the Union army defeated the Confederate army at Shiloh.

**2.** The first sentence in "The First Day" reads:

**With the loss of Forts Henry and Donelson in February, General Johnston withdrew his disheartened Confederate forces into west Tennessee, northern Mississippi and Alabama to reorganize.**

What does the word *disheartened* mean?
F. badly wounded
G. with no interest
H. with low spirits
I. sadly marching

**3.** What is the author's purpose in including the number of soldiers killed, wounded, or missing?
A. to show that the war would not end quickly
B. to show that war is unnecessary and deadly
C. to demonstrate that all of Johnston's army was weak
D. to describe the viciousness of the Confederate army

**4.** Why did General Grant want to seize the Memphis & Charleston Railroad?
F. There were many Confederate soldiers on the train.
G. It was the Confederacy's most important railroad junction.
H. It was where the Confederate troops were most highly concentrated.
I. It was the only all-weather route to transfer supplies to the east coast.

**5.** How did Grant finally defeat the Confederate troops at Shiloh?
A. His surprise attack at Corinth halted the Confederate soldiers.
B. He crossed the river during the night and was met with reinforcements.
C. His fresh troops were able to defeat the Confederate's exhausted troops
D. He gradually drove them from Mississippi into the Swamps of Owl Creek.

**6.** What organizational pattern does the author, James McPherson, use for both of the passages?
F. chronological order of events
G. order of importance of generals
H. circular, ending the story where it began
I. a spatial description of the battle fields

**7.** Which of the following events was an effect of the first day of the battle?
A. General Johnston was killed by a stray bullet.
B. The Confederate army withdrew from Corinth.
C. 23,746 soldiers were killed, wounded, or missing.
D. 43,938 of Johnston's men landed and surprised Grant.

**8.** By looking at the Battle of Shiloh Battle Map, the reader can determine that Breckinridge and his men moved in what direction over the two days?
F. north
G. south
H. east
I. west

**9.** The last paragraph of the article "The First Day" ends with

**The Federal survivors established a solid front before Pittsburg Landing and repulsed the last Confederate charge as dusk ended the first day of fighting.**

In which sentence is the word *repulsed* used as it is in the above sentence?
A. The basketball was repulsed off the backboard.
B. Mary was repulsed by her brother's lack of manners.
C. The giant grandfather clock repulsed once its batteries were replaced.
D. The football team finally repulsed the opposing team to win the game.

**10.** What prediction does the author make about the rest of the Civil War?
F. The Civil War will end without much more fighting.
G. The Civil War would see many more generals killed.
H. The Civil War had reached its turning point in the Battle of Shiloh.
I. The Civil War would not end quickly as many had thought it would.

**11.** What information is supported by both the map and the articles?
A. Grant's troops approached from the South.
B. Elm's army was approaching from the northeast.
C. The Hornet's Nest was surrounded by Confederate Troops.
D. Johnston's troops approached from north of the Hornet's Nest.

**12.** In which source do you find information that General Beauregard ordered his troops to retreat back to Corinth?
F. the article "The First Day" only
G. the article "The Second Day" only
H. the map and the article "The First Day"
I. the map and the article "The Second Day"

**13.** What conclusion can you draw regarding the first day's battle?
A. The Church of Shiloh made this an appropriate place for so many men to die.
B. The "hornet's nest" gave the Confederate troops an advantage over the Union.
C. The Union troops and the Confederate troops were equally matched for the first seven hours.
D. General Johnston planned a surprise attack because he had a grudge against General Grant.

**14.** How did the Federal troops discover Johnston's surprise attack?
F. General Beauregard's troops discovered them.
G. A reconnaissance found the Confederate troops a mile away.
H. The Confederate troops were discovered at Pittsburg Landing.
I. Buell's arrival and Grant's reserve division countered the surprise.

**15.** The primary function of the Battle of Shiloh Battle Map is to help the reader to better understand
A. the location of the Tennessee River.
B. the number of men who were killed during the battle.
C. the placement of the Hornet's Nest compared to the Shiloh Church.
D. the movement of the Confederate and Union forces over the two days.

**Directions:** Read "Prehistoric Survivors" before answering questions 16 through 24 on the answer sheet.

# Prehistoric Survivors
by Andrew Byatt, Alastair Fothergill, and Martha Holmes

Few animals provoke as much fear as sharks. While their speed and fearsome teeth certainly equip them to be efficient predators, their reputation as ruthless, irrational killing machines far exceeds reality. Never has a group of animals been so misunderstood and maligned. True, some sharks do occasionally attack people, but attacks are infrequent and by no means always fatal. More people are kicked to death by donkeys each year than are killed by sharks. We should respect them certainly, but for their extraordinary evolutionary success and their design, rather than because we fear them.

## Sharks and Their Relatives

There are about 1100 species of sharks, rays and skates in the world. They differ from other fishes in that their skeletons are made of cartilage rather than bone, and also they have been around for a very long time. Over 100 million years ago, creatures similar to the sharks we know today were hunting in the ocean. The design was obviously good because, although they have diversified considerably, unlike many of their prehistoric contemporaries, their line did not die out.

Sharks live throughout the oceans at almost all depths. Some, such as the mega mouth, which lives in the deep ocean, are rarely seen. Very occasionally they are brought to the surface in nets, usually dead. Another little-known shark is the smallest, the spiny pygmy shark, which is only 25 cm (10 in) long and also lives at depth. The slow-moving Greenland shark inhabits Artic waters and is seldom encountered. By far the majority of sharks are concentrated in tropical coastal waters where the water is warm and prey is plentiful.

## Jaws

Not all sharks have big teeth. Some, such as whale sharks and basking sharks feed on plankton and do not need substantial teeth. Ironically, these are the largest of the group: whale sharks grow to 12 m (39 feet) (although individuals of 18 m/59 feet have been seen), and basking sharks reach an amazing 10 m (33 feet).

Smaller species, such as horn sharks, which live in temperate waters, have rows of tiny teeth. Similar in size to very coarse sand, they grow so close together that they form a rough, hard plate, perfect for crunching small crustaceans. Stingrays have a similar set of minute teeth.

Nevertheless, the large predatory species, such as bull sharks, tiger sharks and great white sharks, are famous for their teeth, which are triangular, serrated and very sharp. When a tooth gets damaged or lost during feeding, there is always another one just behind ready to replace it. Rows of teeth are continually forming at the back and slowly moving forward to the leading edge of the mouth. Tiger sharks are thought to get through an astonishing 24,000 teeth in ten years.

## Hunting

Sharks have a number of ways of hunting down their prey. They can hear well, detecting sounds many kilometers away. They have an extraordinary good sense of smell, particularly for blood. At distances of 100 m (328 feet) or so they can feel vibrations in the water.

Homing in on any of these cues, they begin to use sight. Their vision is very good, and most of them can see better in dim light than their prey. Great white sharks hunt well in poor visibility by swimming low in the water and watching for the silhouette of an elephant seal or fur seal swimming near the surface.

Close to, sharks pick up very weak electrical charges that radiate from all animals. Even a tiny fish hiding in the sand, moving its gills slightly to breathe produces an electrical signal. A small hammerhead shark scanning the sea floor for any electrical cue can home in on such a signal.

—From *The Blue Planet: A Natural History of the Oceans*
by Andrew Byatt, Alastair Fothergill, and Martha Holmes, 2001

*Answer questions 16 through 24. Base your answers on the passage "Prehistoric Survivors."*

16. According to the passage, what is the largest type of shark?
    F. whale sharks
    G. basking sharks
    H. great white sharks
    I. spiny pigmy sharks

17. What is the main cause of sharks being such effective hunters?
    A. Sharks live and hunt at all depths of the ocean.
    B. Rows of large teeth allow them to capture large and fast-moving prey.
    C. The majority of sharks are found in warm water where there is more prey.
    D. Most of a shark's senses are well developed, helping it hunt its prey.

18. Which of the following opinions would the author of this passage support?
    F. Sharks occasionally attack people; therefore, they should be feared.
    G. There are over 1,100 species of sharks, rays, and skates in the world.
    H. Sharks are irrational killing machines, well-known for their fearsome teeth.
    I. Sharks are misunderstood creatures of the ocean who need to be respected.

19. What is the main idea of this passage?
    A. Sharks have amazing senses that allow them to be vicious and effective hunters.
    B. Because they evolved from prehistoric times, many species of shark are known for their effective designs.
    C. Although sharks have changed somewhat from their prehistoric relatives, their line did not die out.
    D. Large predatory species, such as bull sharks, tiger sharks, and great white sharks, are famous for their teeth, which are triangular, serrated, and very sharp.

**20.** Why is so little known about some species of shark?
   **F.** The sharks' electrical charges prohibit study by humans.
   **G.** The sharks live too deep in the ocean to allow humans to study them.
   **H.** The sharks have too many teeth, and scientists cannot safely get near them.
   **I.** The sharks' vision is too good, and they swim away before scientists can get close.

**21.** Read this sentence from the passage:

**While their speed and fearsome teeth certainly equip them to be efficient predators, their reputation as ruthless, irrational killing machines far exceeds reality.**

What is the meaning of the word *ruthless*?
   **A.** cruel
   **B.** deceiving
   **C.** without rational thought
   **D.** without feelings of happiness

**22.** How do whale sharks compare with basking sharks?
   **F.** Whale sharks grow bigger than basking sharks grow.
   **G.** Whale sharks feed on plankton, and basking sharks do not.
   **H.** Whale sharks have small teeth, while basking sharks have substantial teeth.
   **I.** Whale sharks live in temperate waters, while basking sharks live in Artic waters.

**23.** Based on the main heading and subheadings, the reader can determine that the main organizational structure is
   **A.** an argument with support about the danger of sharks.
   **B.** a listing of the most important information about sharks.
   **C.** a comparing and contrasting of the different types of sharks.
   **D.** a cause and effect listing of why people are threatened by sharks.

**24.** How do the authors support the information they present about sharks?
   **F.** with stereotypes and documented instances of shark attacks
   **G.** with specific facts and statistics about sharks and their habits
   **H.** with personal anecdotes of time they have spent swimming with sharks
   **I.** with common opinions people have concerning the behavior of sharks

**Directions:** Read the passage from "King Arthur and His Knights" before answering questions 25 through 32 on the answer sheet.

# from King Arthur and His Knights
by Thomas Bulfinch

On the decline of the Roman power, about five centuries after Christ, the countries of Northern Europe were left almost destitute of a national government. Numerous chiefs, more or less powerful, held local sway, as far as each could enforce his dominion, and occasionally those chiefs would unite for a common object; but, in ordinary times, they were much more likely to be found in hostility to one another. In such a state of things the rights of the humbler classes of society were at the mercy of every assailant; and it is plain that, without some check upon the lawless power of the chiefs, society must have relapsed into barbarism. Such checks were found, first, in the rivalry of the chiefs themselves, whose mutual jealousy made them restraints upon one another; secondly, in the influence of the Church, which, by every motive, pure or selfish, was pledged to interpose for the protection of the weak; and lastly, in the generosity and sense of the right which, however crushed under the weight of passion and selfishness, dwell naturally in the heart of man. From this last source sprang Chivalry, which framed an ideal of the heroic character, combining invincible strength and valor, justice, modesty, loyalty to supervisors, courtesy to equals, compassion to weakness, and devotedness to the Church; an ideal which, if never met with in real life, was acknowledged by all as the highest model for emulation.

The word "Chivalry" is derived from the French "cheval," a horse. The word "knight," which originally meant boy or servant, was particularly applied to a young man after he was admitted to the privilege of bearing arms. This privilege was conferred on youths of family and fortune only, for the mass of the people were not furnished with arms. The knight then as a mounted warrior, a man of rank, or in the service and maintenance of some man of rank, generally possessing some independent means of support, but often relying mainly on the gratitude of those whom he served for the supply of his wants, and often, no doubt, resorting to the means which power confers on its possessor.

In time of war the knight was, with his followers, in the camp of his sovereign [king], or commanding the field, or holding some castle for him. In time of peace he was often in attendance at his sovereign's court, gracing with his presence the banquets and tournaments with which princes cheered their leisure. Or he was traversing the country in quest of adventure, professedly bent on redressing wrongs and enforcing rights, sometimes in fulfillment of some vows of religion or of love. These wandering knights were so-called knights-errant; they were welcome guests in the castles of the nobility, for their presence enlivened the dullness of those secluded abodes, and they were received with honor at the abbeys, which often owed the best part of their revenues to the patronage of the knights but if no castle or abbey or hermitage were at hand their hardy habits made it not intolerable to them to lie down, supperless, at the foot of some wayside cross, and pass the night. . . .

## The Training of a Knight

The preparatory education of candidates for knighthood was long and arduous. At seven years of age the noble children were usually removed from their father's house to the court or castle of their future patron, and placed under the care of a governor, who taught them the first articles of religion, and respect and reverence for their lords and superiors, and initiated them in the ceremonies of a court. They were called pages, valets, or varlets, and their office was to carve, to wait at table, and to perform other menial services, which were not then considered humiliating. In their leisure hours they learned to dance and play on the harp, were instructed in the mysteries of woods and rivers, that is, in hunting, falconry, and fishing, and in wrestling, tilting with spears, and performing other military exercises on horseback. At fourteen the page became an esquire, and began a course of severer and more laborious exercises. To vault on a horse in heavy armor; to run, to scale walls, and spring over ditches, under the same encumbrance; to wrestle, to wield the battle-axe for a length of time, without raising the visor or taking a breath; to perform with grace all the evolutions of horsemanship,—were necessary preliminaries to the reception of knighthood, which was usually conferred at twenty-one years of age, when the young man's education was supposed to be completed. In the meantime, the esquires were no less assiduously engaged in acquiring all those refinements of civility which formed what was in that age called courtesy. The same castle in which they received their education was usually thronged with young persons of the other sex, and the page was encouraged, at a very early age, to select some lady of the court as the mistress of his heart, to whom he was taught to refer all his sentiments, words, and actions. The service of his mistress was the glory and occupation of a knight, and her smiles, bestowed at once by affection and gratitude, were held out as the recompense of his well-directed valor. Religion united its influence with those of loyalty and love, and the order of knighthood, endowed with all the sanctity and religious awe that attended the priesthood, became an object of ambition to the greatest sovereigns.

The ceremonies of initiation were peculiarly solemn. After undergoing a severe fast, and spending whole nights in prayer, the candidate confessed, and received the sacrament. He then clothed himself in snow-white garment, and repaired to the church, or the hall, where the ceremony was to take place, bearing a knightly sword suspended from his neck, which the officiating priest took and blessed, and then returned to him. The candidate then, with folded arms, knelt before the presiding knight, who, after some questions about his motives and purposes in requesting admission, administered to him the oaths, and granted his request. Some of the knights present, sometimes even ladies and damsels, handed to him in succession the spurs, the coat of mail, the hauberk [coat of mail extending below the knees], the armlet [band worn around the upper arm] and gauntlet [glove with long, wide cuff], and lastly he girded on the sword. He then knelt again before the president, who, rising from his seat, gave him the "accolade," which consisted of three strokes, with the flat of a sword, on the shoulder or neck of the candidate, accompanied by the words: "In the name of God, of St. Michael, and St. George, I make thee a knight; be valiant, courteous, and loyal!" Then he received his helmet, his shield, and spear; and thus the investiture ended.

—From *The Age of Chivalry* by Thomas Bulfinch, 1858

*Answer questions 25 through 32. Base your answers on the passage from "King Arthur and His Knights."*

25. How did the ideals of chivalry and knighthood come about?
   A. Sovereigns needed knights for tournaments and banquets.
   B. King Arthur invented them because the times were so bad.
   C. The Church influenced individuals with money and opportunity to become knights.
   D. The natural goodness that lives in the heart of men created chivalry during a time of need.

26. What was the author's purpose in writing this passage?
   F. to entertain with details of how a man was made a knight
   G. to explain how chivalry and the system of knights came about
   H. to interest the reader in falconry and other knightly occupations
   I. to convince the reader that the system of knights was good and necessary

27. What is the main idea of this passage?
   A. A knight's training was long and arduous, taking over 14 years of his life.
   B. The ceremony of knighthood was both solemn and intense and was attended by both priests and other nobility.
   C. Knights and chivalry were developed out of need in society and were an interesting part of European history.
   D. The privilege of knighthood was conferred on youths of family and fortune only, for the mass of the people were not furnished with arms.

28. How did knights make their living?
   F. Those they served provided for them.
   G. Most had independent means of support.
   H. Mistresses were their glory and occupation.
   I. Hunting, fishing, falconry, wrestling, and other military exercises provided for them.

**29.** Which of the following is a step in the process of becoming a knight?
- **A.** living in secluded homes or abbeys
- **B.** traversing the country in search of adventure
- **C.** serving as a page, mainly waiting on tables and carving food
- **D.** eating and partying the night before the initiation ceremony

**30.** Why were knights-errant so welcome in the houses of nobility?
- **F.** The knights paid a great deal of money to the abbeys.
- **G.** The knights were fulfilling their vows of religion and love.
- **H.** The nobility needed protection from the rivalry of the chiefs.
- **I.** The knights provided some excitement in an otherwise dull time.

**31.** Read the following sentence from the passage:

**On the decline of the Roman power, about five centuries after Christ, the countries of Northern Europe were left almost destitute of a national government.**

What does the word *destitute* mean in this sentence?
- **A.** likely to fail
- **B.** limited of people
- **C.** littered with chaos
- **D.** lacking something needed

**32.** Read this sentence from the passage.

**Numerous chiefs, more or less powerful, held local sway, as far as each could enforce his dominion, and occasionally those chiefs would unite for a common object; but, in ordinary times, they were much more likely to be found in hostility to one another.**

What does the sentence above tell readers about governments of countries in Northern Europe during this time period?
- **F.** There was little to no government because each chief was fighting to have the most power.
- **G.** There was a great deal of government because the chiefs were hostile toward one another.
- **H.** There was a great deal of government because the chiefs often united against common causes.
- **I.** There was little to no government because people of the time preferred to live under the rule of chiefs.

| **Directions:** | Read the excerpt from *The Car* before answering questions 33 through 42 on the answer sheet. |
| --- | --- |

## from *The Car*
### by Gary Paulsen

Breakfast that first morning was normal. Sugar-coated cereal with milk and more sugar sprinkled on it. There was no bread so he couldn't do toast and peanut butter, which he loved, but the cereal filled him so it didn't matter.

Through the day he worked at mowing lawns in a nearby housing development. He loved working with motors and mechanical devices—he sometimes thought it was the only thing he got from his father—and had rebuilt an old rotary lawn mower that he used for cutting grass. The business had started small but had grown, and he had saved almost thirteen hundred dollars over the last two years, which he kept in a jar in his room.

Terry worked all day, and when it was evening he pushed the mower home to find his parents still not there.

Again, this did not surprise him. They were often late, and sometimes his father did not come home at all.

They lived in a rented old two-story house on the edge of an open field at the end of a road near a housing development, and all of it seemed about to break down and die. The house was in need of paint and repair, the street coming from the development was full of potholes and cracks, and the land around was overgrown with weeds and brush.

When he got home Terry put the mower in the garage, went into the house, and turned the TV set on to some rerun of a reran rerun about kids in the sixties, who all wore bell-bottom pants and long-collared shirts. He didn't much like television—it bored him, except for the music videos and some movies—but he kept it on all the time he was in the house because he needed the sound. He'd read something in school about certain people needing background sound like running water or surf or wind in trees—they called it "white" sound—and he thought of television that way. Pretty much worthless except as "white" sound.

He found TV dinners and cooked two of them (one was never enough)—turkey and beef stew—and ate them watching the show about the kids in the sixties. He watched more TV and worked on a model of a '57 Chevy he'd been putting together for two weeks. He liked working on models—when he couldn't work on engines—because it completely occupied his mind, making them look exact, clean, dead perfect. Then somehow it was night and his parents still weren't home, and he went to bed.

The second morning he awakened to the same routine, but now there was wonder—they should have been home and fighting by this time—and he thought about calling somebody like the police. But something stopped him. A little tickle, a happiness at the quiet and peace was there in his mind, and he didn't make the call but went out again to mow lawns.

That evening they were still not home, and he sat quietly working on the model after two more TV dinners, and for the first time he thought of the movie about the kid who was left home by himself. Except that the same tickle was there, the feeling that it was actually nice not having them around.

The first call came at almost exactly eight o'clock.

His mother called first.

"Terry, I'm not coming home. I can't take it any longer. I've taken all my things. Tell your father I won't be there for him to fight any longer. You'll both have to do without me." And she hung up.

He had said almost nothing. Had once more felt a sense of wonder—this time at why he didn't seem to care all that much that his mother had gone. A part of him felt bad—like he ought to feel rotten, only he didn't. She was gone—that thought was there—and there wouldn't be any more fights.

His father called just after nine.

"Tell your mother I'm not coming back—I've got all my stuff, or everything I want. I'm sick of the whole thing." And he hung up.

Terry put the phone back in the cradle and looked out the window at the road in the darkness and thought: *So, they aren't going to be here. Neither one. At least for a little while. Mother thinks I'm staying here with Father and Father thinks I'm staying here with Mother.*

*I'm alone.*

*Just me.*

*And the house.*

*Oh yes,* he thought, and a smile came, widened into a grin. *There's one other thing. The car.*

—From *The Car* by Gary Paulsen, 1994
Copyright © Gary Paulsen.

*Answer questions 33 through 42. Base your answers on the passage from* The Car.

**33.** How does Terry react to the disappearance of both of his parents?
  **A.** with fear
  **B.** with relief
  **C.** with horror
  **D.** with amusement

**34.** What kind of "white noise" made Terry relax and feel comfortable?
  **F.** television
  **G.** running water
  **H.** a lawn mower
  **I.** a '57 Chevy's motor

**35.** What organizational pattern is used in this excerpt from *The Car*?
  **A.** flashback to a time when Terry was happy
  **B.** foreshadowing of what might happen to Terry in the future
  **C.** chronological telling of the events that happened to Terry so far
  **D.** list of causes of why Terry is home alone and how it is affecting him

**36.** Read this sentence from the passage.

**The house was in need of paint and repair, the street coming from the development was full of potholes and cracks, and the land around was overgrown with weeds and brush.**

What type of literary device does the author use in the sentence above?
  **F.** irony, showing Terry's sense of sarcasm
  **G.** metaphor, comparing the house to the land
  **H.** imagery, creating a vivid picture of the setting
  **I.** tone, expressing Terry's attitude toward the house

**37.** The tone of this passage changes from
   **A.** fear to comfort.
   **B.** wonder to delight.
   **C.** sarcasm to reflection.
   **D.** sadness to happiness.

**38.** What conclusion about Terry's family can you draw from this line from the story?

   **. . . they should have been home and fighting by this time . . .**

   **F.** Terry and his parents did not get along and often fought.
   **G.** Terry's parents were verbally and physically abusive toward him.
   **H.** Terry's parents did not get along and spent most of their time fighting.
   **I.** Terry wanted to move out of his house due to the amount of fighting going on there.

**39.** How is Terry's major conflict resolved?
   **A.** He mows lawns to earn money for himself.
   **B.** He decides to call the police to find his parents.
   **C.** His parents call to say they are not coming home.
   **D.** He remembers that he is not totally alone—he has the car.

**40.** Which of the following statements best describes Terry's character?
   **F.** Terry is outgoing and funny.
   **G.** Terry is lazy and spoiled by his parents.
   **H.** Terry is a bit lonely yet very self-sufficient.
   **I.** Terry is a "mama's boy" and never wants to be alone.

**41.** What is the most likely setting of this story?
   **A.** the poor section of a large city
   **B.** a rural, run-down part of a small town
   **C.** a trailer park on the outskirts of a town
   **D.** the upper class side of a typical American town

**42.** Why does Terry enjoy putting together model cars?
   **F.** because it keeps him from thinking about his problems
   **G.** because it keeps him away from the fighting of his parents
   **H.** because it relaxes him after a long day of mowing lawns
   **I.** because cars are his greatest interest and source of enjoyment

**Directions:**  Read the passage "Security Robots" before answering questions 43 through 50 on the answer sheet.

# Security Robots
### by Ellen Thro

Almost all office buildings, stores, and factories have security systems. These are human guards, video camera systems, wall-mounted alarms, or a combination of systems. Good security systems are expensive. Guards can't be everywhere at once. Video cameras and wall alarms aren't always successful in detecting intruders or other problems.

A sentry robot to patrol the building can be an added security tool. In fact, a leading manufacturer of sentry robots and automated security systems, Cybermotion, Inc., says that security managers report high turnover and low quality performance by security workers has been the main motivation for switching to a robotic sentry. A sentry robot is a special type of mobile robot. Besides navigating through its environment, it must have sensors and programming to tell normal from unusual conditions.

When a robot patrols the corridors, its sensors tell it that things are normal, such as office furniture being where it should be, corridor lights turned on but office lights turned off, and the building's temperature at 68 degrees. The robot notes a few ordinary abnormalities, such as the wastebaskets in a different place.

The robot is also programmed to observe out-of-the-ordinary abnormalities, such as a corridor temperature much higher than normal or smoke in the air. These conditions can cause the robot to sound a fire alarm. If the temperature is too low, it could mean an open outer door. The robot can tell if lights are on where they shouldn't be. Under these conditions, the robot may give an intruder alarm.

Security robots need many sensors. Besides light and temperature, they need infrared or light sensors for people or animals. Detectors are needed for smoke and gas. Water detectors respond to flooding from a leaking roof or a broken water pipe. Sound detectors hear footsteps, breaking glass, or voices. Vibrations detectors locate doors being forced or blown open. Ultrasound systems find unexpected obstacles, perhaps equipment or products being removed. The robot may also need radiation detectors.

The detectors must work together as a system, with one backing up another's finding. This is because the robot's controller should not make a judgment based on single occurrences. For instance, home smoke detectors sometimes go off while food is being cooked, after a certain concentration of smoke. It is easy to check immediately to be sure that no fire hazard is involved.

A robotic security system makes a sure judgment by having several types of sensors back each other up. For instance, if the noise and vibration go off at the same time, someone may be trying to break in. Vision, motion, and heat detectors may all have to be set off to indicate an intruder in the halls.

A higher heat level may mean that someone is in the room. But there is a difference between an unauthorized person and, for example, a mouse. The controller may be set to sound an alarm if the heat's radiation is high enough to indicate a person, but not a mouse. It may also compare what the sensors have detected with past patterns. If conditions are above normal patterns, the computer signals building security or telephones for the police.

Security and surveillance are tasks that sophisticated robots can perform as well. The U.S. military probably uses more of them than the commercial world does. The *2001 World*

*Robotics Survey,* by the United Nations Economic Commission for Europe, in cooperation with the International Federation of Robotics, lists just 60 worldwide in 2000. However, it projects 1,800 by the year 2004.

Security robots are not just for offices and factories. At least one became available in 2000 for patrolling at home, ready to sound an alarm or call the police in case of intrusion. Spy-Cye, built and sold by personal robots.com, is a package ($2995) consisting of a core robotic unit, a spy camera, Ma-N-Zap mapping software, and a Cye T-shirt.

The nine-pound Spy-Cye is controlled through a graphic interface with any PC. Point-and-click controls allow the user to create a map of the premises by dragging an icon along the desired path. It has an on-board, 16-bit, 16-Mhz controller that handles serial communications with the PC, motion control, dead-reckoning navigation, and obstacle detection sensors. Its batteries recharge at a home-base unit. It moves at three feet per second, can run on any floor surface, and can move between carpeted and bare floors. Its 12 servo-motors have a 38.3:1 gear ratio.

—From *Robotics: Intelligent Machines for the New Century* by Ellen Thro, ©2003 by Ellen Thro. Reprinted with permission by Facts On File.

*Answer questions 43 through 50. Base your answers on the passage "Security Robots."*

**43.** A major difference between a security robot and a human guard is
   **A.** a robot can be everywhere.
   **B.** a robot has programmable sensors.
   **C.** a robot can detect noises and changes in furniture.
   **D.** a robot moves throughout the building in a particular pattern.

**44.** What is the author's opinion of security robots?
   **F.** They are too expensive for home use.
   **G.** They are as or more effective than human guards.
   **H.** Many conditions can set off a robot's alarm unnecessarily.
   **I.** One out-of-the-ordinary occurrence is enough for a sentry robot to alarm the police.

**45.** What do the paragraphs about the Spy-Cye reveal to readers about security robots?
   **A.** Security robots are not just for businesses.
   **B.** Security robots have several types of sensors.
   **C.** There will be 1,800 security robots by the year 2004.
   **D.** Security robots are more effective than human security guards.

**46.** What evidence in the passage would lead you to believe that the use of robot sentries will grow in the future?

    **F.** The International Federation of Robotics made large projections for the year 2004.

    **G.** The International Federation of Robotics listed 60 robots in the world in 2000.

    **H.** Spy-Cye, a personal robot, is currently being marketed for personal home use.

    **I.** Good security systems are expensive, and guards cannot be everywhere at once.

**47.** Which of the following statements correctly reflects why a person might buy a security robot for his or her business?

    **A.** No one has quit his job as a security guard in over five years.

    **B.** Human security guards have not been doing an adequate job.

    **C.** A decrease in sales has resulted in less money to spend on security.

    **D.** Video cameras and alarms have kept the business safe since it opened.

**48.** The controlling idea of this passage is

    **F.** sentry robots are able to sense many abnormalities.

    **G.** sentry robots are more effective than human guards.

    **H.** sentry robots are an effective and growing trend in security.

    **I.** sentry robots, like Spy-Cye, are being used in homes throughout the world.

**49.** Read the following sentence from the passage:

    **A sentry robot to patrol the building can be an added security tool.**

    The word *sentry* as it is used in this sentence means

    **A.** general

    **B.** grandiose

    **C.** grave

    **D.** guard

**50.** According to the passage, what kinds of abnormalities might a sentry robot detect?

    **F.** PC motion control

    **G.** ultrasound sensors

    **H.** temperature changes

    **I.** dead-reckoning navigation

**Directions:**       Read the following passage from *Of Mice and Men* by John Steinbeck before answering questions 51 through 59 on the answer sheet.

## from *Of Mice and Men*
### by John Steinbeck

Evening of a hot day started the little wind to moving among the leaves. The shade climbed up the hills toward the top. On the sand banks the rabbits sat as quietly as little gray, sculptured stones. And then from the direction of the state highway came the sound of footsteps on crisp sycamore leaves. The rabbits hurried noiselessly for cover. A stilted heron labored up into the air and pounded down river. For a moment the place was lifeless, and then two men emerged from the path and came into the opening by the green pool.

They had walked in single file down the path, and even in the open one stayed behind the other. Both were dressed in denim trousers and in denim coats with brass buttons. Both wore black, shapeless hats and both carried tight blanket rolls slung over their shoulders. The first man was small and quick, dark of face, with restless eyes and sharp, strong features. Every part of him was defined: small, strong hands, slender arms, a thin and bony nose. Behind him walked his opposite, a huge man, shapeless of face, with large, pale eyes, with wide, sloping shoulders; and he walked heavily, dragging his feet a little, the way a bear drags his paws. His arms did not swing at his sides, but hung loosely.

The first man stopped short in the clearing, and the follower nearly ran over him. He took off his hat and wiped the sweat-band with his forefinger and snapped the moisture off. His huge companion dropped his blankets and flung himself down and drank from the surface of the green pool; drank with long gulps, snorting into the water like a horse. The small man stepped nervously beside him.

"Lennie!" he said sharply. "Lennie, for God's sakes don't drink so much." Lennie continued to snort into the pool. The small man leaned over and shook him by the shoulder. "Lennie. You gonna be sick like you was last night."

Lennie dipped his whole head under, hat and all, and then he sat up on the bank and his hat dripped down on his blue coat and ran down his back. "Tha's good," he said. "You drink some, George. You take a good big drink." He smiled happily.

George unslung his bindle and dropped it gently on the bank. "I ain't sure it's good water," he said. "Looks kinda scummy."

Lennie dabbed his big paw in the water and wiggled his fingers so the water arose in little splashes; rings widened across the pool to the other side and came back again. Lennie watched them go. "Look, George. Look what I done."

George knelt beside the pool and drank from his hand with quick scoops. "Tastes all right," he admitted. "Don't really seem to be running, though. You never oughta drink water when it ain't running, Lennie," he said hopelessly. "You'd drink out of a gutter if you was thirsty." He threw a scoop of water into his face and rubbed it about with his hand, under his chin and around the back of his neck. Then he replaced his hat, pushed himself back from the river, drew up his knees and embraced them. Lennie, who had been watching, imitated George exactly. He pushed himself back, drew up his knees, embraced them, looked over to George to see whether he had it just right. He pulled his hat down a little more over his eyes, the way George's hat was.

*Answer questions 51 through 59. Base your answers on the passage from John Steinbeck's*
Of Mice and Men.

**51.** What can you infer about the character of Lennie from this passage?
   **A.** He is a very simpleminded man, perhaps mentally retarded.
   **B.** He is a man who is sure of himself and an independent thinker.
   **C.** He is a man who spends a great deal of time outside, in nature.
   **D.** He is a man who is pretending to be slow-witted to get a laugh from George.

**52.** Read the following sentence from the passage:

**George unslung his bindle and dropped it gently on the bank.**

What is the meaning of *bindle* as it is used in this sentence?
   **F.** suspenders
   **G.** bag of food
   **H.** rolled up coat
   **I.** bundle of blankets

**53.** What is the tone suggested by the nature images at the beginning of the passage?
   **A.** calm and serene
   **B.** joyful and carefree
   **C.** nervous and watchful
   **D.** serious and afraid

**54.** What is the main reason that George scolds Lennie?
   **F.** He does not want Lennie to continue to imitate him.
   **G.** He does not want Lennie to scare away all of the animals.
   **H.** He does not want Lennie to get sick from drinking the water.
   **I.** He does not want Lennie to make rude horse noises as he drinks.

**55.** How does the author develop the passage?
   **A.** by cause and effect
   **B.** by compare and contrast
   **C.** by description and dialogue
   **D.** by flashback and foreshadowing

**56.** Read the sentence from the passage.

**The shade climbed up the hills toward the top.**

What type of literary device does the author use in the sentence above?
   **F.** simile, comparing the shade to a climber
   **G.** hyperbole, exaggerating how the shade moved
   **H.** onomatopoeia, using words that imitate sounds
   **I.** personification, giving human qualities to the shade

**57.** The major difference in the physical appearances of Lennie and George is that
   **A.** Lennie is big and George is small.
   **B.** Lennie is smart and George is not.
   **C.** Lennie wears a hat and George does not.
   **D.** Lennie wears a denim coat and George wears denim pants.

58. Why does the author have the characters speak with a particular dialect?
    F. It makes the characters easier to understand.
    G. It adds more authenticity to the setting of the story.
    H. It makes the characters more realistic to the reader.
    I. It shows what area of the United States they are from.

59. At the beginning of the reading passage, why did the animals suddenly run away?
    A. They heard Lennie and George approaching.
    B. It is unclear from the reading why they ran away.
    C. They heard the flapping of a predator from above.
    D. The sounds of the cars from the highway frightened them.

# ANSWERS TO PRACTICE TEST #1

1.  **D**  *(Main Idea)*
2.  **H**  *(Context Clues)*
3.  **A**  *(Author's Purpose)*
4.  **I**  *(Cause and Effect)*
5.  **C**  *(Details)*
6.  **A**  *(Organizational Patterns)*
7.  **D**  *(Cause and Effect)*
8.  **G**  *(Text Features—Informational Text)*
9.  **D**  *(Multiple Meanings)*
10.  **I**  *(Author's Perspective)*
11.  **C**  *(Synthesis)*
12.  **G**  *(Analyze and Evaluate)*
13.  **C**  *(Synthesis)*
14.  **G**  *(Details)*
15.  **D**  *(Text Features—Informational Text)*
16.  **F**  *(Details)*
17.  **D**  *(Cause and Effect)*
18.  **I**  *(Author's Perspective)*
19.  **B**  *(Main Idea)*
20.  **G**  *(Cause and Effect)*
21.  **A**  *(Context Clues)*
22.  **F**  *(Compare and Contrast)*
23.  **B**  *(Organizational Patterns)*
24.  **G**  *(Validity and Reliability)*
25.  **D**  *(Cause and Effect)*
26.  **G**  *(Author's Purpose)*
27.  **C**  *(Main Idea)*
28.  **F**  *(Cause and Effect)*
29.  **C**  *(Details)*
30.  **I**  *(Cause and Effect)*
31.  **D**  *(Context Clues)*
32.  **F**  *(Word Relationships)*

33.  **B**  *(Literary Elements—Character Development)*
34.  **F**  *(Details)*
35.  **C**  *(Organizational Patterns)*
36.  **H**  *(Literary Devices)*
37.  **B**  *(Literary Devices)*
38.  **H**  *(Word Relationships)*
39.  **C**  *(Literary Elements— Conflict/Resolution)*
40.  **H**  *(Literary Devices)*
41.  **B**  *(Literary Elements—Setting)*
42.  **F**  *(Cause and Effect)*
43.  **B**  *(Compare and Contrast)*
44.  **G**  *(Author's Perspective)*
45.  **A**  *(Word Relationships)*
46.  **F**  *(Validity and Reliability)*
47.  **B**  *(Synthesis)*
48.  **H**  *(Main Idea)*
49.  **D**  *(Context Clues)*
50.  **H**  *(Details)*
51.  **A**  *(Literary Element—Character Development)*
52.  **I**  *(Context Clues)*
53.  **A**  *(Literary Devices)*
54.  **H**  *(Cause and Effect)*
55.  **C**  *(Organizational Patterns)*
56.  **I**  *(Literary Devices)*
57.  **A**  *(Compare and Contrast)*
58.  **H**  *(Literary Elements—Character Development)*
59.  **A**  *(Cause and Effect)*

# ANSWER SHEET: PRACTICE TEST 2

1. Ⓐ Ⓑ Ⓒ Ⓓ
2. Ⓕ Ⓖ Ⓗ Ⓘ
3. Ⓐ Ⓑ Ⓒ Ⓓ
4. Ⓕ Ⓖ Ⓗ Ⓘ
5. Ⓐ Ⓑ Ⓒ Ⓓ
6. Ⓕ Ⓖ Ⓗ Ⓘ
7. Ⓐ Ⓑ Ⓒ Ⓓ
8. Ⓕ Ⓖ Ⓗ Ⓘ
9. Ⓐ Ⓑ Ⓒ Ⓓ
10. Ⓕ Ⓖ Ⓗ Ⓘ
11. Ⓐ Ⓑ Ⓒ Ⓓ
12. Ⓕ Ⓖ Ⓗ Ⓘ
13. Ⓐ Ⓑ Ⓒ Ⓓ
14. Ⓕ Ⓖ Ⓗ Ⓘ
15. Ⓐ Ⓑ Ⓒ Ⓓ
16. Ⓕ Ⓖ Ⓗ Ⓘ
17. Ⓐ Ⓑ Ⓒ Ⓓ
18. Ⓕ Ⓖ Ⓗ Ⓘ
19. Ⓐ Ⓑ Ⓒ Ⓓ
20. Ⓕ Ⓖ Ⓗ Ⓘ

21. Ⓐ Ⓑ Ⓒ Ⓓ
22. Ⓕ Ⓖ Ⓗ Ⓘ
23. Ⓐ Ⓑ Ⓒ Ⓓ
24. Ⓕ Ⓖ Ⓗ Ⓘ
25. Ⓐ Ⓑ Ⓒ Ⓓ
26. Ⓕ Ⓖ Ⓗ Ⓘ
27. Ⓐ Ⓑ Ⓒ Ⓓ
28. Ⓕ Ⓖ Ⓗ Ⓘ
29. Ⓐ Ⓑ Ⓒ Ⓓ
30. Ⓕ Ⓖ Ⓗ Ⓘ
31. Ⓐ Ⓑ Ⓒ Ⓓ
32. Ⓕ Ⓖ Ⓗ Ⓘ
33. Ⓐ Ⓑ Ⓒ Ⓓ
34. Ⓕ Ⓖ Ⓗ Ⓘ
35. Ⓐ Ⓑ Ⓒ Ⓓ
36. Ⓕ Ⓖ Ⓗ Ⓘ
37. Ⓐ Ⓑ Ⓒ Ⓓ
38. Ⓕ Ⓖ Ⓗ Ⓘ
39. Ⓐ Ⓑ Ⓒ Ⓓ
40. Ⓕ Ⓖ Ⓗ Ⓘ

41. Ⓐ Ⓑ Ⓒ Ⓓ
42. Ⓕ Ⓖ Ⓗ Ⓘ
43. Ⓐ Ⓑ Ⓒ Ⓓ
44. Ⓕ Ⓖ Ⓗ Ⓘ
45. Ⓐ Ⓑ Ⓒ Ⓓ
46. Ⓕ Ⓖ Ⓗ Ⓘ
47. Ⓐ Ⓑ Ⓒ Ⓓ
48. Ⓕ Ⓖ Ⓗ Ⓘ
49. Ⓐ Ⓑ Ⓒ Ⓓ
50. Ⓕ Ⓖ Ⓗ Ⓘ
51. Ⓐ Ⓑ Ⓒ Ⓓ
52. Ⓕ Ⓖ Ⓗ Ⓘ
53. Ⓐ Ⓑ Ⓒ Ⓓ
54. Ⓕ Ⓖ Ⓗ Ⓘ
55. Ⓐ Ⓑ Ⓒ Ⓓ
56. Ⓕ Ⓖ Ⓗ Ⓘ
57. Ⓐ Ⓑ Ⓒ Ⓓ
58. Ⓕ Ⓖ Ⓗ Ⓘ
59. Ⓐ Ⓑ Ⓒ Ⓓ
60. Ⓕ Ⓖ Ⓗ Ⓘ

# PRACTICE FCAT READING TEST #2

**Directions:**   Read "Battling Economies" before answering questions 1 though 9 on the answer sheet.

## Battling Economies
### by Duane Damon

In 1861, the North and South were much like two separate and distinct countries. With 90 percent of the nation's factories, the North was an industrial powerhouse. Massachusetts alone produced one-and-a-half times as many goods as the entire Confederacy. From the fertile farmlands of the Midwest came enough grain to feed the North with huge amounts left over for export to Europe. The North's population of 20 million people in 23 states was more than double of that of the South.

Their very lifestyles put the soon-to-be Confederates at a serious disadvantage. Theirs was an agricultural society, not an industrial one. The South enjoyed a wealth of raw materials but was poor in factories, skilled labor, and machinery. The region's economy rested on the sale of its major crops—particularly cotton—to countries across the Atlantic Ocean.

To make matters more difficult, more than one-third of the South's nine million people were black slaves. At first this ratio benefited the plantation owners and farmers of the Confederacy. Since only white men were allowed to serve in the Southern army, slaves stayed at home to work the fields. But as the war dragged on and Confederate forces dwindled, the South would sorely miss this neglected source of military manpower.

All of these differences meant that the North was better prepared to wage war than the South. By the time war broke out, smoke-belching factories in Northern states were already turning out an impressive array of labor-saving machines for the farm. Mowers, reapers, harrows, threshers, and cultivators allowed Northerners to maintain their farms with fewer hands than ever before. Gearing up to manufacture rifles, cannons, ammunition, and uniforms would be a fairly simple matter.

The South, on the other hand, clung stubbornly to its old methods and traditions. "When the war began," wrote historian Bruce Catton in *The Civil War,* "the Confederacy had almost nothing but men. The men were as good as the very best, but their country simply could not support them." To meet the needs of its armies, the South was forced to switch from its century-old economy based on cotton production to one based on manufacturing. It was a nearly impossible task.

Adding to those woes was the sorry state of the South's transportation system. In all of the Confederacy there were only 9,000 miles of railroad track, and much of that was in poor repair. By comparison, the North boasted some 22,000 miles of track. Producing enough goods in the Southern states would become difficult. Moving these goods from factory or farm to consumers would become a nightmare.

Outnumbered, outgunned, and outmanned, the South entered the conflict as determined as the North was confident. But while the North's economy would thrive on the demands of the war, the South's economy was fated to be crushed by them.

—From *When This Cruel War Is Over: The Civil War Home Front*
by Duane Damon. © 1996 by Duane Damon. Used by permission of the publisher,
Lerner Publications Co., a division of Lerner Publishing Group.
All rights reserved.

*Answer questions 1 through 9. Base your answers on the passage "Battling Economies."*

1. What is the main idea of this passage?
   A. The South was mainly an agricultural society with land rich in raw materials.
   B. In 1861, the North and South were much like two separate and distinct countries.
   C. The North was an industrial powerhouse with 90 percent of the nation's factories.
   D. The North's economy would grow as a result of the war, while the South's would be devastated.

2. According to the passage, the South's population was more than one-third black slaves. How did this put the South at a disadvantage during the war?
   F. The South was poor in factories, skilled labor, and machinery.
   G. The South could not provide enough cotton to export to Europe.
   H. The South was not able to use the slaves as a source of military manpower.
   I. Slaves stayed at home to work in the fields while the white men fought in the war.

3. Consider the similarities and differences between the economies of the North and the South. Who had the advantage and why?
   A. The North had the advantage because of its industry.
   B. The South had the advantage because of its agriculture.
   C. The South had the advantage because of its large transportation system.
   D. The North had the advantage because of the money from its large cotton crop.

4. How did the author develop the ideas discussed in the passage?
   F. The author discussed the causes and effects of the war.
   G. The author compared and contrasted the North and the South.
   H. The author made an argument and gave support that the North was stronger.
   I. The author stated the main idea and supported it with details about the North and South.

5. What was the author's purpose in writing this passage?
   A. The author wished to express his opinions about why the North succeeded in winning the Civil War.
   B. The author wished to persuade the readers that the South deserved to lose the Civil War as a result of its struggling economy.
   C. The author wished to inform the readers about how the economies of the North and South played a part in who won the Civil War.
   D. The author wished to entertain the readers with specific facts and details about the economies of the North and South during the war.

**6.** In what way is Bruce Catton a reliable source of information concerning the Civil War?
   **F.** He lived and fought during the Civil War.
   **G.** He studied the men of the Confederacy.
   **H.** He is a Civil War historian and wrote a book on the subject.
   **I.** He lived in the South during the switch from cotton production to manufacturing.

**7.** In what way did the North surpass the South in agriculture?
   **A.** The North had more factories and skilled laborers to produce their food.
   **B.** The North could maintain their farms due to new developments in machinery.
   **C.** The North enjoyed a wealth of raw materials with less manpower than the South.
   **D.** The North did not have to grow their own grain as the Midwest provided it to them.

**8.** How was the South's economy affected by the war in contrast with the North's economy?
   **F.** The South's economy flourished while the North's faltered.
   **G.** The South's economy grew although the North's grew larger.
   **H.** The South's economy was broken down while the North's grew stronger.
   **I.** The South's economy was based on cotton while the North's was based on manufacturing.

**9.** Read the following sentence from the passage:

   **By the time war broke out, smoke-belching factories in Northern states were already turning out an impressive array of labor-saving machines for the farm.**

   In this sentence, the word *array* means
   **A.** agriculture
   **B.** fortune
   **C.** machinery
   **D.** variety

**Directions:** Read the passage "Shipping Out" from *Thar She Blows: American Whaling in the Nineteenth Century* and the excerpt from *Moby Dick* before answering questions 10 through 20 on the answer sheet.

# Shipping Out
### by Stephen Currie

*God knows I shall be glad when this cruise is ended. I would not suffer again as I have the last 3 months for all the Whales on the North West.*

—Whaleman Joseph Eayrs, 1844

Eayrs's lament was a common one among the American men who went whaling in the nineteenth century. Although whaling involved travel to exotic islands and battling enormous creatures, whalers spent most of their time exhausted, bored, or terrified. Worse yet, voyages were often long and the work was smelly, dirty, and dangerous. Whaling ships often did not return home for four or five years. "It's a rough, tough life full of toil and strife/We whalemen undergo," is the verse of a popular whaling song, and few whalers would have disagreed.

Why, then, did Americans hunt and kill whales? In a word, money. Whales were valuable. All whales have a layer of blubber, or fat, that helps protect them from cold water. Nineteenth-century American whalers were especially interested in sperm, right, and bowhead whales because these three species had a particularly thick layer of blubber. When melted down into liquid, the blubber became oil, which could be burned to provide light and heat. In nineteenth century America, whale oil was one of the best sources of fuel available. Many households burned whale candles and whale lamps. The sperm whale also carried a supply of purer oil in its head. This high-grade oil was used to make expensive candles.

Whales were useful for other reasons, too. Right and bowhead whales were prized for their baleen. Commonly called "whalebone" by the whaling crews, baleen consists of hard yet flexible strips of cartilage that hang inside a whale's mouth. Whalebone helps the whale filter plankton and other tiny creatures out of the water. In the nineteenth century, strong, thin baleen was used to make fishing rods, buggy whips, and stays for corsets—the constricting undergarments that women wore around their waists to keep them fashionably small.

Whalers were also after ambergris—a pulply, gray substance found in the stomach of some sperm whales. Little is known about its biological purpose in whales. According to one theory, ambergris forms around things that whales swallow and cannot digest. Outside the whale, the substance was worth more than its weight in gold. Processed ambergris was added to perfume in very small amounts to keep the scent fresh and strong. Collecting enough ambergris could make a ship's owner very wealthy indeed.

The desire for light, beauty, and material goods all helped bring about the slaughter of whales. Products harvested from whales were in high demand until alternative sources became available in the late nineteenth century. Until then, catching and killing whales filled that need.

—From *Thar She Blows* by Stephen Currie. © 2001 Lerner Publications Co., a division of Lerner Publishing Group. Used by permission. All rights reserved.

## from *Moby Dick*
by Herman Melville

BOOK I. (FOLIO), CHAPTER I. (SPERM WHALE).—This whale, among the English of old vaguely known as the Trumpa whale, and the Physeter whale, and the Anvil Headed Whale, is the present Cachalot of the French, and the Pottsfich of the Germans, and the Macrocephalus of the Long Words. He is, without doubt, the largest inhabitant of the globe; the most formidable of all whales to encounter; the most majestic in aspect; and lastly, by the far the most valuable in commerce; he being the only creature from which that valuable substance, spermaceti, is obtained. All his peculiarities will, in many other places, be enlarged upon. It is chiefly with his name that I now have to do. Philologically considered, it is absurd. Some centuries ago, when the Sperm whale was almost wholly unknown in his own proper individuality, and when his oil was only accidentally obtained from the stranded fish; in those days spermaceti, it would seem, was supposed to be derived from a creature identical with the one then known in England as the Greenland or Right Whale. It was the idea also, that this same spermaceti was that quickening humor of the Greenland Whale which the first syllable of the word literally expresses. In those times, also, spermaceti was exceedingly scarce, not being used for light, but only as an ointment and medicament. It was only to be had from the druggists as you nowadays buy an ounce of rhubarb. When, as I opine, in the course of time, the true nature of spermaceti became known, its original name was still retained by the dealers; no doubt to enhance its value by notion so strangely significant of its scarcity. And so the appellation must at last have come to be bestowed upon the whale from which this spermaceti was really derived.

BOOK I. (FOLIO), CHAPTER II. (RIGHT WHALE).—In one respect this is the most venerable of the leviathans, being the one first regularly hunted by man. It yields the article commonly known as whalebone or baleen; and the oil specially known as "whale oil," an inferior designated by all the following titles: The Whale; the Greenland Whale; the Black Whale; the Great Whale; the True Whale; the Right Whale. There is a great deal of obscurity concerning the identity of the species thus multitudinously baptized. What then is the whale, which I include in the species of my Folios? It is the Great Mysticetus of the English naturalists; the Greenland Whale of the Growlands Walfish of the Swedes. It is the whale which from more than two centuries past has been hunted by the Dutch and English in the Arctic seas; it is the whale which the American fishermen have long pursued in the Indian ocean, on the Brazil Banks, on the North West Coast, and various other parts of the world, designated by them Right Whale Cruising Grounds.

Some pretend to see a difference between the Greenland whale of the English and the right whale of the Americans. But they precisely agree in all their grand features; nor has there been presented a single determinate fact upon which to ground a radical distinction. It is by endless subdivisions based upon the most inconclusive differences, that some departments of natural history become so repellingly intricate. The right whale will be elsewhere treated of at some length, with reference to elucidating the sperm whale.

—From *Moby Dick* by Herman Melville, 1851

*Answer questions 10 through 20. Base your answers on the passage "Shipping Out" and the excerpt from* Moby Dick.

10. What is the author's purpose in writing the passage "Shipping Out"?
    F.  to provide information about baleen and its many uses
    G.  to tell readers about the dangers of nineteenth-century whaling
    H.  to describe the many uses of the products harvested from whales
    I.  to convince readers that the catching and killing of whales needed to be stopped

11. According to the reading, what were the original uses for the oil of the sperm whale?
    A.  light and heat
    B.  ointment and medicine
    C.  whale oil and rhubarb
    D.  preservative and perfume

12. What is Melville's purpose in writing the excerpt from *Moby Dick*?
    F.  to provide information to the reader about the sperm and right whales
    G.  to tell the reader about the baleen and spermaceti of various whales
    H.  to show how the same whales were referred to by many different names
    I.  to educate the reader about the Trumpa whale and the Anvil Headed whale

13. How does Stephen Currie organize the information in the passage "Shipping Out"?
    A.  He gives the causes and effects of whaling.
    B.  He tells a story of whaling in chronological order.
    C.  He compares and contrasts whaling to other fishing industries.
    D.  He states his main idea and then supports it with details about whaling.

14. What is the main idea of "Shipping Out"?
    F.  Whalers spent most of their time exhausted, bored, or terrified.
    G.  Whalers traveled to exotic islands and battled enormous creatures.
    H.  The desire for light, beauty, and material goods all helped to bring about the slaughter of whales.
    I.  Nineteenth-century American whalers were especially interested in sperm, right, and bowhead whales.

15. The use of capitalized words in the excerpt from *Moby Dick* helps the reader to
    A.  identify particular characters.
    B.  locate chapters and chapter topics.
    C.  understand the facts presented by the author.
    D.  see the differences between vocabulary terms.

16. Eayrs seems to be qualified to make a statement about whaling in the nineteenth century because he
    F. spent three months on a ship whaling in 1844.
    G. cultivated and sold ambergris during the 1800s.
    H. captured and killed sperm, right, and bowhead whales.
    I. studied whales and their uses for more than three years.

17. What words best describe whalers of the nineteenth century?
    A. brave and happy
    B. exotic and afraid
    C. greedy and adventurous
    D. tired and bored

18. The use of the quote in italicized print at the beginning of "Shipping Out" helps the reader to
    F. locate specific details about the different uses of whale blubber.
    G. gain perspective from someone who experienced the whaling industry.
    H. understand differences between pleasure cruising and hunting for whales.
    I. identify important information about why Americans hunt and kill whales.

19. What whale was the first regularly hunted by people?
    A. the right whale
    B. the sperm whale
    C. the Physeter whale
    D. the bowhead whale

20. Both the authors of "Shipping Out" and of *Moby Dick* would agree that
    F. the bowhead whale is the greatest of all whales.
    G. baleen was the most valuable product of a harvested whale.
    H. whales are enormous, valuable creatures to be treated with respect.
    I. whalers were money-hungry men, looking out for only their own gain.

**Directions:** Read "Lincoln's Autobiographies of 1858–1859" before answering questions 21 through 28 on the answer sheet.

# Lincoln's Autobiographies of 1858–1859

*Lincoln wrote three autobiographies in a two-year period. This first, terse effort was prepared at the request of Charles Lanman, who was compiling the Dictionary of Congress.*

## June 1858

Born, February 12, 1809, in Hardin County, Kentucky.

Education defective.

Profession, a lawyer.

Have been a captain of volunteers in Black Hawk war.

Postmaster at a very small office.

Four times a member of the Illinois legislature, and was a member of the lower house of Congress.

*Lincoln wrote this second autobiography for Jesse Fell, a long-time Illinois Republican friend who was a native of Pennsylvania. Fell used his influence to get the piece incorporated in an article appearing in a Pennsylvania newspaper on February 11, 1860. Lincoln enclosed the autobiography in a letter to Fell, which said, "There is not much of it, for the reason, I suppose, that there is not much of me."*

## December 20, 1859

I was born Feb. 12, 1809, in Hardin Kentucky. My parents were both born in Virginia, of undistinguished families—second families, perhaps I should say. My mother, who died in my tenth year, was of a family of the name of Hanks, some of whom now reside in Adams, and others in Macon Counties, Illinois. My paternal grandfather, Abraham Lincoln, emigrated from Rockingham County, Virginia, to Kentucky, about 1781 or 2, where, a year or two later, he was killed by indians [sic], not in battle, but by stealth, when he was laboring to open a farm in the forest. His ancestors, who were Quakers, went to Virginia from Berks County, Pennsylvania. An effort to identify them with the New-England family of the same name ended in nothing more definite, than a similarity of Christian names in both families, such as Enoch, Levi, Mordecai, Solomon, Abraham, and the like.

My father, at the death of his father, was but six years of age; and he grew up litterally [*sic*] without education. He removed from Kentucky to what is now Spencer County, Indiana, in my eighth year. We reached our new home about the same time the State came into the Union. It was a wild region, with many bears and other wild animals, still in the woods. There I grew up. There were some schools, so called; but no qualification was ever required of a teacher beyond "readin, writin, and cipherin" to the Rule of Three. If a straggler supposed to understand latin [*sic*] happened to sojourn in the neighborhood, he was looked upon as a wizzard [*sic*]. There was absolutely nothing to excite ambition for education. Of course when I came of age I did not know much. Still somehow, I could read, write, and cipher to the Rule of Three; but that was all. I have not been to school since. The little advance I now have upon this store of education, I have picked up from time to time under the pressure of necessity.

I was raised to farm work, which I continued till I was twenty-two. At twenty-one I came to Illinois, and passed the first year in Macon County. Then I got to New-Salem (at that time in Sangamon, now in Menard County), where I remained a year as a sort of Clerk in a store. Then came the Black-Hawk war; and I was elected Captain of Volunteers—a success which gave me more pleasure than any I have had since. I went the campaign, was elated, ran for the Legislature in the same year (1832) and was beaten—the only time I ever have been beaten by the people. The next, and three succeeding biennial elections, I was elected to the Legislature. I was not a candidate afterwards. During this Legislative period I had studied law, and removed to Springfield to practise [sic] it. In 1846 I was once elected to the lower House of Congress. Was not a candidate for re-election. From 1849 to 1854, both inclusive, practiced law more assiduously than ever before. Always a whig in politics, and generally on the whig electoral tickets, making active canvasses—I was losing interest in politics, when the repeal of the Missouri Compromise aroused me again. What I have done since then is pretty well known.

If any personal description of me is thought desirable, it may be said, I am, in height, six feet, four inches, nearly; lean in flesh, weighing on an average one hundred and eighty pounds; dark complexion, with coarse black hair, and grey eyes—no other marks or brands recollected.

—Source: *Abraham Lincoln Online*

*Answer questions 21 through 28. Base your answers on the entries "Lincoln's Autobiographies of 1858–1859."*

**21.** The use of bold-print words in the articles helps the reader to
    **A.** locate important vocabulary terms.
    **B.** identify when Lincoln was writing.
    **C.** understand Lincoln's life more thoroughly.
    **D.** create a specific image of Lincoln's character.

**22.** What was it that rearoused Lincoln's interest in politics?
    **F.** his interest in and practice of law
    **G.** reelection to the House of Congress
    **H.** the repeal of the Missouri Compromise
    **I.** becoming a member of the Whig Party

**23.** What did Lincoln include in his December 1859 autobiography that he did not include in his June 1858 autobiography?

   **A.** his date of birth

   **B.** a description of his appearance

   **C.** his involvement in the Black Hawk War

   **D.** his professions as a lawyer and a politician

**24.** According to both of Lincoln's autobiographies, he considers his education

   **F.** excessive

   **G.** formal

   **H.** ineffective

   **I.** sparse

**25.** What can you infer about Abraham Lincoln from his description of his family?

   **A.** Lincoln's family as well as its history is important to him.

   **B.** Lincoln was devastated by the killing of his father by Indians.

   **C.** Lincoln was ashamed at his lower class family background.

   **D.** Lincoln was grateful to his family for raising him in the wild country.

**26.** During his years in Congress, Lincoln was a member of what political party?

   **F.** the Whigs

   **G.** the Quakers

   **H.** the Mordecai

   **I.** the Captain of Volunteers

**27.** What was the reason for Lincoln's writing of the 1858 autobiography?

   **A.** Fell requested it for a Pennsylvania newspaper article.

   **B.** Lincoln wanted people to know about his life and his family.

   **C.** Lanman requested it for an entry in the *Dictionary of Congress*.

   **D.** It was a request from a fellow Republican to provide support for the party.

**28.** What job did Lincoln hold before he went into the Black Hawk War?

   **F.** postmaster

   **G.** clerk in a store

   **H.** Captain of Volunteers

   **I.** member of Congress

| **Directions:** | Read "Chapter I" from the story *Danger; or, Wounded in the House of a Friend* before answering questions 29 through 36 on the answer sheet. |
|---|---|

# Chapter I

from *Danger; or, Wounded in the House of a Friend*

by T. S. Arthur

Snow had been falling for more than three hours, the large flakes dropping silently through the still air until the earth was covered with an even carpet many inches in depth.

It was past midnight. The air, which had been so still, was growing restless and beginning to whirl the snow into eddies and drive it about in an angry kind of way, whistling around sharp corners and rattling every loose sign and shutter upon which it could lay its invisible hands.

In front of an elegant residence stood half a dozen carriages. The glare of light from hall and windows and the sound of music and dancing told of a festival within. The door opened, and a group of young girls, wrapped in shawls and waterproofs, came out and ran, merrily laughing, across the snow-covered pavement, and crowding into one of the carriages, were driven off at a rapid speed. Following them came a young man on whose lip and cheeks the downy beard had scarcely thrown a shadow. The strong light of the vestibule lamp fell upon a handsome face, but it wore an unnatural flush.

There was an unsteadiness about his movements as he descended the marble steps, and he grasped the iron railing like one in danger of falling. A waiter who had followed him to the door stood looking at him with a half-pitying, half-amused expression on his face as he went off, staggering through the blind drift.

The storm was one of the fiercest of the season, and the air since midnight had become intensely cold. The snow fell no longer in soft and filmy flakes, but in small hard pellets that cut like sand and sifted in through every crack and crevice against which the wild winds drove it.

The young man—boy, we might better say, for, he was only nineteen—moved off in the very teeth of the storm, the small granules of ice smiting him in the face and taking his breath. The wind set itself against him with wide obstructing arms, and he reeled, staggered and plunged forward or from side to side, in a sort of blind desperation.

"Ugh!" he ejaculated, catching his breath and standing still as a fierce blast struck him. Then, shaking himself like one trying to cast aside an impediment, he moved forward with quicker steps, and kept onward, for a distance or two or three blocks. Here, in crossing the street, his foot struck against some obstruction which the snow had concealed, and he fell with his face downward. It took some time for him to struggle to his feet again, and then he seemed to be in state of complete bewilderment, for he started along one street, going for a short distance, and then crossing back and going in an opposite direction. He was in no condition to get right after once going wrong. With every few steps he would stop and look up and down the street and at the houses on each side vainly trying to make out his locality.

"Police!" he cried two or three times; but the faint, alarmed call reached no ear of nightly guardian. Then, with a shiver as the storm swept down upon him more angrily, he started forward again, going he knew not whither.

The cold benumbed him; the snow choked and blinded him; fear and anxiety, so far as he was capable of feeling them, bewildered and oppressed him. A helmless ship in storm and darkness was in no more pitiable condition than this poor lad.

On, on he went, falling sometimes, but struggling to his feet again and blindly moving forward. All at once he came out from the narrow rows of houses and stood on the edge of what seemed a great white field that stretched away level as a floor. Onward a few paces, and then—Alas for the waiting mother at home! She did not hear the cry of terror that cut the stormy air and lost itself in the louder shriek of the tempest as her son went over the treacherous line of snow and dropped, with a quick plunge, into the river, sinking instantly out of sight, for the tide was up and the ice broken and drifting close to the water's edge.

—From "Chapter I" in *Danger; or, Wounded in the House of a Friend* by T. S. Arthur, 1875

*Answer questions 29 through 36. Base your answers on "Chapter I" from* Danger; or, Wounded in the House of a Friend.

29. The mood of the story changes from
    A. terror to pity.
    B. safety to disillusionment.
    C. restlessness to bewilderment.
    D. peace and festivity to danger.

30. At the end of "Chapter 1," what conflict has the reader been left to resolve?
    F. The reader must determine if the mother will hear her son's cries for help.
    G. The reader must determine what will happen to the young man who fell in the river.
    H. The reader must determine if the snow storm will cause more death and destruction.
    I. The reader must determine if the police will arrive to arrest the young man.

31. What causes the young man to fall into the snow?
    A. an icy step
    B. something unseen in the snow
    C. the snow and wind in the man's face
    D. he just loses his balance and falls face first

32. What does the following sentence from the passage tell the reader about the young man?

    **Following them came a young man on whose lip and cheeks the downy beard had scarcely thrown a shadow.**

    F. He is quite young, barely a man.
    G. He is a very handsome gentleman.
    H. He is upset to leave the party alone.
    I. He is cold from the snow and wind.

**33.** How does the author organize the events of "Chapter I"?
   **A.** with a flashback to events before the party
   **B.** with foreshadowing of events yet to happen
   **C.** by telling the story chronologically in the order of time
   **D.** by telling the main idea of the story and then supporting it with details

**34.** The author's purpose in mentioning the young man's mother at the end of the chapter is to
   **F.** create suspense and drama for the reader.
   **G.** alert the readers that she has called the police.
   **H.** show how the intense storm has affected her.
   **I.** let the reader know that the young man has family.

**35.** To make his writing more realistic to the reader, many of the descriptions in the chapter are filled with
   **A.** hyperbole, exaggerating the effects of the snowstorm.
   **B.** personification, giving human qualities to the snowstorm.
   **C.** allusion, giving references to well-known events or ideas.
   **D.** imagery, creating descriptions of winter cheer that appeal to the senses.

**36.** What does the author's attitude toward the young man seem to be?
   **F.** sarcastic
   **G.** scared
   **H.** sorrowful
   **I.** sympathetic

**Directions:** Read the fables "The Fox and the Crow" and "The Fox and the Goat" before answering questions 37 through 45 on the answer sheet.

# The Fox and the Crow
## by Aesop

A crow who had stolen a piece of cheese was flying toward the top of a tall tree where she hoped to enjoy her prize, when a fox spied her. "If I plan this right," said the fox to himself, "I shall have cheese for supper."

So, as he sat under the tree, he began to speak in his politest tones: "Good day, mistress crow, how well you are looking today! How glossy your wings, and your breast is the breast of an eagle. And your claws—I beg pardon—your talons are as strong as steel. I have not heard your voice, but I am certain that it must surpass that of any other bird just as your beauty does."

The vain crow was pleased by all this flattery. She believed every word of it and waggled her tail and flapped her wings to show her pleasure. She liked especially what friend fox had said about her voice, for she had sometimes been told that her caw was a bit rusty. So, chuckling to think how she was going to surprise the fox with her most beautiful caw, she opened wide her mouth.

Down dropped the piece of cheese! The wily fox snatched it before it touched the ground, and as he walked away, licking his chops, he offered these words of advice to the silly crow: "The next time someone praises your beauty be sure to hold your tongue."

*Application: FLATTERERS ARE NOT TO BE TRUSTED.*

—From *Aesop's Fables* by Aesop

# The Fox and the Goat
by Aesop

A fox had the misfortune to fall into a well from which, try as he might, he could not escape. Just as he was beginning to be worried a goat came along intent on quenching his thirst.

"Why, friend fox, what are you doing down there?" he cried.

"Do you mean to say that you haven't heard about the great drought, friend goat?" the fox said. "Just as soon as I heard I jumped down here where the water is plentiful. I would advise you to come down, too. It is the best water I have ever tasted. I have drunk so much that I can scarcely move."

When the goat heard this he leaped in to the well without any more ado. The fox immediately jumped to the goat's back and using his long horns was able to scramble out of the well to safety. Then he called down to the unhappy goat the following advice: "The next time, friend goat, be sure to look before you leap!"

*Application: IT IS NOT SAFE TO TRUST*
*THE ADVICE OF A MAN IN DIFFICULTIES.*

—From *Aesop's Fables* by Aesop

*Answer questions 37 through 45. Base your answers on the fables "The Fox and the Crow" and "The Fox and the Goat."*

**37.** In the fable "The Fox and the Goat," why does the goat jump into the well?
  **A.** He was extremely thirsty.
  **B.** He wanted to swim with the fox.
  **C.** He wanted to help friend fox get out of the well.
  **D.** He wanted to be near water in case it all dried up.

**38.** Read this sentence from the passage:

**The vain crow was pleased by all this flattery.**

What does *flattery* mean?
F. compliments
G. foolery
H. happiness
I. words

**39.** The foxes in the fables are similar in that
A. both foxes love to please other animals.
B. both foxes praise the beauty of the other animal.
C. both foxes use clever tricks to get what they want.
D. both foxes desire to eat and drink as much as possible.

**40.** The author's opinion of the character of a fox is
F. foxes are generally friendly creatures.
G. foxes are sneaky and not to be trusted.
H. foxes are always looking for food and drink from others.
I. foxes are unhappy animals who prey upon the misfortune of others.

**41.** In the fable "The Fox and the Crow," why does the crow sing?
A. to call the goat for help
B. to feed the fox the cheese
C. to show off her singing voice
D. to tell the fox to leave her alone

**42.** The use of italics and capitalization at the end of each fable helps the reader to
F. identify the author of each story.
G. locate the title and topic of each story.
H. locate the main characters of each story.
I. identify the moral, or application, of each story.

**43.** What does the fox mean when he tells the goat to "be sure to look before you leap!"?
A. Do not trust flattery; it could be a trick.
B. Before you drink water, be sure it is safe.
C. Jumping too quickly can cause you to land in a well.
D. Before you make a decision, consider the consequences.

**44.** Why does the crow believe what the fox tells her?
F. She really is a beautiful singer.
G. Her voice really sounded rusty and unappealing.
H. She wants to believe that she is a wonderful singer.
I. The fox has paid her truthful compliments in the past.

**45.** Why did Aesop write these fables?
A. to teach his readers simple lessons in humanity
B. to warn people of the dangers of particular animals
C. to instruct his readers in the wily character of the fox
D. to impassion people to read more stories about animals

> **Directions:** Read the passage "The Declaration of Independence" before answering questions 46 through 54 on the answer sheet.

# The Declaration of Independence

The Declaration of Independence is one of the most important documents in the history of the United States. It signifies the colonies' break from England and the rule of George III. The Second Continental Congress formed a committee to write the Declaration, but the Committee thought it would be better for only one man to write the document. It took Thomas Jefferson seventeen days to write the Declaration of Independence. On July 2, 1776, the Congress voted to declare independence from England. After two days of debate and some changes to the document, on July 4, the Congress voted to accept the Declaration of Independence. This is why we celebrate July 4th as Independence Day.

## About the Declaration of Independence

During the American Revolution, many delegates to the Second Continental Congress were instructed by constituents to argue for the independence of the thirteen colonies from Great Britain. On June 7, 1776, Richard Henry Lee called for a resolution of independence. On June 11, John Adams, Benjamin Franklin, Thomas Jefferson, Robert R. Livingston, and Roger Sherman were instructed to draft just such a resolution.

The actual writing of the document was entrusted to Thomas Jefferson. Benjamin Franklin, John Adams, and Jefferson then revised the first draft. It was sent to Congress on July 2, 1776. After two days of debate and revision, the final draft of the Declaration of Independence was adopted. This represents the formal separation of the American colonies from Great Britain.

The Declaration contains a justification for the American Revolution. It is a unique combination of general principles and an abstract theory of government. The fundamental American ideal of government given is based upon the theory of natural rights. The opening paragraphs of the document outline the "natural rights" afforded to all people, calling them "self-evident truths," and using them to form the basis of a governmental system. The second portion of the document outlines how George III had infringed upon those natural rights to establish a tyranny over the colonies, thereby justifying the American Revolution to the world.

The Declaration of Independence, along with the Constitution and the Bill of Rights, is on public display at the Rotunda of the National Archives.

Photo courtesy of the National Archives and Records Administration
*http://bensguide.gpo.gov/9-12/documents/declaration/about.html*

**Signing the Declaration of Independence**

The Declaration of Independence was approved by the Second Continental Congress on July 4, 1776, but it was not signed until almost a month later. The Congress did not have the approval of all thirteen colonies until July 9. On July 19, Congress ordered that an official copy of the document be created. The order called for handwritten ornamental script to be used on parchment paper with the title "The unanimous declaration of the thirteen United States of America." Using a quill pen, this took some time to finish. Therefore, the actual signing finally took place on August 2.

As president of the Congress, John Hancock was the first to sign this historic document. He used large bold script and signed under the text in the center of the page. At that time, a general practice was to sign below text on the right and by geographic location. Using this protocol, signatures of the New Hampshire delegates began the list. Delegates from Georgia, the southernmost state, ended the list. Some of the delegates were not in Philadelphia on that day, but signed the document later. Not all delegates signed the document.

*http://bensguide.gpo.gov/documents/declaration_of_independence.htm*

The fifty-six signers of the Declaration of Independence included two future presidents, three vice presidents, and ten members of the United States Congress. Below are the names of the men who signed the Declaration of Independence:

*[Column 1]*
**Georgia:** Button Gwinnett, Lyman Hall, George Walton

*[Column 2]*
**North Carolina:** William Hooper, Joseph Hewes, John Penn
**South Carolina:** Edward Rutledge, Thomas Heyward, Jr., Thomas Lynch, Jr., Arthur Middleton

*[Column 3]*
**Massachusetts:** John Hancock
**Maryland:** Samuel Chase, William Paca, Thomas Stone, Charles Carroll of Carrollton
**Virginia:** George Wythe, Richard Henry Lee, Thomas Jefferson, Benjamin Harrison, Thomas Nelson, Jr., Francis Lightfoot Lee, Carter Braxton

*[Column 4]*
**Pennsylvania:** Robert Morris, Benjamin Rush, Benjamin Franklin, John Morton, George Clymer, James Smith, George Taylor, James Wilson, George Ross
**Delaware:** Caesar Rodney, George Read, Thomas McKean

*[Column 5]*
**New York:** William Floyd, Philip Livingston, Francis Lewis, Lewis Morris
**New Jersey:** Richard Stockton, John Witherspoon, Francis Hopkinson, John Hart, Abraham Clark

*[Column 6]*
**New Hampshire:** Josiah Bartlett, William Whipple
**Massachusetts:** Samuel Adams, John Adams, Robert Treat Paine, Elbridge Gerry
**Rhode Island:** Stephen Hopkins, William Ellery
**Connecticut:** Roger Sherman, Samuel Huntington, William Williams, Oliver Wolcott
**New Hampshire:** Matthew Thornton

—Source: Ben's Guide to U.S. Government for Kids (9–12):
"The Declaration of Independence."
(Washington, DC: The U.S. Government Printing Office.
*http://bensguide.gpo.gov/9-12/documents/declaration/index.html*)

*Answer numbers 46 through 54. Base your answers on the passages and pictures from "The Declaration of Independence."*

**46.** What caused the American colonies to write the Declaration of Independence?
   **F.** They felt that England was infringing on their rights as people, and they wanted to create their own government.
   **G.** They knew that they had to seek approval from all the different countries around the world after the revolution.
   **H.** King George III demanded a document outlining their new government and the "natural rights" of all people.
   **I.** John Adams, Benjamin Franklin, Thomas Jefferson, Robert R. Livingston, and Roger Sherman wanted to unite all Americans.

**47.** On what date was the Declaration of Independence signed?
   **A.** July 2, 1776
   **B.** July 4, 1776
   **C.** July 19, 1776
   **D.** August 2, 1776

**48.** The picture of the actual Declaration of Independence helps the reader to
   **F.** see how the real signatures looked and how they were organized.
   **G.** notice who was the first signer of the Declaration of Independence.
   **H.** gain a better understanding of the words included in the Declaration.
   **I.** see where the Declaration of Independence is kept on public display.

**49.** What conclusion can you draw based on the fact that the Declaration of Independence was handwritten in ornamental script on parchment paper with the title "The unanimous declaration of the thirteen United States of America"?

    **A.** There probably was a law that all official government documents be written on parchment.

    **B.** The Declaration of Independence was a very important document to the American colonists.

    **C.** The government officials did not really care how long it took to create the final document.

    **D.** The colonists wanted to give the Declaration a title that would confuse the British king yet unite the Americans.

**50.** Which statement best reflects the author's purpose in writing this passage?

    **F.** to persuade more Americans to read the Declaration of Independence

    **G.** to inform readers about the history of the Declaration of Independence

    **H.** to explain to readers how King George III felt about the Declaration

    **I.** to express great admiration for the writers of the Declaration of Independence

**51.** Read the following sentence from the passage:

**On June 11, John Adams, Benjamin Franklin, Thomas Jefferson, Robert R. Livingston, and Roger Sherman were instructed to draft just such a resolution.**

In which sentence does "draft" have the same meaning as used in the excerpt above?

    **A.** She took a long draft of milk after eating the very spicy chicken wings.

    **B.** The U.S. government was drafting men into the various branches of the military.

    **C.** The race car driver would draft behind the closest car in order to increase his speed.

    **D.** The students drafted their first essay and then gave them to the teacher for comments.

**52.** Why was John Hancock the first to sign the Declaration of Independence?

    **F.** He was the president of Congress.

    **G.** He was the writer of the Declaration.

    **H.** He was the first by geographic location.

    **I.** He called for the resolution of independence.

**53.** What does the following statement from the passage mean?

**"It [The Declaration of Independence] is a unique combination of general principles and an abstract theory of government."**

    **A.** The Declaration was written by both government theorists and abstract lawmakers.

    **B.** The Declaration combines very specific concepts of both freedom and government.

    **C.** The Declaration brings together both basic ideas and complicated government beliefs.

    **D.** The Declaration is a very complex piece of writing created by a brave combination of men.

**54.** Which if the following men is a delegate from South Carolina who signed the Declaration?

    **F.** Caesar Rodney

    **G.** Joseph Hewes

    **H.** Thomas Lynch, Jr.

    **I.** Thomas Nelson, Jr.

| **Directions:** | Read the passage "Chemical Warfare" before answering questions 55 through 60 on the answer sheet. |
|---|---|

# Chemical Warfare

Bombardier beetles, such as *Brachinus* species, deter would-be predators by spraying them with boiling hot quinones—noxious chemicals that blister the skin and frighten off both ants and toads. The beetle itself suffers no ill effects because the quinones are present only briefly in its body. The quinones' precursors, hydroquinone and hydrogen peroxide, are produced by special glands and stored in a cuticle-lined abdominal chamber. They are discharged as required into a second "combustion" chamber, where they are acted upon by the enzyme peroxidase. The reaction that follows produces quinones, water, and oxygen, and also considerable heat. The oxygen allows the quinones to be expelled, with some force and an audible "pop," from a nozzle at the tip of the abdomen. The heat, an added deterrent, causes much of the liquid to be converted to an irritating gaseous cloud resembling a tiny puff of smoke.

By swiveling the mobile abdomen tip, the beetle can aim its spray to either side, both forward and backward, with remarkable accuracy. It releases spray in tiny pulses, and can continue spraying for some time before its reservoir is exhausted.

Many darkling beetles also use quinone sprays. Some *Eleodes* species, less mobile than bombardier beetles, lower the head and raise the abdomen to direct the spray at the face of a vertebrate attacker. Since the rest of the beetle is not distasteful, certain mice have adopted a method for getting around the defense mechanism. The beetle is snatched up and its abdomen rapidly inserted into sand, where the quinones discharge harmlessly; the mice then eat it from the head downward.

—Source: *Firefly Encyclopedia of Insects
and Spiders* edited by Christopher O'Toole.
©Brown Reference Group, 2002.

*Answer questions 55 through 60. Base your answers on the passage "Chemical Warfare."*

**55.** What is the main idea of the passage "Chemical Warfare"?
   **A.** Darkling beetles spray quinones into their attackers' faces.
   **B.** Some species of beetle use heat and gas to ward off their enemies.
   **C.** Mice have adapted a way to overcome the beetle's quinone spray.
   **D.** Bombardier beetles spray their enemies with a pulse of hot quinones that "pop" as they are expelled.

**56.** Why do bombardier beetles require a second chamber in order to discharge the quinones?
   **F.** to allow the quinones to react with peroxidase
   **G.** to allow the quinones to react with hydroquinone
   **H.** to allow the quinones to react with hydrogen peroxide
   **I.** to allow the quinones to react with other noxious chemicals

**57.** How have some mice adapted in order to avoid the beetles' chemical spray?
A. The mice always eat the beetles from the head downward.
B. The mice have developed a body chemical that keeps their skin from blistering.
C. The mice move from side to side and forward and backward to avoid being sprayed.
D. The mice shove the beetle's spraying abdomen into the ground to avoid the chemicals.

**58.** What is one major difference between the bombardier beetle and the darkling beetle?
F. The bombardier beetle uses quinine spray, while the darkling beetle does not.
G. The bombardier beetle is often eaten by mice, while the darkling beetle is not.
H. The bombardier beetle is affected by its own toxic chemicals, while the darkling beetle is not.
I. The bombardier beetle can swivel and aim its spray in any direction, while the darkling beetle cannot.

**59.** Read the following sentence from the passage:

**Bombardier beetles, such as *Brachinus* species, deter would-be predators by spraying them with boiling hot quinones—noxious chemicals that blister the skin and frighten off both ants and toads.**

What does *noxious* mean?
A. boiling hot
B. harmful
C. notorious
D. obnoxious

**60.** What effect does the quinone spray have on the beetles' enemies?
F. It scares them away.
G. It hinders their breathing.
H. It attracts them to the beetle.
I. It allows the enemies to eat the beetles' head first.

## ANSWERS TO PRACTICE TEST #2

1.  **D** *(Main Idea)*
2.  **H** *(Cause and Effect)*
3.  **A** *(Compare and Contrast)*
4.  **G** *(Organizational Patterns)*
5.  **C** *(Author's Purpose)*
6.  **H** *(Validity and Reliability)*
7.  **D** *(Details)*
8.  **H** *(Cause and Effect)*
9.  **D** *(Context Clues)*
10. **H** *(Author's Purpose)*
11. **A** *(Synthesis)*
12. **F** *(Author's Purpose)*
13. **D** *(Organizational Patterns)*
14. **I** *(Main Idea)*
15. **B** *(Text Features—Literary Text)*
16. **F** *(Validity and Reliability)*
17. **C** *(Word Relationships)*
18. **G** *(Text Features—Informational Text)*
19. **A** *(Details)*
20. **H** *(Synthesis)*
21. **B** *(Text Features—Informational Text)*
22. **H** *(Details)*
23. **B** *(Compare and Contrast)*
24. **I** *(Synthesis)*
25. **A** *(Conclusions/Inferences)*
26. **F** *(Details)*
27. **C** *(Cause and Effect)*
28. **G** *(Details)*
29. **D** *(Literary Elements—Mood)*
30. **G** *(Literary Elements—Conflict and Resolution)*

31. **B** *(Cause and Effect)*
32. **F** *(Word Relationships)*
33. **C** *(Organizational Patterns)*
34. **F** *(Author's Purpose)*
35. **B** *(Literary Devices)*
36. **I** *(Literary Elements—Tone)*
37. **D** *(Cause and Effect)*
38. **F** *(Context Clues)*
39. **C** *(Compare and Contrast)*
40. **G** *(Author's Perspective)*
41. **C** *(Cause and Effect)*
42. **I** *(Text Features—Literary Text)*
43. **D** *(Word Relationships)*
44. **H** *(Cause and Effect)*
45. **A** *(Author's Purpose)*
46. **F** *(Cause and Effect)*
47. **D** *(Details)*
48. **F** *(Text Features—Informational Text)*
49. **B** *(Conclusions/Inferences)*
50. **G** *(Author's Purpose)*
51. **D** *(Multiple Meanings)*
52. **F** *(Cause/Effect)*
53. **C** *(Word Relationships)*
54. **H** *(Text Features—Informational Text)*
55. **B** *(Main Idea)*
56. **F** *(Cause and Effect)*
57. **D** *(Details)*
58. **I** *(Compare and Contrast)*
59. **B** *(Context Clues)*
60. **F** *(Cause and Effect)*

# UNIT TWO

# FCAT WRITING

| Chapter 5 | # What You Need to Know |

---

## ANOTHER TIMED TEST?

FCAT Writing is indeed another timed test, but it is considerably different and shorter (yea!) than FCAT Reading. Like FCAT Reading, FCAT Writing is administered in the spring term, usually during February. FCAT Writing is a test of what is known as *demand writing*. Demand writing is a kind of writing in which a specific topic is given and then you are expected to, upon demand, write about that topic within a certain amount of time. During FCAT Writing, you will be given 45 minutes to write either an expository or persuasive essay upon an assigned topic. A writing folder in which you are to write your essay will be provided for you. The only things you need to bring to the test are a pencil or two and your brain.

## A Passing Score?

Currently, the state of Florida does not use this test as a graduation requirement for students. The state mainly uses this test as part of its school grading system in order to evaluate how well students are learning and teachers are teaching. A score of 4.0 on the writing rubric is considered passing for this test and helps schools earn points for a passing grade. Hopefully, you will earn a score of at least a 4.0 in order to show that you are a capable and competent writer and to help your school earn a good grade.

## Upcoming Changes to the FCAT Writing?

You may be aware that in 2006, the FCAT writing test was changed to be called FCAT Writing+. A multiple-choice portion was added to the test, and scores were calculated by combining a student's performance on both the multiple-choice questions and the writing prompt. However, in the 2008–2009 school year, the multiple-choice portion was removed, and the test name was changed to FCAT Writing. At this time, it does not seem as if the multiple-choice section will be again added to the test. You can check on the FCAT Writing developments by visiting the Florida Department of Education's website at *http://fcat.fldoe.org/fwinfopg.asp*.

## It's Just a Draft!

If 45 minutes seems like a short time in which to write a complete, well-developed essay, you are right—it is! The good news is that the state of Florida understands that as well. What the state is really asking you to do is to write a draft. A draft, as you probably already know, is a first attempt at writing on a topic. It is not perfect, but the ideas are there and can be organized and focused. The state is not looking to see that you have spelled every word correctly or have placed every comma where it needs to be. However, it does expect you write using good grammar and usage of the English language. Most important, the state expects you to be able to support your ideas by using good reasons, examples, details, and facts.

## Getting Ready

How do you prepare for FCAT Writing? You prepare in the same way that you prepare for the reading test. In order to get better at doing anything, you have to practice. So in order to earn a good score on the writing test, you need to write. You must have strategies anytime you try something difficult. Here are some tips and strategies to help you score well on FCAT Writing. Some strategies need to be started weeks to months before taking the test, and some are for during the test itself. You should recognize some of these tips from Chapter 1 of this book.

## Weeks Before the Test

1. Write as Much as Possible: Since this part of the FCAT is a writing test, the better your writing skills, the better you will do. Anything you write will prepare you for the test. The more you write, the better a writer you will become. In particular, you should practice writing expository and persuasive essays, as that is what you will be asked to write on the test.
2. Read: In addition to writing, you need to read. By reading, you will be exposed to examples of good writing that you can emulate (imitate). Look at the styles that different writers have. Notice their use of humor, description, and persuasion. Imitating these styles and incorporating them into your own writing can make your writing more effective.
3. Improve Your Vocabulary: Using precise and mature vocabulary will definitely improve your score on this test and make any writing you do better. Even if you are not sure how to spell a particular word, try to use it anyway. You will be rewarded for a good vocabulary even if your spelling on those words is a little shaky.
4. Familiarize Yourself with the Test: Just knowing how the test is set up and what kinds of questions are on it will allow you to do better on the FCAT. Reading this chapter of this book should help you feel more comfortable about the test.

## Days Before the Test

1. Get Rested: You know that you do not really do anything very well when you are tired. So make sure that you rest up the few days before the test. Get a good eight hours of sleep or more!
2. Eat Well: Not only does your body need to be rested to perform well, it also needs to be fortified. Eat lots of "good for you food" days before the test, and your body will get those nutrients into your system.
3. Hydrate Yourself: Drink lots of water! This is also good for your body and, specifically, your brain. Just do not wait until the night before or day of the test to do this. You will succeed in only making yourself have to go to the bathroom during the test!
4. Keep Writing. Just because the test is getting close does not mean you should stop preparing. Write, write, write!

## The Morning of the Test

1. Eat a Good Breakfast: If you are hungry during the test, you will only be distracted by the growling of your stomach. You will also have difficulty concentrating on the writing prompt, and your body will not have the energy it needs.

2. Do Not Drink Too Much: Again, if you have to go to the bathroom during the test, you will not be able to concentrate on what you are doing. Also, you will break your concentration and use up valuable time if you have to get up and leave the room to use the restroom.

3. Be Comfortable: Dress in layers. This may seem like silly advice, but sometimes testing rooms are very cold or very hot. If you are uncomfortable because of the temperature, you will have difficulty concentrating on what you are doing.

4. Bring Pencils: Just like FCAT Reading, the writing test also requires you to answer with a number 2 pencil. The test will be scored by a real person, but it will be scanned into a machine first. The machine can read only number 2 pencil marks. Be sure that your pencils have erasers so that you can erase any mistakes you make.

5. Stay Calm: You will not help yourself at all if you are very nervous. Relax, you have prepared. Just do your best.

6. Know Where and When to Report: Every school is different, so be sure that you know what time and what room to report to on the day of testing. You do not want to create more stress for yourself by running around at the last minute, not knowing where to go.

## During the Test

1. Listen to the Directions: On the FCAT test, a monitor will read the instructions to you. Pay attention, even if you think you know what you are doing. Better safe than sorry. Also, do not be afraid to ask questions if you are not sure what to do.

2. The Writing Folder: Before the testing begins, the proctor will hand out writing folders to each student. This folder is the only thing you will have to write on for the test.

   • The first page is just personal information about yourself (name, school, gender, background, and so on). This information may already be filled in, or you may have to fill it in yourself. Listen to your proctor for instructions.
   • The next page of the folder will be your writing prompt. On this page, you will find out the topic about which you will write.
   • The next page is the planning page. You can use this page to plan before you write. However, **anything that you write on this page WILL NOT be scored**. This is very important to know. In the past, students have begun their actual essays on the planning sheet and have earned poor grades since anything on this page is not scored.
   • The last two pages of the folder are for writing your essay. You will have no more than these two pages to write on, so plan accordingly. These are the only two pages of the writing folder that will be scored.

3. Read the Prompt Carefully: You need to be 100 percent sure about what your writing topic is. You do not want to write a wonderful essay about the wrong topic—it would be unscorable.

4. Use Time Wisely: Since you only have 45 minutes in which to write your essay, you must use your time wisely. The following is a good breakdown of *approximately* how much time you should use for the test:

   • **Reading the Prompt and Planning: 10 Minutes:** Be sure you understand the topic and plan what you are going to write. Generally speaking, students who plan their essays (by outlining, creating webs, listing, and so on) write more focused, better organized, and better supported essays.

- **Writing the Essay: 25–30 minutes:** Write steadily. Try not to get bogged down by worrying too much about spelling and grammar. Get your ideas onto paper, and support them as best you can.
- **Proofreading and Editing: 5–10 minutes:** Not too many people enjoy proofreading and editing their own essays, but it is an important step that should not be left out. You may find some general spelling or grammar errors that can be easily fixed or realize that the order of your paragraphs needs to be changed. You can simply draw an X through the error if this is the case. Remember, this is a draft. You can make corrections. Your essay is not going to be perfect, but you can do your best in the time given to make the essay the best you can.

The time breakdown above is only a suggestion, especially since every person writes differently. However, every person needs to take the time to read the prompt and plan, write the essay, and proofread. You do not want to look at the clock and realize that you have been planning for 30 minutes and now you have only 15 minutes left to write.

5. Write Neatly. Even though your essay will be machine-scanned into a computer, it will be graded by real people. If your writing cannot be read, then it will not be scored. You can print or write in cursive, just as long as it is readable. Also keep in mind that you only have two pages on which to write your essay. If you have big, loopy handwriting, you may want to try and tone it down so you can fit your entire essay in the space given.

6. Consider Your Audience: Anytime you write, you need to think about your audience. This essay is being written for the state of Florida's Department of Education and will be scored by adults. Therefore, you should not use slang or derogatory language. You should not write offensive or inappropriate ideas. Extreme and/or questionable essays can and have been tagged by the graders and sent back to the school's district office and to the school, where the writer of the essay has been questioned. Do not let this happen to you.

7. Use Standard English with Proper Grammar and Usage: Since this is a writing test, one of the items that is being graded is how well you can write using the standard English language. Although you will not be penalized for small errors in spelling and grammar, too many errors can make your essay unreadable, which will be reflected by a low score.

# TWO TYPES OF WRITING

There are many different kinds of writing. On FCAT Writing, though, you will be asked to write in only one of two possible ways: expository or persuasive. This is good news for you because you can practice both of these kinds of writing until you feel you can very effectively produce a good essay in either format.

## Expository Essays

> An expository essay is one in which you explain something.

To produce an exposition is to produce an explanation. You might be asked to explain how, why, when, who, what, or where about anything. Expository writing can also be used to give information about something.

> **Use your imagination!**

What if you receive an expository prompt (or topic) and the topic is one for which you have no explanation or the prompt does not really apply to you? For example, what if you get a prompt that asks you to explain the effects video games have on teenagers? What if you have never played a video game, you do not like video games, and you really do not care about video games? Well, even if you know nothing about the topic, it is perfectly acceptable to make up something. PRETEND! Pretend that you do know something about the topic and make it up! Have some fun with it, and write a good essay that may not be truthful or based on fact but is a good essay nonetheless. FCAT Writing is not testing what you know but, instead, how well you can write.

## Persuasive Essays

> **A persuasive essay is an essay in which you try to persuade or convince someone that your viewpoint or idea is best.**

> **Pick a Side!**

When writing a persuasive essay, you should pick one side or the other to write about. For example, if the writing prompt asks you to persuade your principal whether uniforms should or should not be mandatory at your school, then you would first have to decide what side of the debate you are on: for or against uniforms. Then you would write to persuade or convince your principal that your side is the best. You CANNOT write about both sides of the issue even if you see benefits or problems with each side. You MUST choose a side!

> **Choose wisely!**

Also, remember that the side that you feel most strongly about may *not* be the side that is easiest to write about. For example, you may feel strongly that uniforms should not be in public school but find you could more easily write and support a persuasive essay that is *for* uniforms instead of against them. Again, this test is about how well you can write, not necessarily about your true feelings on the topic. In other words, you can write in favor of an issue you do not truly support.

> **And in the end . . .**

Even if you have no opinion on the topic, pick a side and *pretend* you care. Be outrageous, be funny, pretend you are arguing about something that you have very strong feelings for—you might be surprised at what a good essay you can produce!

## RUBRICS TO REMEMBER

A rubric is a way to measure how well someone completes a job. It is a set of expectations with a value attached to a level of achievement. For example, if you were in a physical fitness class and the coach wanted to measure how well you had achieved the skills of basketball, she might develop a rubric like this to measure your skills:

| Skills | High Level of Achievement: 5 points | Medium Level of Achievement: 3 points | Low Level of Achievement: 1 point |
|---|---|---|---|
| **Dribbling** | | | |
| **Free Throws** | | | |
| **Passing** | | | |

Depending on how well honed (or developed) your skills are, you could earn a high, medium, or low level of achievement. The highest score you could earn in this exercise would be 15 if you earned 5 points for each skill. The lowest score you could earn would be 3.

As we have already discussed, if you are going to write something, it is a good idea to know, *before you write*, how it is going to be evaluated. By having this information first, you can be sure to include all of the elements that are going to be evaluated. Looking at the rubric for the FCAT Writing essay will allow you to see how your writing is going to be evaluated, before you even write it!

## Holistic Scoring

The essay you will be writing for FCAT Writing will be graded *holistically*. Holistic scoring means that someone will read your essay and grade it on its **overall impression**, without picking it apart.

The evaluators will be looking at four major areas. The following are the items that are on the scoring rubric:

- Focus
- Organization
- Support
- Conventions

For each of these four items, you will be rated from a 1 to a 6. So the highest overall score you can achieve on the FCAT writing essay is a 6 and the lowest is unscorable (or 0).

# A Look at the Rubric

The FCAT Writing rubric below has been reworded so that you can more easily understand it and use it when practicing for the test. The formal or actual rubric that will be used by the state has been included in the appendix at the end of this book along with the rubric below. The rubric is quite long, but read it and discuss it with your teacher and classmates until you fully understand what the state expects you to do. Understanding the rubric will allow you to earn a much higher score than if you just write without knowing what is expected of you.

|   | Focus | Organization | Support | Conventions |
|---|---|---|---|---|
| 6 | _____ Focused on topic, insightful, purposeful | _____ Logically organized, effective use of transitions, smooth flow | _____ Relevant, specific, substantial, committed to subject, may include creative writing | _____ Few, if any, errors, mature language, fresh expressions, varied sentence structure |
| 5 | _____ Focused on topic | _____ Logically organized, effective use of transitions | _____ Ample use of specific examples and details | _____ Few errors, mature language, varied sentence structure |
| 4 | _____ Focused on topic, few—if any— loosely related ideas | _____ Organized, some use of transitions | _____ Support is consistently developed but may not be specific | _____ Some errors in grammar, adequate word choice, variety in sentence structure |
| 3 | _____ Focused on topic but contains loosely related ideas | _____ Some organization but may not be logical | _____ Uneven development of support | _____ Some errors in grammar, adequate word choice, some variety in sentence structure |
| 2 | _____ Addresses topic but may lose focus | _____ Beginning, middle, and end but may be brief | _____ Nonspecific support, erratic, ideas may be repeated | _____ Errors in basic grammar, common words spelled correctly, word choice is limited, predictable, vague |
| 1 | _____ Addresses topic but includes ideas that are only loosely related, may also include ideas not related to topic | _____ Weak organization, may be incomplete | _____ Little to no development of support, may only be fragmented lists or general information | _____ Limited or inappropriate word choice, many and obvious mistakes in grammar, common words misspelled |

# Moving On

Now that you are familiar with the structure of the test, the writing you will be expected to do, and the scoring of the essay, it is time to move on to the actual writing process. There are many ways for you to be sure that you perform well on this test. Read on to find out how!

# Chapter 6 | The Writing Process

Writing almost always requires some kind of writing process. The writing process can be different for different kinds of writing. This chapter deals with the process for the demand writing that is required on FCAT Writing.

## READING THE PROMPT—GET THE T'n'T!

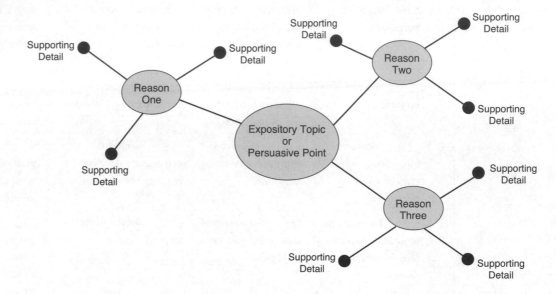

One of the most important things you can do before you write anything is to be sure you understand the topic about which you will be writing. On FCAT Writing, the topic presented is called the writing prompt. The prompt on the FCAT test will always be set up in the same way: with a **writing situation** followed by **directions for writing**. It is here you will find out the T'n'T, or *topic and type,* of writing required for the test.

## The Writing Situation

The writing situation is the first part of the prompt for FCAT Writing. In the writing situation you will find the topic about which you will be expected to write. You should be looking for a key word or group of words in the writing situation that will give you an idea about what you will be writing.

## Directions for Writing

The directions for writing are the most important part of the writing prompt. They always come after the writing situation and give specific instructions about what you are to write. Making sure that you follow the directions for writing is the first step in ensuring a high score on FCAT Writing.

The directions for writing will normally be separated into two parts. One part will ask you to think personally about the topic from the writing situation. The other part will ask you either to explain or to persuade. *It is in the second part of the directions for writing you will find out whether you will be writing an expository or persuasive draft.* Look for clue words that indicate what type of writing you will be doing.

---

**For expository writing, look for the words**

- explain *why*
- explain *how*
- explain *what*

**and be sure that you answer accordingly**.

---

For example, if the prompt asks you to explain *why* you go to the movies, do not spend the entire essay writing about *what* movies you like to see (although that might be a part of the essay). Making sure you know what the prompt is asking is a key to FCAT Writing.

---

**For persuasive writing look for the words**

- convince
- persuade
- why
- opinion
- point of view

---

The presence of some of these words should clearly alert you to the fact that you will be writing a persuasive draft. Once you have ascertained (figured out) that you will be writing a persuasive piece, you should then be sure that you know two more things: the **topic** of persuasion and who your **audience** will be. In most persuasive prompts, the directions for writing will indicate who your audience will be.

Example: The prompt has indicated that you are to persuade someone to let you borrow his car. You might write a different essay if you were trying to persuade your mom than if you were trying to persuade your best friend.

## Examples of Writing Prompts

*Here are some sample prompts to give you an idea of what FCAT Writing will look like.*

### 1. Writing Situation
*The governor has decided to allow individual counties to decide whether or not seat belts should be required by law for front seat passengers of a vehicle. A committee will be taking opinions from the community at their next meeting.*

### Directions for Writing
*Think about whether or not you think seat belts should be required by law for front seat passengers. Now write to convince the committee members to accept your point of view on whether or not seat belts should be required by law for front seat passengers.*

**2. Writing Situation**

*Many teens have ideas about what they would like to do someday as a career.*

**Directions for Writing**

*Think about what you would like to do someday as a career. Now explain why you would like this particular career someday.*

# EXERCISE: PRACTICE WITH PROMPTS

*Answer the following questions for each of the prompts above.*

1. What is the topic of prompt #1?

   _____

2. What type of writing is being asked of you in prompt #1?

   _____

3. What words indicate the type of writing in prompt #1?

   _____

4. What is the topic of prompt #2?

   _____

5. What type of writing is being asked of you in prompt #2?

   _____

6. What words indicate the type of writing in prompt #2?

   _____

## *Check Your Answers*

1. Topic: Should seat belts for front seat passengers be required by law?
2. Type of Writing: persuasive
3. Words that Indicate Type of Writing: "convince," "point of view"
4. Topic: career choice
5. Type of Writing: expository
6. Words that Indicate: "explain why"

**Remember:** Read the prompt carefully to be sure of the topic and type of writing (expository or persuasive) that you will be doing! Get the T'n'T!

## PLANNING

Once you are sure of the T'n'T, then you can begin to plan your essay. Although this process should not take you more than about ten minutes, it is an important phase in the writing process. Writing that has been planned in some way, especially demand writing, is usually much better than writing that is just thrown onto the page. There is no one correct way to plan for your essay. There are many different methods for planning. Ultimately, though, you should choose the method that allows *you* to plan and write most effectively.

### Planning for Expository Essays

One you have figured out that you will be writing an expository essay, you will need to follow some steps to be sure your essay is complete.

**Step One:** Choose your topic.

Although the general topic will be given to you, first you still need to figure out how you are going to respond to the topic. Use the topic from above on a career choice as an example. The first step for this essay would be to figure out what career you want to write about. Remember, you should choose an idea that you have a genuine interest in because it will be easier for you to write about. If you cannot think of a topic that truly interests you, make up something. Use your imagination and pretend. Once you have chosen your topic, pretend that you *really, really* care about it, and write in a way that reflects that!

**Step Two:** Think of reasons.

In any expository essay, the prompt will be asking you to explain something. The prompt may ask you to explain *what, how,* or *why*. Make sure you are answering the right question, and then think of reasons. As an example, think again about the career prompt. Once you have decided on what career you want to write about, the next step is to think of reasons *why* you would choose this career. You should try to think of two or three good reasons.

**Step Three:** Explain and support your reasons.

Once you have thought up some good reasons that explain what, how, or why, you next need to think of support—good support—for your reasons. Support for your reasons can come in the form of facts, incidents, reasons, examples, statistics, or personal anecdotes. Good support is a key ingredient to a well-written essay.

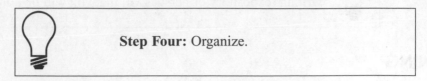

**Step Four:** Organize.

Once your have all the key components, you will need to decide how to organize them. You should think of some ideas for your introduction, the order in which you will present your reasons, and ideas for your conclusion. Further on you will see some sample graphic organizers that can help you with your organization.

# EXERCISE

*Try following these four steps as if you were planning for the expository prompt on careers. Use the samples to help you. Here is the prompt again in case you have forgotten it:*

### Writing Situation
*Many teens have ideas about what they would like to do someday as a career.*

### Directions for Writing
*Think about what you would like to do someday as a career. Now write to explain why you would like this particular career someday.*

**Step One**—Choose your career:

_____

*Sample Choice: Police Officer*

**Step Two**—Reasons why you would like this career (two or three):

1.
2.
3.

*Sample Reasons:*

1. *Like to help people*
2. *Rewarding job*
3. *Like to take risks*

**Step Three**—Support your reasons:

1. Reason One

_____

   A.  Support One:
   B.  Support Two:
   C.  Support Three:

2. Reason Two

_____

A. Support One:
B. Support Two:
C. Support Three:

3. Reason Three

_____

A. Support One:
B. Support Two:
C. Support Three:

*Sample Support:*

1. *Reason One: Like to help people*
   A. *Support One: Have helped people in the past (give example(s) or personal anecdote—personal story)*
   B. *Support Two: Police officers help people (give examples of how)*
   C. *Support Three: (none necessary for this sample)*
2. *Reason Two: Rewarding job*
   A. *Support One: Get to help others (refer to examples from above)*
   B. *Support Two: Get to stop criminals (give a specific example)*
   C. *Support Three: Get respect of others (children, some adults, statistics)*
3. *Reason Three: Like to take risks*
   A. *Support One: Have taken risks in the past (give examples/personal anecdote)*
   B. *Support Two: Officers take risks every day (give examples)*
   C. *Support Three: Get rewarded for taking risks (tell how)*

**Step Four**—Organize:

1. Introduction:
2. Body Paragraph #1:
3. Body Paragraph #2:
4. Body Paragraph #3:
5. Conclusion:

*Sample Organization:*

1. *Introduction: Include topic and all three reasons, start with question*
2. *Body Paragraph #1: Like to take risks*
3. *Body Paragraph #2: Like to help people*
4. *Body Paragraph #3: Rewarding job*
5. *Conclusion: Sum up, answer question from introduction, just imagine . . .*

 **Remember:** Organization is key in any writing!

# Planning for a Persuasive Essay

Just as you need to plan for an expository essay, you also need to plan for a persuasive essay if that is what you are assigned. Doing so will ensure you include all components of a well-written essay.

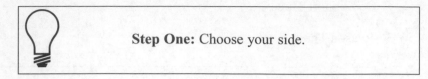

**Step One:** Choose your side.

Writing a persuasive essay means that you will have to choose one side that you will support with your writing. There are different ways to choose the side you want. You may decide to choose the side that you feel most strongly about, or you may choose the side that you can best support (which may not be the side that you actually agree with!). No matter what side you choose, YOU MUST **NOT** SUPPORT BOTH SIDES OF THE ISSUE. The key to persuasive writing is to try to convince your readers to come to your side of the issue.

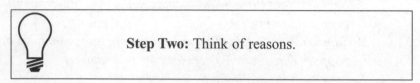

**Step Two:** Think of reasons.

Now that you have chosen your side, you need to come up with reasons to support your side. For example, if the sample topic is the seat belt issue, you would need to come up with reasons why seat belts should OR should not be required by law for front seat passengers (depending on the side of the issue you choose). You should try to think of two to three good reasons to support your opinion.

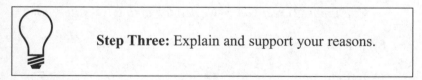

**Step Three:** Explain and support your reasons.

Once you have your reasons, you must now explain and support your ideas to your readers. Try to convince them to side with your opinion. Use good logical reasoning and as many statistics, facts, examples, personal anecdotes, and any other support as you can come up with. Since this is demand writing, you cannot research this topic in order to come up with actual statistics. So it is perfectly acceptable to make these up in your essay. (The same applies to statistics used in an expository essay.)

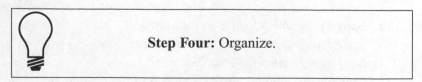

**Step Four:** Organize.

Once your have all the key components, you will need to decide how to organize them. You should think of some ideas for your introduction, the order in which you will present your reasons, and ideas for your conclusion. A good, well-supported essay should be four to five paragraphs for FCAT Writing. Further on, you will see some sample graphic organizers that can help you with your organization.

## *Choose Your Planner*

In order for you to complete all or most of these steps in about a ten-minute time period, using some sort of organizer to sketch out your ideas will be helpful. By doing so, you will not only get your ideas on paper, but you can organize them at the same time.

1. Brainstorm or List: In a brainstorming session, you would just write down any ideas that come to mind and choose the ones that are the best. A list is similar in that you would just make a list of your ideas and then write. Although brainstorming or listing is not enough planning for some people, others, especially advanced writers, are able to think and organize quite well in their heads. They therefore need nothing more than a brainstorming session or quick list. However, most people need more than just this.

2. Outline: This form of planning is much more detailed than brainstorming or listing. An outline is an excellent way to plan. In order for it to be effective for this type of demand writing, it would have to be brief and done quickly. Going through each writing step as you practice the above would be outlining.

3. Cluster: Clustering is what most students use to plan quickly and effectively for FCAT Writing. It is shorter than outlining and more complete than listing or brainstorming. A cluster uses circles and/or lines to organize ideas. The most central idea is in the center, and the reasons and support stem out from there. A blank cluster might look like this:

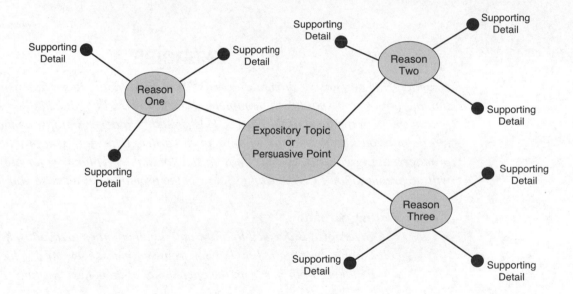

The central circle is where you put your topic. Then you continue to cluster out with reasons followed by supporting details. This is a quick and easy way to get your ideas on paper in an organized fashion. As you look at your cluster, you can then figure out which reason you want to put in which paragraph and how you plan to organize your thoughts and ideas.

**Example:** A cluster on a sample expository essay about the career of a police officer might look something like this:

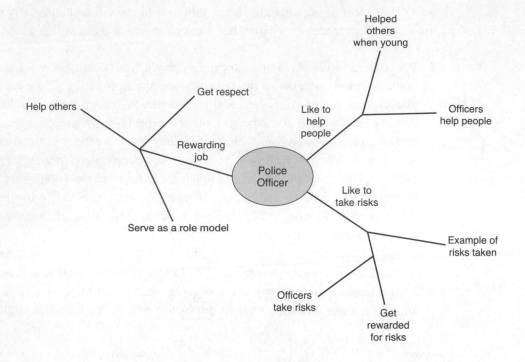

# EXERCISE

*Use the prior persuasive prompt on seat belts to try a planning session using a cluster like the one above. You should still complete all of the steps, but you should complete them by putting them in the form of the cluster. This should be quicker, but just as thorough, as writing them in outline format (as you practiced earlier). The more you practice the steps and practice putting your ideas down in a cluster (or some preplanning format), the better you will be prepared for FCAT Writing. Below is the prompt again in case you forgot!*

### Writing Situation
*The governor has decided to allow individual counties to decide whether or not seat belts should be required by law for front seat passengers of a vehicle. A committee will be taking opinions from the community at their next meeting.*

### Directions for Writing
*Think about whether or not you think seat belts should be required by law for front seat passengers. Now write to convince the committee members to accept your point of view on whether or not seat belts should be required by law for front seat passengers.*

Draw your cluster below.

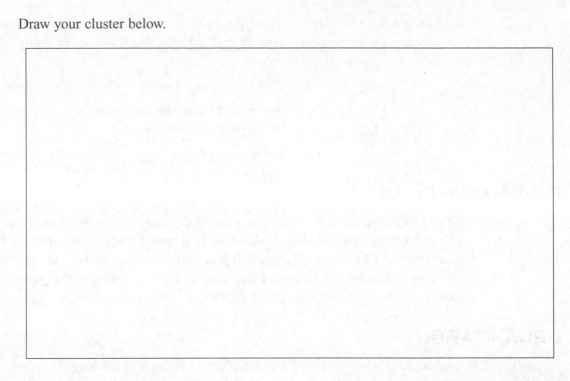

Once you are finished planning your essay, it is time to start writing. Since you have 45 minutes for your FCAT Writing essay, at this point, after reading the prompt and planning your essay, you should have approximately 35 minutes left to write and proofread.

# FOCUS

As you already know, the rubric for FCAT Writing measures four different areas, the first one being the **focus**. So what exactly does focus mean when it comes to writing? Well, it really is not much different from when you focus your eyes. Think of what you do when you focus your eyes on an object—you narrow them, limiting your scope of sight to just that object so you are able to see it better and more clearly. The same is true when you focus on a topic for writing.

## Focusing on Focus

In writing, focusing includes a variety of things.

1. Writing About the Topic: You need to make absolutely sure that you are actually writing about the topic given and not something close to the topic. For an expository essay, be sure you are explaining what the prompt is asking for. Do not explain *what* your favorite pet is if the prompt asks *why* your pet is your favorite. For a persuasive essay, be sure you are writing about only one side of the argument and that all of your reasons support your side or opinion.
2. Writing with a Purpose: If your writing is focused, then it should also be purposeful. Writing that has a purpose means that there is a reason behind the words. Even if you do not really care for writing or do not care for the topic you have been assigned, you need to move beyond your feelings and *write with purpose*. Write as though the issue or topic really means something to you, as though you have a real purpose and stake in what you are writing about.
3. Not Going Off Topic: Sometimes as people write (just as when they speak), they start by writing about one topic and then somehow end up on anther. Be very careful that

throughout your essay you are writing only about the topic itself and that any support you include in your essay also directly relates to the topic. Do not be guilty of getting side-tracked or going off on a tangent!

> **Remember: Focus on the Topic.**
> Do not get sidetracked!

## Proofread for Focus

After you finish writing your essay, you should have five to ten minutes left for a quick proofread. As you are reading, look critically at your writing to be sure everything that you have written is focused on the topic. If you find something that seems off topic, erase it or cross it out. Remember, this is demand writing, and you are expected to create a good draft. Crossing something out is perfectly acceptable and is certainly better than leaving it there.

# ORGANIZATION

You can have great ideas and a wonderful writing style, but without good organization your essay will be difficult to understand and ineffective. Organization is another key ingredient to a well-written essay and another one of the four major elements that the FCAT Writing rubric will be measuring.

## Organizational Road Map

For both the persuasive and the expository essay, you can easily organize your ideas and thoughts into a logical order. You can think of this organizational style as a road map or formula. The basic format for either type of essay looks like the following:

- **Paragraph One—Introduction:** Every well-written essay needs an introduction. It is here that you will make your reader aware of the topic about which you are writing and the major points that you are going to include in your essay. Some things that you will want to include in your introduction include:

  An interesting opening
  The topic about which you are writing (This is easily incorporated into your essay by rewriting the directions for writing into a statement.)
  The reasons that support your topic

- **Paragraph Two—Body Paragraph #1:** The second paragraph in your essay should be one of the reasons that you thought up during your planning session. You should decide which reason should most logically come first. In some essays, the order of the reasons will matter, and in others, it will not. You must decide if the order of the reasons makes a differ-ence or enhances your essay in any way. You should include in this first body paragraph:

  Your first reason
  An explanation of the reason
  Support for your reason: facts, incidents, statistics, personal anecdotes, examples, and so on.

- **Paragraph Three—Body Paragraph #2:** The paragraph should be just like paragraph two except with your second reason, logically placed of course. It should also include an explanation of the second reason along with all of the necessary support to make your ideas understood.

- **Paragraph Four—Body Paragraph #3:** If you have been following along, you should easily realize that in this next paragraph should go your third and, probably, final reason along with all of the necessary explanations and support. However, you may not have a third reason. If you could not think of a good third reason during your planning and still do not have a good third reason by the time you get to your fourth paragraph, *then do not put one in.* You should really not include a third reason just to have a five-paragraph essay. A weak reason or a reason that cannot be supported will only decrease the effectiveness of your essay. It is perfectly acceptable to have only a four-paragraph essay, especially if it is very well written. There is a perfectly good chance that you can earn a score of 5 or even 6 with a four-paragraph essay. If you do not have a third reason, proceed directly to the conclusion.

- **Paragraph Five—Conclusion:** The conclusion is just as important to your essay as your introduction, so do not leave it out! Your conclusion should touch again on the topic of your essay as well as sum up all of the major points in your essay. Do not, however, just reword your introduction; your reader will find this boring. Try to end with a bang—or at least with something that will leave your audience thinking. You should include in your conclusion:

> Your topic or opinion
> Your major points (reasons)
> A clincher (closing statement or thought)

The basic map or formula for organizing your essay should look something like this:

---

**INTRODUCTION (Essay Paragraph 1):**
Interesting Opener, Topic, Reasons

---

**BODY PARAGRAPH #1 (Essay Paragraph 2):**
First Reason, Explanation, Support

---

**BODY PARAGRAPH #2 (Essay Paragraph 3):**
Second Reason, Explanation, Support

---

**\*BODY PARAGRAPH #3 (Essay Paragraph 4):**
Third Reason, Explanation, Support
\*If you do not have a third reason, proceed to conclusion

---

**CONCLUSION (Essay Paragraph 5):**
Topic or Opinion, Major Points, Clincher

---

## Transitions

Transitions, words that allow writing to flow more smoothly and logically from one point to the next, are another important part of organization. There are many different types and uses of transitions. Turn to Chapter 7 to read more about transitions and how to use them.

## SUPPORT

Now that you have planned and organized your essay, you need to focus on yet another important aspect of the essay: support. Support is the place where students can and should spend much more time with their essays. Focused and specific support can turn your essay from average to exceptional.

## Types of Support

As you write your essay, realize that you can include many different kinds of support. Depending on your topic and your audience, you will want to include different types of support. As you write, consider the following:

- **Facts:** Facts are one type of support you may want to include. A fact is a statement that can be looked up and proven right or wrong. Facts lend credibility to your essay; they make your essay more believable. Remember, you are free to include facts *even if you are not sure if they are true*. Since this is demand writing and you have no time or way to research for the essay, you are welcome to make up what you need to!

- **Incidents:** An incident is an event that has occurred. The event is separate unto itself and has importance by itself. For example, if you are writing an essay about the benefits of exercise, you might want to include a specific incident in which you had started an exercise program of jogging every morning and explain how it improved your overall health. Incidents make your essay more interesting while adding credibility as well.

- **Reasons:** Most of you already know what a reason is—a statement offered as explanation for something. A reason tells *why* something happened. As you write your essay, include reasons when you want to explain *why* to your audience, especially when making a specific point about your topic.

- **Examples:** When students think of types of support, most think of *examples*. Examples are excellent ways of supporting what you are trying to say. They add clarity to your writing. If you use examples, though, be sure they are specific and concrete. Do not be afraid to use more than one or two examples and to add explanations, incidents, and personal anecdotes to your examples.

- **Statistics:** Statistics are numbers that come from research. Statistics almost always make your writing more believable because they are based on research; they are factual. Often students do not think of using statistics in an FCAT Writing situation because they do not have access to research materials. However, this does not matter! Feel free to make up your own statistics to add to your essay. It is an easy and effective way to make your support much more credible and effective.

- **Personal Anecdotes:** A personal anecdote is a little story that you can include in your essay that adds interest, credibility, and perhaps even humor. Because it is a personal anecdote, it should be a little story about something that happened to you. Does that mean, though, it REALLY has to have happened? Absolutely not. Just like the other types of support that we have discussed, personal anecdotes can be made up as well.

- **Quotes:** Quotes are words and/or statements that someone else has said that you include in your essay. When you add a quote to your writing, you need to include quotation marks (" ") around the statement so that your readers know that these words are not your own. You are, in fact, borrowing them from someone else. Why include quotes? Well, just like the other forms of support, quotes add credibility to your writing. If you are writing an essay about the benefits of exercise and you include a quote from an Olympic medalist, people will be more likely to believe what you are saying—would not an Olympic medalist know the benefits of exercise? Quotes can also be an interesting way to begin or end your essay. Again, the quotes do not have to be real—you can make them up.

## Support Should Be . . .

According to the FCAT Writing rubric, there are very specific ideas about the support you create in your essay. You need to be aware of four major areas when you are thinking about support for your FCAT Writing essay.

1. Support Should Be Substantial: You need to include enough support to make your ideas clearly understood by your readers. This means that, most likely, you will have to write more than you feel is enough to get your ideas across. Remember, it is always clear to the author of *any* piece of writing what he or she is trying to say. What is important, though, is that the writer convey to the reader exactly what he or she means. In order to do this, you need to have substantial—more than enough—support in your essay.

2. Support Should Be Specific: You need to be sure that, even if you do have enough support, the support is specific. A whole bunch of generalizations just will not do! For example, if you are writing about why you want to be a police officer and you say it is an exciting job, that is not enough. You need to be specific about exactly what in the job is exciting. Give examples, explain them, give statistics, provide details, include anything that will help your audience understand exactly what you mean by "excitement."

3. Support Should Be Relevant: Even if you have many examples that are very specific, you still need to consider another aspect: relevancy. In order to be relevant, the support must be important to the writing topic. For example, if you are writing a persuasive essay about why dogs are the best pet to have, it would not be relevant to include information about the good qualities of cats. It would not be important to the topic. So do NOT just arbitrarily add details to writing just to make it longer or just because… anything! Be sure all your support is important and adds information to the topic at hand.

4. Support Should Be Concrete: Once you are sure that your support is substantial, specific, and relevant, there is one more area left to consider: Is your support concrete? By concrete,

evaluators are looking for items that are measurable and that are real. Concrete items are specific, particular, and tangible (able to be touched). Does this mean that the support that you include in your essay needs to be true or really have happened to you? No. However, it does mean that any support you include in your essay should be realistic on some level and should lend stability to your essay.

## CONVENTIONS

The last aspect you need to consider when writing your essay is the area of conventions. Conventions are what most people think of when they think of English class: punctuation, spelling, capitalization, and the general grammar or mechanics of writing.

## And the Good News Is . . .

The good news is that you can have some errors in the area of conventions and still get the highest score possible on your FCAT Writing essay. Since essay scorers realize that this is demand writing and that you are writing under a time constraint, you are naturally going to have some errors in your writing. You start to lose points, however, when the errors in your writing interfere with the readers' understanding of what is being said.

## Punctuation

The following are just a couple of reminders about the rules of punctuation.

- **Ending Punctuation:** First of all, be sure that you include the correct punctuation at the end of each sentence. Periods need to come at the end of every complete thought. Questions and exclamatory remarks add variety to your writing, so do not forget to put question marks and exclamation points at the ends of those sentences.
- **Comma Use:** As for commas, use them only when needed. Commas are NOT like spices that you just sprinkle in to add something extra to your writing. Commas are used to make writing more clear to the reader. You should really use commas when you want your reader to pause. Finally, do NOT connect two complete sentences with a comma. This is called a comma splice and is incorrect. Use a semicolon (;) to connect two complete sentences or a comma and a conjunction, such as *and, but,* or *or*.
- **Apostrophes:** There are basically two times you need to use an apostrophe. One is when you are dropping something out of a word or number, as when you write a contraction. Some examples of this include:

  '94 (1994)
  'cause (because)
  don't (do not)
  I'm (I am)

The other time that you use an apostrophe is when you are showing ownership. Think of the apostrophe as a little arm attached to the word saying, "It is mine!" For example, *the girl's shoe* means the shoe belongs to the girl; it is hers. The general rule for adding apostrophes to show ownership is: if the possessive word does NOT end in *s*, add an apostrophe and *s*. If the word showing possession already ends in s, just add an apostrophe. This rule works about 95 percent of the time and will do in a pinch for demand writing.

## Spelling

Unfortunately, you will not have access to a dictionary or be able to spell-check when you write your FCAT essay. The best advice concerning spelling is just to do the best that you can! Not knowing how to spell a word should NOT keep you from using it. You will get more points for using sophisticated vocabulary, even if you spell some words wrong, than you would for using simplistic vocabulary, even if all of those words are spelled correctly. In other words, the FCAT writing test rewards you for trying, even if you spell the words incorrectly.

## Capitalization

Most people are well versed in the rules of capitalization. Here are just a couple of quick reminders about those rules. You should capitalize:

- Words at the beginning of a sentence
- The pronoun "I"
- Names of people
- Days of the month and months of the year
- Languages
- Names of places: countries, towns, cities, counties, buildings, and so on
- Names of particular things: names of ships, boats, airplanes, airlines, music groups, and so on.

## General Grammar and Usage

The English language has so many grammar and usage rules that we would need a whole other textbook to cover them. However, we can still look at some of the most common mistakes that students make in their writing so that you can be sure that *you* will not make them in *your* writing.

- **Noun/Verb Agreement:** When you write, you need to be sure that you have agreement between your nouns and verbs. A singular noun (naming one thing) needs to be with a singular verb, and a plural noun (naming more than one thing) needs to be with a plural noun. This is especially tricky when other nouns or a prepositional phrase are separating the noun and verb. Try covering up the extra nouns or prepositional phrase to get the correct answer.
- **Noun/Pronoun Agreement:** Again, be sure that the pronoun that you are using agrees with the noun it modifies (in both gender and number). If you have trouble in this area, review the rules of agreement in your classroom grammar book or on the Internet.
- **Sentence Fragments:** Make sure that, as you write, all of your sentences are complete. A complete sentence has both a subject and a predicate (a verb).
- **Run-on Sentences:** On the other hand, make sure that, as you write your sentences, you put correct punctuation at the end of them to avoid run-on sentences. Do not string a bunch of complete sentences together with commas either. Sentences that are too long can be difficult to understand.
- **Text Talk:** In today's world it is common for students (and even adults!) to incorporate text talk—shortened language used in texting or in instant messaging—into formal writing. Although you may be tempted to do so, do not use text talk in your FCAT Writing essay. Since this is a formal writing experience, text talk, a type of informal

writing, is not appropriate. Additionally, you run the risk of your evaluator not understanding your abbreviations or of thinking you do not know how to spell or use correct grammar. Some of the most common text talk to avoid are:

- i—use "I"
- u—use "you"
- lol—describe the situation
- dropping vowels

# PROOFREADING

From reading the prompt to planning to writing the essay, you have finally come to the end of the writing process. Even when you actually finish your essay, though, you still have one more step to be sure your essay is the best that it can be. That step is proofreading.

## The Truth

The truth of the matter is that no one really likes to proofread, especially after a session of grueling writing—like demand writing. When time is available, it is often best to let the writing sit for a while—a day, a week, for example—and then look at it again. However, since the FCAT Writing test is demand writing and you have only 45 minutes to complete your essay, you have no time to let your essay sit. You must proofread it right then and there or run the risk of leaving many mistakes that can lower your score.

## Final Considerations

Even though you would like nothing better than just to flip your paper over and never see it again, after you finish your essay, take five to ten minutes to make a final reading. If you find mistakes, fix them. Since this is a demand writing situation, it is perfectly acceptable to cross things out or add things in. You may even need to draw arrows to reorganize or add in other ideas. However, be neat as you make your corrections. During that final reading, you should consider a few last things:

1. Topic: Take just a minute to reread the prompt. Be sure that you have answered everything that has been asked of you.
2. Organization: As you reread your essay, check your organizational pattern. Did you write a complete and engaging introduction? Are your body paragraphs logically organized? Did you include a conclusion that effectively wraps up your ideas?
3. Support: Be very critical of your support. Did you include enough facts, statistics, anecdotes, examples, and explanations to demonstrate your ideas clearly to the reader?
4. Focus: Is what you wrote focused on the topic? Did you go off on a tangent in any places? If so, cross out those sections.
5. Conventions: Check your spelling, punctuation, capitalization, grammar, and usage. Correct any mistakes that you find.

# Chapter 7 | *Taking It Higher*

Now that you have spent time learning how to write a basic essay in a demand writing session, you can concentrate on making your writing even better. Take a look at the following strategies that can easily move your writing from mediocre to outstanding.

## LEAD IN; LEAD OUT

Think about the last time you met a stranger. It would probably be a fair assumption that you made some sort of judgment about that person based on your first impression. The same is true of any writing that you do. What you say in the beginning will affect your readers as to how they respond to the rest of your writing. Equally important is how you leave your readers. You want to end your writing in such a way that your readers remember what you have said. Therefore, you should pay special attention to both the introduction and conclusion of your essay.

## Lead In

Everyone knows the importance of a good introduction. If you were a famous person (and maybe someday you will be!), you would want to have an impressive introduction.

Write an introduction of your "famous self" below.

_____

- What kinds of words did you use in your introduction?
- What kind of effect were you trying to create?
- Who did you see as your audience?

Those are the same kinds of questions you should ask yourself when you write the introduction to your FCAT essay. There are all kinds of ways to get your audience's attention. Some of the more common "oldies but goodies" include:

1. a question
2. a relevant quote
3. a startling statistic

4. a personal anecdote, perhaps a humorous one
5. a detailed description (may use sensory language)
6. a dialogue
7. a strong statement of your position (especially for a persuasive essay)

As you consider what to write for that first sentence of your essay, consider the same questions that you addressed above.

- Who is the audience of your essay?
- What overall effect do you want your essay to have?
- What kind of tone (or attitude) do you want your essay to have?

You should consider all of those things when you write your opening sentence and paragraph. Remember, just because you do not have access to the Internet or to reference books to get that famous quote or great statistic does not mean you cannot use one. This is demand writing—use your imagination and make one up!

Starting your essay in an interesting way will not only draw your readers into what you have to say and make them want to read more, but it should also give your readers some idea of what your essay is going to be about. **The introduction should lead the readers into the rest of your essay.** Therefore, don't forget to pay attention to the rest of the introductory paragraph. With the information from your introduction, the readers should also be able to tell what your essay is going to be about: what you will be explaining if it is an expository essay or what side of the argument you will be writing for if it is a persuasive essay.

As mentioned before, the only way to get better at something is to practice it, and certainly writing is no exception. However, you do not need to write full essays every time just to get better at writing introductions. Try writing just the introduction to many different topics so you can get good at writing interesting openings more quickly and more effectively.

# EXERCISE

*Write just the introductory paragraph to the prompt below.*

### Writing Situation
*Your parents have just bought the car of YOUR dreams, but not for you—for them!*

### Directions for Writing
*Naturally, you would like to drive your parents' new car to the prom. Now write to persuade your parents to let you drive their new car to the prom.*

---

_____

_____

_____

_____

_____

_____

_____

_____

_____

 **Remember:** An introduction should include:
- an interesting opening sentence
- a thesis statement of some sort that tells what your essay will be about
- points that you will be expanding on in the body paragraphs

## Lead Out

Just as important as the introduction is the conclusion of your essay. If you do not end with something strong, it is doubtful that your readers will remember you or your point. There are many ways to end an essay. Just consider the possibilities.

1. Restate Something from the Introduction: If you started your essay with a statistic, question, or quote, consider coming back to that idea. Comment on the statistic or quote; answer the question. This will bring your essay back full circle and make your essay complete.

2. Use a Transition: So your readers know that they are coming to the end of the essay, you may want to use a transition to bring your essay to a close. Look at the transitions of conclusion in the next section for ideas.

3. Think About It: If you choose not to end your concluding paragraph with a transition, you may want to start with a "think about it" statement. This can be more powerful than a transition, and it is exactly what you want to leave your reader doing: thinking. Some ways you could begin include:

   - Just think about it . . .
   - Imagine . . .
   - Pretend . . .
   - What if . . .

Finish the statement with the main point of your essay. This is a good way to leave your reader with a powerful image of what you are trying to say.

For example, if you were writing to persuade your principal *not* to consider mandatory uniforms, you might begin your conclusion this way:

Just think about it, every student in the exact same clothes, sitting like little robots at their desks. Is this what we want for public education? No personal expression, no personal thought? Well, by requiring students to wear uniforms, that is exactly the direction in which we are heading.

4. Wrap It Up: No matter what way you choose to begin your conclusion, you should try to wrap up the major points of your essay. This will remind your reader of what is most important in your writing. However, just because you are restating the ideas does not mean you need to use the exact same words. Recopying whole sentences (or your whole introduction) is a very bad idea. This will succeed only in putting your reader to sleep!

# TRANSITIONS

Transitions are what we use in writing to connect ideas together. Transitions make writing flow and allow the reader to understand better what the writer is trying to say. When writing, you can use many different kinds of transitions in many different places.

## Transitions of Time or Importance

These transitions are what you can use in your writing when you are putting items in chronological order (the order of time). These transitions help your reader understand how something logically occurred.

### Some Common Time Transitions

| First | Next | Then |
|---|---|---|
| Second | Finally | Last |
| Third (and so on) | In the end | |

## Transitions of Contrast

Sometimes in your writing you many want to compare items or tell how they are different. Some transitions help your reader more easily distinguish the comparisons or contrasts that you are trying to make.

### Some Common Transitions of Comparison or Contrast

| However | In contrast | Thus |
|---|---|---|
| Therefore | In comparison | Likewise |
| Similarly | On the other hand | In other words |
| But | Yet | Although |
| Nevertheless | On the contrary | Likewise |

## Transitions of Addition

Often when writing, you may list items. You may be giving reasons, examples, details—anything! Your writing will sound smoother and will flow better if you add in some transitions.

### Some Common Transitions of Addition

| Besides | Also | Too |
|---|---|---|
| In addition | Additionally | Plus |
| Another | Furthermore | For example |
| For instance | Equally important | To illustrate |

## Transitions of Conclusion

Sometimes the ending can be one of the most difficult parts of writing an essay. Transitions can help make your ending sound smoother and pull all of your ideas together for the reader.

### Some Common Transitions of Conclusion

| In conclusion | In summary | To wrap up |
|---|---|---|
| Therefore | To summarize | As you can see |
| Finally | In short | Consequently |
| All in all | With all this in mind | |

## Transitional Sentences

As you write your essay, you will want something to connect the ideas in your different paragraphs. This is where transitional sentences come into play. A transitional sentence is a sentence either at the end of one paragraph or at the beginning of another that allows the ideas between the two paragraphs to be connected. These sentences keep the writing flowing smoothly and prevent it from sounding jerky as you jump from one idea to the next. Transitional sentences are typically harder to use than transitional words. With some practice, though, you will have no problem writing them.

## Points to Remember

There are a few rules of thumb to remember when using transitions. The first is that, more often than not, a transition is set off by a comma. Second, do not use the same one or two transitional words over and over again. Try to vary your transitions just as you vary anything else in your writing. No one wants to read the same words again and again.

## USE OF HUMOR

Humor can be a very powerful tool in writing. It can engage your reader or make your point more easily. Humor is also a sign of intellect, so using it in your FCAT writing essay can move up your writing score.

## Where to Use It

If you decide to use humor in your writing, where do you put it? There are many opportunities to use humor in your essay. Take a look at these possibilities.

1. The Introduction: You may want to start off your introduction with a funny quote or story. This will easily engage your readers in your essay and make them want to keep reading.
2. As Support: A humorous story might be a good way to add a little something lighthearted to your essay. It will also be a change of pace for your readers and may even make your point clearer.
3. The Conclusion: As you wrap up your essay, you may want to leave your readers on a light note. Something humorous may do that. It may also leave your readers feeling good about your essay and the point you were trying to make.

## Just Remember This

You have to be careful about only one thing when using humor in your writing. You must be sure that the humor you are using is appropriate for your audience. Since this is an essay that you are writing in school, anything that you write in your FCAT essay should be appropriate for school. If you have to question yourself or think twice about your choice of humor, leave it out. It is probably inappropriate. In this situation, it is best to err on the side of caution and use only humor that is appropriate for school.

## CHANGE IT UP!

Another way to make your writing more sophisticated is by changing both your style and your sentence structure. By adding some creativity and variety to your essay, your readers will stay engaged in what you are saying and will enjoy reading your writing!

## Sentence Structure

An easy way to change your writing from monotonous to interesting is to change the structure of some of your sentences. Think about it: if every one of your sentences sounded exactly the same, it would be easy for your readers to drift away from what they were reading. A writing sample without any variety in its sentence structure might sound like this:

> My best friend is Lisa. I like Lisa because she is smart and funny. I like her because she makes me laugh. Lisa is a kind person. She is the type of person who is honest in any situation. She would never hurt my feelings. Anyone would be glad to have Lisa for a friend. I am certainly glad she is my best friend. I hope I never lose her.

What do you notice about this paragraph? Well, you should notice that every sentence is written with the same structure—first the subject of the sentence, then the verb. Also, all of the sentences are relatively short, and they are all simple sentences. Finally, there is a great deal of repetition in the words used: Lisa, her, person, friend. However, there are some easy ways to change this boring paragraph to something much better.

1. Combine Sentences: If you are the type of person who always writes simple, short sentences, then you probably want to have some longer, more complex sentences in your

essay. An easy way to accomplish that is to combine sentences that fit together. Do not do this to all of your sentences, though, or you will have the same problem: all complex sentences with no simple ones!

For example, combine the second and third sentence from above to form this longer, more complex sentence: *I like Lisa because she is smart and funny and because she makes me laugh.* That was easy to do, but it changed the sound of the paragraph and added variety to the sentences.

2. New Beginnings: Another way to add variety to your sentence structure is by beginning your sentences differently. The easiest way to do this is by starting your sentence with one of the following:

- A participial, a gerund, or a participial or gerund phrase (start with an *-ing* or *-ed* word). Example: *Laughing* is our favorite pastime!
- A prepositional phrase (start with a preposition: *on, in, through, between, among, upon, over, under, of, about . . .*). Example: *In any situation,* she is the type of person who is honest.
- An infinitive phrase (*to* + a verb). Example: *To tell the truth,* I like her because she makes me laugh.
- A transition word. Example: *In addition,* Lisa is a kind person.
- An adverb (word ending in *-ly*) Example: *Certainly,* I am glad that she is my best friend.
- An adverbial clause (begin with words like *because, if, although* and include a noun and a verb). Example: *Because she is smart and funny,* I like Lisa.

3. Sentence Types: When you write, you will probably find that most of your sentences are declarative sentences or statements. Add variety to your writing by including questions, commands, and exclamations. Use them sparingly to have the greatest effect.

4. New Words: As you write, try not to use the same words over and over. Try to vary your vocabulary so that your readers do not get bored by hearing the same words and phrases repeatedly. Try to use as many descriptive words as possible (adjectives and adverbs). Adding specific details to your writing will help you with this.

## Another Look

Now take another look at the "boring" paragraph from above with just a few changes in the variety of the sentences, phrases, and words.

Do you have a best friend? My best friend is Lisa. Because she is so smart and so funny, she is also my oldest friend. To tell the truth, the best part of our friendship is that she makes me laugh. Laughing is our favorite pastime! In addition, Lisa is kind. Also, in any situation, she is honest, but she would never hurt my feelings. Anyone would be glad to have Lisa for a friend. Certainly, I am glad that she is my best friend, and I hope never to lose her!

Although the paragraph could still use some work, it is a great improvement over what we started with.

# EXERCISE

*Now write a paragraph about your best friend. Try to use some of the strategies that we have discussed. Share your writing when you are finished to get feedback from your peers, parents, and teachers.*

## VOCABULARY

Another way to make a higher score on FCAT Writing is to use a more sophisticated and precise vocabulary. That does not mean you need to sound like Einstein, but you do need to have maturity in your choice of language. That can mean a variety of things.

## Ample Adjectives and Adverbs

One way to make any kind of writing better is to add adjectives and adverbs. Adjective and adverbs change the picture that your reader is making in his or her mind. They make writing more descriptive and more vivid. Adjectives and adverbs can address our senses of sight, smell, hearing, touch, and even taste. They elicit emotions, and so they add to the tone of the writing as well!

For example, look at this sentence: *The girl walked into the room.*

Now add some adjectives and adverbs to see how the picture changes. The adjectives are underlined. The adverbs are double underlined. Think about which of your senses are addressed with the changes in word choice, and see how the tone changes as a result.

The tall, beautiful, blonde girl walked slowly into the dimly lit room.

OR

The short, smelly girl walked happily into the loud room.

OR

The brown, athletic girl walked jauntily into the math room.

You can easily see that adjective and adverbs address our senses and thus can paint very different pictures for the reader.

## Nouns and Verbs

Some other parts of speech that you should pay attention to are your choices for nouns and verbs. Simply removing a bland noun or verb and substituting one with much more energy and pizzazz can make the most simple sentence stand out.

Let's look again at the sentence from above. The main nouns are *girl* and *room*, and the main verb is *walked*. Those verbs are quite ordinary. Take a look at how the sentences change if we substitute *girl, room,* and *walked* with some different nouns and verbs. The nouns are underlined. The verbs are double underlined.

The tall, beautiful, blonde actress sauntered slowly into the dimly lit auditorium.

OR

The short, smelly toddler trotted happily into the quiet library.

OR

The brown, athletic student strolled jauntily into the math classroom.

When looking at these sentences now, it should be difficult to recognize the original: *The girl walked into the room.* Now we have three very different sentences that express three very different ideas. Each has a different tone, and each addresses different senses. This makes each sentence unique.

## EXERCISE: TRY SOME ON YOUR OWN

*Use some of the ideas from above to take the following sentences from ordinary to extraordinary.*

1. The dog ate the food.
2. The doctor saw the patient.
3. The students carried the books.
4. People talked about the problem.
5. The officer gave a ticket to the driver.

## Specific and Sophisticated Word Choice

Regardless of whether they are nouns, verbs, adjectives, adverbs, or any other part of speech, you should always be very specific in your word choice. Think about what you are trying to say, and choose a particular word that expresses that idea. Also think about yourself. You are a young adult. The words that you choose when you write your essay should reflect the vocabulary of a young adult. In addition, do not be afraid to use some words that are a little more sophisticated, even if you are not sure how to spell them. In a demand writing situation, it is perfectly acceptable if your spelling is a little shaky on difficult words.

## TONE (OF VOICE)

Creating tone in your writing is another way to make your writing stand out and move it away from the mediocre. Tone is the attitude in the writing that comes through to the readers. Tone can be created most dramatically through word choice. Punctuation can also add to the tone, as can the structure of your sentences. The best way to create tone is to think about the attitude you are trying to convey. Do you want your readers to feel happy? Sad? Angry? Do you want your readers to laugh? Cry? Shudder with disgust? Just as the way you say a word creates an attitude, the way you choose particular words in your writing can create an attitude as well. By choosing carefully, the reader will be able to *hear your words* and, thus, hear your tone of voice. This is a very powerful tool in writing. However, accomplishing it does take practice.

## EXERCISE

*This is your writing topic: Spiders.*

1. Write a paragraph about spiders, and create a tone of horror and disgust.
2. Write a paragraph about spiders, and create a tone of humor.
3. Write a paragraph about spiders, and create a tone of romance.
4. Write a paragraph about spiders, and create a tone of sadness.
5. Write a paragraph about spiders with no tone; make it purely informational.

# COLOR IT IN

Often when you write, you try to create a picture for your reader. Once the picture is "drawn," you need to "color it in"—make it come alive as much as possible for the readers. You want to draw in your audience so that they feel as though they are really there. A couple of ways to create this feeling in your writing is by using imagery and figurative language. Even though you have a mere 45 minutes to complete your FCAT essay, you can incorporate some of these strategies into your writing and bring your writing from mediocre to excellent.

## Imagery

When you are writing, you must make your readers feel as though they are there with you in the writing. You need to pull them into your writing, and one way to do so is by using imagery. Most people do describe some things as they write, but often they forget to use description that goes beyond the sense of sight.

> **Imagery is language that appeals to any of the five senses.**

- **Speaking of Sight:** The sense of sight is the one sense that most people think of when describing something or someone. The way something or someone looks is important. When you write about anything pertaining to the sense of sight, consider some of the following:

    Color: Do not be afraid to use some different colors and shades, like *cobalt* instead of just *blue* or *crimson* instead of just *red*.

    Texture: You can describe the texture as it appeals to the sense of sight—for example, *fluffy* clouds or *shiny* hair.

    Shape: This is self-explanatory—for example, the *oblong* room or the *perfectly square* pair of glasses.

- **The Nose Knows:** The sense of smell is a sense often overlooked in description. However, smell is the sense that is most closely linked to memory. Do you remember the way your grandma's kitchen smells during the holidays or the smell of Mom's perfume when you were younger or the even the smell of your elementary school? (If you go back there now, you will remember!) The sense of smell has many emotions attached to it, so include it in your descriptive writing when you can.

- **Do You Hear What I Hear?** Describing the way something sounds is sometimes difficult. However, the beauty of describing a sound is that you can use all those great sound words, for example, *crash, sizzle, plop, snap, clink, clang, ring, clatter,* or *pop*. Using onomatopoeia (words that imitate sound) is a super way to incorporate the sense of sound into your description.

- **Tastes Like Chicken!** You do not often get to incorporate the sense of taste into your description. However, if you get a chance, obviously if food is a part of your essay, then you should utilize the sense of taste. Taste is also closely linked to memory, so you may be able to bring your reader into your essay more easily. Does the food taste nutty, salty, sweet, spicy, or bitter? Think about hot buttered sweet rolls or gooey chocolate chip cookies. If your mouth waters just thinking about it, imagine what it will do for your readers!

- **Tingly Touch:** Touch is another sense that is often overlooked in description. More often than people realize, describing the way something feels is easy. Is it soft, fluffy, scratchy, cold, or mushy? Touch is also a good way to bring forth your reader's emotions. Imagine in your persuasive essay that you are describing the school uniforms (that you are against) as *tight* and *scratchy wool* skirts and *hot polyester* pants that could prohibit students from learning due to their discomfort. This is a much more effective argument than just "uniforms are uncomfortable so students do not learn."

## Figurative Language

In addition to imagery, try using some figurative language in your writing. Figurative language is language that is not meant to be taken literally. For example, if someone says, "It is raining cats and dogs," you can be pretty safe in assuming that cats and dogs are not literally falling from the sky! That phrase is a common figure of speech (or example of figurative language) that means it is really raining hard outside. Take a look at some of the different types of figurative language that you may want to incorporate into your FCAT Writing essay.

- **Similes:** Similes are an easy and common type of figurative language. You probably use them all the time in your speech and in your writing and do not even realize it. A simile is a comparison between two unlike things that uses specific words, most commonly *like* or *as*. Similes are simple to use and are effective in writing. For example, it sounds better to say that *Tom eats like a pig during dinner* than it does to say *Tom is a sloppy eater*.
- **Metaphors:** Metaphors are very similar to similes in that they compare two unlike things. However, metaphors do not use any specific comparison words. So instead of saying that *Tom eats like a pig at dinner* (as a simile does), a metaphor would simply say *Tom is a pig at dinner*. It really is the same comparison, just using different phrasing. Anytime you are making comparisons in your writing, using similes and metaphors not only makes your writing sound better, but it also makes your writing more sophisticated, thus increasing your FCAT score.
- **Hyperbole:** Another kind of figurative language that many people are not familiar with is called hyperbole (pronounced high-PER-bowl-ee). Hyperbole is extreme exaggeration for effect. If you are trying to get a specific point across to someone, sometimes using exaggeration is effective. For example, if you are writing an expository essay explaining why your dog is your favorite pet, you might use hyperbole.

> My dog is so wonderful. He willfully does anything I ask him to do. In fact,
> I think he would fetch the very moon for me if I asked him to!

This is an example of hyperbole that effectively gets across the point of just how much the writer's dog loves her. Hyperbole also is useful in lightening the mood of the writing or even in creating humor.

- **Personification:** Personification is the process of giving human qualities or characteristics to nonhuman entities. This is very useful in description. Personification gives life to otherwise inanimate objects and can help to pull the readers into the writing. See for yourself. Look at the difference between these two descriptions, one using personification and the other using no figurative language.

  1. The icy wind made my back cold. *(No personification)*
  2. The wind blew its icy breath down my back. *(Personification)*

The difference between the two sentences is obvious. Personification just makes the writing more vivid for the reader. Look at another example.

1. I got scratched by the tree branches as I ran through the dark forest. *(No personification)*
2. The tree limbs reached out, grabbed, and scratched my face as I ran through the dark forest. *(Personification)*

As you can see, using personification does not take many more words, and it really is not a difficult concept. You just have to be aware of its existence as you write and take advantage of opportunities to use it.

## Bringing It All Together

Now you should have many good ideas about how to take your basic FCAT writing from just ordinary to extraordinary. There are so many ways to improve your writing; do not be overwhelmed by all the choices. Just know that the choices are there, and when you get the opportunity to use them—go for it! Take advantage of what you have learned, ranging from interesting introductions to riveting conclusions, from simple to complex sentences, from transitions to vocabulary, from imagery to figurative language. You should now have everything you need in your writing toolbox to take your writing higher!

# Chapter 8

# Some Sample Essays

As you learned in Chapter 5, the actual FCAT Writing consists only of a simple prompt for you to write about. So, how better to prepare you for the real test than to show you some actual prompts, along with some examples of quality responses that were submitted by students like you? By looking at sample essays, you should be able to get an idea of what a good, high-scoring essay looks like. Use these examples to get ideas for your own writing.

## PERSUASIVE ESSAY SAMPLES

## THE PROMPT

### Writing Situation
*The principal of your school is deciding if students should be required to stand for the recitation of the Pledge of Allegiance. He has asked for student feedback before he makes his decision.*

### Directions for Writing
*Decide if you think that students should or should not be required to stand for the Pledge of Allegiance. Now write to convince your principal that students should or should not be required to stand for the pledge.*

## Student Samples

### Score: 6

At the start of every morning, students all around the country stand to recite our nation's Pledge of Allegiance. Some of these students, however, don't want to do so, but stand anyway merely because they are told to. Whether or not these students "should" stand has been an ongoing issue in America for a long time. It is my personal belief that every student in America should possess the choice whether or not they stand for the pledge or not; students should not have to stand for the Pledge of Allegiance. An entire body of students cannot conform to performing a single action, due to the varying "characters" of students. Unfortunately, the result ends in the compromising of beliefs and values.

The Pledge of Allegiance is a verbal symbol of devotion and respect to the United States. Though it may be hard for some to understand why, there are some students who can't (or won't) say the Pledge of Allegiance. We have to understand that the Pledge of Allegiance may conflict with the differing beliefs and ideas of certain students. If you really think about it, it would be ridiculous to believe that everyone values or respects the same ideals as another.

This dispute truly arises in all Americans, not just students. Last year, a man wanted the Pledge of Allegiance altered without the mention of "God" appearing in it. He felt that the class recitations of the pledge would violate the constitutional clause preventing government establishment of religion. Though some people were appalled with this idea, he was still entitled to his right to choose whether or not he accepted the issue of widespread principles. This proves that a single, confining ascendancy should not, and cannot instill a sole idea or presupposition into a group of people, and expect them to peacefully conform. A recent survey was taken, asking over two-hundred thousand American students whether or not they stand for the Pledge of Allegiance and recite it. Unfortunately, over seventy-two percent answered either of two ways: either they stand, but don't really want to, or they flat out refuse.

In closing, I believe that the Pledge of Allegiance is an admirable veneration that every America-loving student should recite. It is unfair, however, to make everyone, including those with differing ideals and beliefs, stand and recite it against their will, forcing them to compromise their principles.

## Score: 5

". . . One Nation, under God, Indivisible with Liberty and justice for all." It's Friday morning, and once again the whole school stands to recite the pledge. But is it right to make students stand and pledge their allegiance to a country that is overflowing with every shape, size, and color? Yes.

The Pledge of Allegiance is a tradition that has been carried out for over a lifetime. Everyone should stand and say it whether they were born in America or not. If students have a problem with it than maybe they shouldn't be here in the first place. When students refuse to say the Pledge it is a sign of disrespect to not only the country, but also to everyone who has lived or fought for America. Students should not have the choice of sitting during the Pledge.

Some students may present the arguement that the Pledge is against their religion or that since they weren't born here they don't have to say it. Just because the pledge says, ". . . one nation under God . . ." does not mean you have to believe in or worship God. It just so happened that the founding fathers were Christian. No one is trying to force any religion on anyone. Also, if you moved to or are visiting America, you should still say the pledge. Students need to be respectful of our customs and traditions.

Students may also say that the Pledge is useless and out-dated, but it isn't. Even tough times have changed over the years, the pledge still is a symbol of patriotism and the citizens love for their country.

I used to think the Pledge was overrated and boring. Now I understand that it is said as a way to unite the country, and to show that through it all, Americans stay loyal. I'm glad it is said in the school system, because the new generations need to know that a country is nothing without and unity from its people.

To sum it up, the pledge should be said in school and by every student, because it represents loyalty, unity, respect, and trust.

**Score: 5**

"I pledge allegiance . . ." rings through students' ears morning after morning, but why must we all say it? Why do we stand up? Is it because we're required to or is it because we're afraid to get in trouble for not respecting other people by standing up? Many students refuse to stand up for reasons such as being athiest, not believing in this country, and not being an American, but of a different nationality.

First off, not every single student in the United States of America believes in God. There are many students out there that have been raised to believe that there is no God. The "under God" part in the pledge can be highly offensive. No athiest should ever have to go against thier religion and stand up for something they don't believe in.

Second of all, not all students believe in this country. In my personal opinion, we shouldn't have to stand up for this country if we don't believe in it. The big impact of the Pledge argument started with the after effects of September 11. Americans started becoming more patriotic and the Pledge was now something everyone stood for. But some people feel that we could have been this patriotic without the attacks. The strong emphasis of this was that every "true" American started to stand and say the Pledge and those who didn't were looked down on.

Last, not every American is American born. A lot of students and their families came to America for a better life. But just because they're living here doesn't mean they don't respect their own country. Why should they have to stand and say the pledge of Allegiance when they would prefer to say the Pledge of their own country to show respect. Even if they don't stand, it doesn't mean they have no respect for the United States and Americans.

Overall, there is really no good reason for students to stand up for something they don't believe in. This issue is stronger for some than others. If it was required to stand for the Pledge of Allegiance because the President said so, would you do it if you were a non-believer? What if the President told the country to jump off a bridge if they didn't like the pledge? So if a student doesn't want to stand and say the pledge then they shouldn't have to.

# EXPOSITORY ESSAY SAMPLES

## THE PROMPT

### Writing Situation
*You have been offered the chance to spend a year in a country outside your own.*

### Directions for Writing
*Decide in what country you would like to spend a year. Now write to explain why you would like to spend a year in this country.*

## Student Samples

*Score: 6*

A chance to live anywhere. . . . Spend time outside the United States on a year sabbatical enjoying whatever the world has to offer. So many choices. . . . Where would I go if I was offered the chance, the chance for a year outside the United States? No question about it. The choice would definitely have to be warm, sunny, salty, and, of course, romantic. I would choose Italy.

Italy, the land of the Mediterranean. One of the reasons that I would love to live in Italy is its proximity to the Mediterranean Sea. Living in Florida, I have become accustomed to living near the ocean. I don't think that I could live anywhere in the world without having a body of salt water near me. The sound of the waves lapping on the shore or the breakers crashing on the beach is a lullaby to my ears. I can imagine the romance of the Italian coast, lying on the sandy shores, listening to the lilt of the Italian language all around.

For me, another draw to Italy is its rich and complex history. Being Catholic, I would of course want to spend time in Vatican City, perhaps catching a glimpse of His Holiness, the pope. I would also love to spend time in Rome, Florence, Vienna, all of the great cities. I would want to see the Coliseum, would close my eyes and hear the roar of the crowds and the lions, see the brave, strong gladiators. I would want to see where the great and horrible Mussolini lived, and visit the cemeteries of World Wars I and II.

Finally, having a quarter percentage Italian blood running in my veins and a certain penchant for Mafia movies, I feel the calling of Italy in my very soul. I want to live in Italy and suck up some of the very essence of the culture. I want to eat the rich, wonderful food, spend time rowing down the Riviera, and party at Carnivale. I want to know what makes the Italian people tick. I want to meet the townspeople and the city folk and feel that, at least for a while, I have 100 percent Italian blood coursing in my veins.

So if anytime in the next year you come looking for me, know that you won't find me here in the good old United States. Although I love my home, for a year my home will be Italy, Italia as the Italians call it. Don't worry about me, though; just close your eyes and imagine a quiet Italian countryside or a bustling Italian city, and know that I will be there, searching for my Italian soul.

*Score: 5*

A long time ago, I started to learn about Egypt, it's agriculture, and it's burial rights. I realized, that the more I learned, the more fascinated I became. So when I received this offer, I didn't think twice about which country I would spend a year in. If the chance arose, that I would be able to spend a year in any country of my choice, (beside the U.S) I would most definitely choose Egypt.

Egypt is located in northeastern Africa, and southwestern Asia, and is the cradle of one of the world's greatest ancient civilizations. The climate in Egypt is similar to our climate here in Florida, but it is extremely humid. I remember asking a former teacher of mine who had previously visited Egypt what it was like. She said that the culture was mostly Muslim, and the people over there were extremely kind. She explained to me how on her tour of the pyramids, a man had dropped his camera off of his camel. A boy had been working nearby, but had stopped what he was doing, ran over, picked up the camera, and handed it back to it's owner. It amazed me that someone would do that, seeing as here in the U.S. that rarely happens! But it fascinated me and I couldn't help but want to learn more!

Because I spent most of my childhood on a farm on eastern Long Island, I decided to study Egypt's agriculture. I was surprised to find that about 40 percent of the labor force engaged in crop farming or herding. Because I spent most of my time on the farm, I was excited to hear that farming was popular in Egypt. It only made me want to go check it out!

Aside from the country itself and its agriculture, there was one major part of Egypt that blew me away with fascination, its astonishing burial rituals. Burying the dead was of religious concern in Egypt. Because of this, they developed elaborate funeral rites. They made every effort to preserve the corpse with embalming and mummifying and then placed them in exceedingly elaborate tombs. All the necessities for a paradisiacal existence, from furniture to reading matter, were, therefore, put into tombs.

I was immediately interested in learning many new things about Egypt. That, I would say, would be my main reason to travel to Egypt for a year. I was never too interested in most things that involved in enhancing the mind. But the interest level I had for Egypt was very high, and it made me yearn to learn so much more about the country. So I am very sure that if I had to spend a year in a country other than the U.S, I would choose Egypt; And now you know why!

▼▲▼▲▼▲▼▲▼▲▼▲▼▲▼▲▼▲▼▲▼▲▼▲▼▲▼▲▼▲▼▲▼▲▼▲▼▲▼

## PERSUASIVE PROMPTS
## The Directions

The following are persuasive writing prompts for you to use. As you practice, remember the following things:

1. Paper: You should have three sheets of notebook paper when you practice for FCAT Writing. Label the first sheet "planning." This is where you brainstorm your ideas. Remember that anything you write on this paper is not graded. The other two papers are for writing your actual essay. Your essay may NOT be more than *two pages* long.
2. Time: You should give yourself no longer than *45 minutes* to write the essay, starting when you begin reading the prompt.
3. Resources: Write the paper using *no extra resources* such as a dictionary, thesaurus, or computer. Unless you have a special circumstance, these items are not allowed during the actual test. The essay must be written entirely on your own as it is during the testing situation.

## THE PROMPTS

**1. Writing Situation**

*Your sophomore class is planning a trip to Europe over Spring Break, but the trip must be approved by the Board of Education.*

**Directions for Writing**

*Decide whether or not you believe that this trip would be a good idea for your sophomore class. Now write to convince the Board of Education why they should or should not approve this trip to Europe.*

**2. Writing Situation**

*The school board is considering changing the school week from the traditional five days a week, 8:00–3:00, to four days a week, 8:00–5:00, with a three-day weekend.*

**Directions for Writing**

*Decide whether you think the school board should or should not go from a five-day school week to a four-day school week. Now write to persuade the school board that your decision is the best for your school.*

3. **Writing Situation**

*The city council where you live is about to instill a curfew for teenagers stating that they need to be off the streets by 8:00 P.M. every night.*

**Directions for Writing**

*Decide if you agree with an 8:00 P.M. curfew for teenagers. Write to the city council and convince them of your views concerning the 8:00 city curfew.*

4. **Writing Situation**

*Your local television station is running a contest searching for the best amateur newscaster.*

**Direction for Writing**

*You have decided that you will enter the contest to be "newscaster of the day." Write to convince the television station that you would be the best candidate to win the contest.*

5. **Writing Situation**

*There has been a great deal of controversy over free downloading of music on the Internet.*

**Directions for Writing**

*Decide whether or not you agree with downloading music for free on the Internet. Write to persuade the public that your views on downloading free music are the best.*

6. **Writing Situation**

*A female friend of yours is thinking about entering a beauty pageant and would like your opinion.*

**Directions for Writing**

*Consider your opinion on females and beauty pageants. Write to convince your friend to enter or not to enter the beauty pageant.*

# EXPOSITORY PROMPTS
## The Directions

Remember that expository writing is writing that explains. Review the directions for persuasive prompts before you begin the expository prompts to be sure that you understand the conditions for paper, time, and resources.

1. **Writing Situation**

*NASA has just selected you for an experiment in which you will spend a year alone on Mars. You will be allowed to bring one item.*

**Directions for Writing**

*Decide what item you will bring with you to Mars. Write to explain why you will bring that particular item.*

**2. Writing Situation**

*People choose pets for many different reasons.*

**Directions for Writing**

*Decide what pet you would choose if you were given the option. Write to explain why you would choose that particular pet.*

**3. Writing Situation**

*Exercise and healthy eating should be a part of every person's life.*

**Directions for Writing**

*Consider your own exercise and healthy eating habits. Write to explain how exercise and healthy eating have or have not affected your life.*

**4. Writing Situation**

*Hearing, seeing, smelling, touching, tasting: the five senses are important in the life of a human.*

**Directions for Writing**

*Decide what sense you consider to be most important to your life. Write to explain why this sense is most important in your life.*

**5. Writing Situation**

*Everyone has a person who he or she admires.*

**Directions for Writing**

*Decide whom you most admire. Write to explain why you admire this person.*

**6. Writing Situation**

*Technology is an important part of life in the 21$^{st}$ century.*

**Directions for Writing**

*Think about how technology affects your own everyday life. Write to explain how technology is part of your everyday life.*

# UNIT THREE

## FOR TEACHERS AND PARENTS

# Chapter 10 | FCAT Reading

I f you are a teacher or a parent, you can do many simple things in your classroom or at your home to encourage your teenager(s) to read and to improve upon their reading skills.

## READING TIPS FOR TEACHERS

One of every teacher's responsibilities is to teach and encourage students to read. There are many easy strategies for teachers to use in order to improve their students' reading abilities. These strategies will not only improve students' performance on the FCAT, they will also improve students' performance in class and in life.

## Tips for Teachers

1. Read Informational Text: One of the reasons that students do so poorly on the FCAT is because they are not accustomed to reading informational text. Informational text often requires a different level of concentration than literary text does, and it also requires different reading strategies. So much informational text is readily available at the high school level that students should have no problem practicing with this type of text.

2. Ask FCAT-Type Questions: As a teacher, you should recognize that the FCAT Reading is NOT an English test; instead, it is a reading test. Therefore, since reading should occur in all high school disciplines, you should be familiar with the reading standards for the FCAT. Once you know the standards, write questions for your own tests and homework that mimic the FCAT. By practicing these types of questions, students will be familiar and competent with them when they get to the FCAT.

3. Short and Extended Response: Another way to prepare students for the FCAT is to have them practice short- and extended-response questions. Even though these types of questions are no longer on the FCAT, all students can benefit from the type of thinking required by these questions. A student who is able to do well on short- and extended-response questions can definitely master a multiple-choice question on the same topic.

4. Grade with a Rubric: When students do answer short- and extended-response questions in class, be sure to grade their answers with a rubric. By doing so, students will know what kinds of answers are acceptable.

5. Individual and Peer Grading: Assigning short- and extended-response questions can mean a great deal more grading for the teacher. However, you can cut down on your own grading and teach students at the same time by having students grade their own answers and by having their peers grade their answers. Of course, you need to teach your students how to do this by teaching and modeling with the rubrics, and you need to monitor their performance. This will also provide students with a number of examples to compare their own answers with as well as immediate feedback.

6. Read to Students: One mistake that many teachers make is forcing students to read aloud in class. Many students feel very uncomfortable in this situation. Quite honestly, many students are not proficient enough readers to read aloud to the rest of the class. The best example you can give to your students is to read aloud to them yourself. This will provide an excellent example for your students, show them that you think reading is important, and allow them to become more proficient readers themselves.

7. Practice Upper-Level Thinking: Since 70 percent of the FCAT reading and writing exam tests higher-level thinking skills, these are the kinds of skills you should practice with your students in class. Try moving away from the classic "memorize and return" teaching that many of us are guilty of using with our students. Make more opportunities in class for students to conclude, infer, synthesize, and evaluate.

8. Model Reading: Since students see teachers almost as much as they see their parents (and sometimes more) and often admire their teachers (although they might never admit it), teachers can be valuable models for students. Let your students see you reading, especially material beyond your subject matter (which is what they expect you to be reading). Share with them an interesting article you read in the newspaper or the latest novel you are involved in or the gossip from your favorite magazine or online source.

9. Time Assignments: The FCAT is a timed test for tenth graders, so students need to get used to feeling the pressure of working under a timed situation. Occasionally require students to read an assignment and answer questions within an allotted time period. After enough practice, students will feel more comfortable and thus work more efficiently when taking a timed test.

## READING TIPS FOR PARENTS

Many parents despair because their children, especially teenage children, do not like to read. Since the only way to get better at reading and to improve reading skills like those tested on the FCAT is to read, here are some tips that should encourage your child to read and even improve their reading skills.

## Tips for Parents

1. Set the Example: This is the single most important thing you can do to encourage your child to read. If children never see their parents reading, then they will have no idea that reading is important. One of the easiest ways to show the importance of reading to your child is to read yourself. Read the newspaper, a magazine, a novel—what it is really does not matter. Once your child sees you reading, he or she will understand that reading is important in more than just the school world.

2. Share: Do not be afraid to share what you are reading with the other members of your family. If you are interested in something and you share it with someone else, that person may get interested too. Even discussing something you have read with your child may

pique his or her interest. You may actually get your child to read something by showing him or her how interesting it is.

3. Take a Trip: The local public library is a place that many parents and teenagers never venture to, especially together. However, the library is a great, free place to get books for both yourself and your child. If you are not keen on the library, how about a trip to the bookstore? In today's society, bookstores have become a "cool" place to go. Take a trip with your teen, have a soda or a cup of coffee together, and read. Share what you are reading. If you are feeling generous, you may even offer to buy your child a new book or magazine (as well as one for yourself!).

4. Daily News: If you get the newspaper, you may want to start this activity with your child: you can each find an article from the paper that is interesting and then discuss them with one another. Discuss the main points, why the article is interesting, and what you think about it. Even if your child will read only the sports page or the comics, there are still opportunities for reading and sharing. You have to start somewhere!

5. Television Too: If there is one thing that teens do, it is watch television. Even though watching TV is a far cry from reading, there are still some ways you can improve your child's thinking abilities. If you watch television together, discuss some of the elements of the television shows (the elements that can also be found in reading selections). For example, you might discuss the characters, events, conflicts and resolutions, and setting. You can also discuss what the main point of the show was as well as the show's main purpose (to entertain, to inform, and so on). Finally, ask your child to make predictions about what is going to happen next while you are watching and how he or she can apply the events from the show to his or her own life.

6. Review School: Of course, much of what your child reads will come from school. Therefore, you should question your child about schoolwork. Ask about what he or she has read or is reading. From textbooks to novels, sharing what your child has read will reinforce the importance as well as the subject matter of the reading. It will also show your child that you are interested in him or her—improving your child's self-confidence will improve everything he or she does.

7. Homework: Many teachers assign chapters in texts and novels as homework. Be sure you ask your child about his or her homework. Provide a quiet place for reading, and ask about what was read. You may even ask to read it yourself, then you could discuss it together. In addition, if you want to read the homework, you may encourage your child to read it.

8. Magazines and Such: Keep in mind that relevant reading does not just include books. Magazines and newspapers have much of the same kinds of informational text as the FCAT. Feed your child's specific interests by subscribing to a magazine or two. For example, if your teen is already absorbed in skateboarding, subscribe to a skateboarding magazine. You can be sure that he or she will read it and understand it!

9. Do Not Forget the Internet: The Internet also provides many opportunities for reading. So many different kinds of informational text are available on the Internet, and students are constantly spending time there anyway! Discuss what kinds of articles and blogs your student is reading. This is a great way to make connections, discuss text, and monitor what your teen is seeing on the Internet.

As you can see, you can encourage reading and improve your child's reading abilities in so many ways. The most important is just to spend time with your son or daughter in all kinds of activities, including reading.

# Chapter 11 | **FCAT Writing**

▬▬▬▬▬▬▬▬▬▬▬▬▬▬▬▬▬▬▬▬▬▬▬▬▬▬▬▬▬▬▬

I f you are a teacher or a parent, you can do many simple things in your classroom or at your home to encourage your teenager(s) to write and to improve upon their writing skills.

## WRITING TIPS FOR TEACHERS

Although many teachers consider writing to be the job of only the English teacher, every teacher can help students become better writers. Just as students need to read to become better readers, students need to write to become better writers. Since all teachers graduated from college in order to earn a degree, all teachers know how to write. All teachers can share their ideas and style of writing with their students to help improve writing overall.

## Writing Tips for Teachers

1. **Assign Writing:** You do not have to be an English teacher to have writing assignments in your class. Any kind of writing assignment will help students prepare for FCAT Writing. From paragraphs to essays to research papers, students use the same basic skills for writing. The more students practice these skills, the better writers they will become.

2. **Ask for Support:** One of the biggest problems students have when they write is providing adequate support. When you require students to write in your class, be sure to require that they support what they are saying. You may want to discuss the assignment beforehand and/or brainstorm ideas before starting them on the assignment. Try to stress that their support be relevant, specific, substantial, and concrete.

3. **Model for Students:** When you ask students to write in class, it is always helpful if you provide a model answer. You may want to write the actual answer together as a class on the board or overhead the first time or two you try a new type of writing assignment.

4. **Assign Persuasive and Expository Essays:** Of course, the best way for students to get ready for the actual FCAT writing test is to practice persuasive and expository prompts. You can write prompts in the same fashion that the FCAT does but use topics that are relevant to your subject matter.

5. **Provide Feedback:** If students are not provided feedback on their writing, they tend to make the same mistakes over and over. Although it takes a little more time, it is very valuable if you provide some feedback to the students about their writing. Ideally, you should provide students with one thing they are doing well and one thing they could improve on. If you point out too many mistakes, students may be overwhelmed and not know where to begin (and therefore do nothing). However, students can work on one mistake and make some real changes.

6. **Grade with the Rubric:** Grading with the FCAT Writing rubric is very important. Students need to get used to what is required of them by the rubric and where their writing falls within the rubric.

7. **Self and Peer Grading:** Students should always be expected to evaluate their own work. By having students assess their own writing, as well as the writing of their peers, you encourage them to think critically. You should provide some sort of training for them, however; students will not know how to do this on their own. Introduce them to the rubric, and show them how to grade. If they become familiar enough with the rubric to grade their own writing, they should be more capable of writing to the requirements.

8. **Timed Assignments:** FCAT Writing is a timed test, so you should provide ample opportunities for students to practice writing the same kinds of prompts under the same kind of time constraint. This will teach them how to utilize their time and to feel more comfortable under pressure.

9. **Break It Down:** Students do not always have to write a full essay in order to prepare for FCAT Writing. Sometimes it is more effective just to work on one part of the essay. For example, you may want to work just on writing a good introduction so students can get a handle on this part of the essay. Students will be much more receptive to writing just a paragraph than they would be to writing a whole essay and thus will put more effort into the shorter assignment (hopefully!). By teaching in this way, you can move from one part of the essay to another or from one element of the rubric to another. For example, you may focus on organization, support, or conventions.

10. **Internet:** Students always write better for an audience. In that way the writing is more authentic and relevant. Many students who do not consider themselves writers blossom in this environment. Encourage students to comment and give feedback on one another's posts. Consider easy, safe-for-school sites like *http://edublogs.org* and *http://pbworks.com*.

## WRITING TIPS FOR PARENTS

There are not as many opportunities for your child to write at home as there are for him or her to read. However, you can do some things at home to improve your child's writing.

## Tips for Parents

1. **Ask to See School Writing:** One way to let your child know you care, and thus to improve his or her performance, is to let your child know you are interested. Look at the writing your teen does at school. Read it. Comment on it. Ask how he or she feels about it.

2. **Have Your Child Put Requests in Writing:** All kids, especially teenagers, have all kinds of requests for their parents. From extending the curfew to wanting to borrow the car, have your teenager put his or her requests into writing. This way, the writing will be authentic, meaningful, and carry more weight than just a grade at school.

3. **Diaries and Journals:** Teens are naturally filled with emotions and sometimes anguish at this time of their lives. Buy your son or daughter a diary or journal so he or she can express feelings with the written word. Although this kind of writing is not the same as FCAT writing, any practice at writing will improve writing skills.

4. **Newspapers:** Newspapers, believe it or not, offer some opportunities for writing. Encourage your son or daughter to write letters to the editor and work on the crossword puzzle. This will make the writing more realistic and improve vocabulary skills.

5. **Internet:** Web 2.0 offers many opportunities for students to write and share thoughts with a worldwide audience. Encourage your children to participate in blogs and wikis. Read what they have written and make comments. Additionally, this a  great way to get insight into your teenager's thoughts and feelings—often difficult during these years!

6. **Encourage Reading:** The more a child reads, the more likely his or her writing skills will improve. Most published writing is, at a minimum, good. Therefore, a reading child will improve both his or her reading and writing skills.

# Appendix | FCAT Writing: Formal and Informal Rubrics

## FCAT Writing Formal Rubric

*This is the rubric put out by the state and used by the FCAT graders.*

| 6 Points | The writing is focused and purposeful, and it reflects insight into the writing situation. The organizational pattern provides for a logical progression of ideas. Effective use of transitional devices contributes to a sense of completeness. The development of the support is substantial, specific, relevant, and concrete. The writer shows commitment to and involvement with the subject and may use creative writing strategies. The writing demonstrates a mature command of language with freshness of expression. Sentence structure is varied, and few, if any, conventional errors occur in mechanics, usage, punctuation, and spelling. |
|---|---|
| 5 Points | The writing is focused on the topic, and its organizational pattern provides for a logical progression of ideas. Effective use of transitional devices contributes to a sense of completeness. The support is developed through ample use of specific details and examples. The writing demonstrates a mature command of language, and there is variation in sentence structure. The response generally follows the conventions of mechanics, usage, punctuation, and spelling. |
| 4 Points | The writing is focused on the topic and includes few, if any, loosely related ideas. An organizational pattern is apparent, and it is strengthened by the use of transitional devices. The support is consistently developed, but it may lack specificity. Word choice is adequate, and variation in the sentence structure is demonstrated. The response generally follows the conventions of mechanics, usage, punctuation, and spelling. |
| 3 Points | The writing is focused on the topic but may contain ideas that are loosely connected to the topic. An organizational pattern is demonstrated, but the response may lack a logical progression of ideas. Development of support is uneven. Word choice is adequate, and some variation in sentence structure is demonstrated. The response generally follows the conventions of mechanics, usage, punctuation, and spelling. |

# FCAT Writing Formal Rubric (continued)

| | |
|---|---|
| **2 Points** | The writing addresses the topic but may lose focus by including extraneous or loosely related ideas. The organizational pattern usually includes a beginning, middle, and ending, but these elements may be brief. The development of the support may be erratic and nonspecific, and ideas may be repeated. Word choice may be limited, predictable, or vague. Errors may occur in the basic conventions of sentence structure, mechanics, usage, and punctuation, but commonly used words are usually spelled correctly. |
| **1 Point** | The writing addresses the topic but may lose focus by including extraneous or loosely related ideas. The response may have an organizational pattern, but it may lack a sense of completeness or closure. There is little, if any, development of the supporting ideas, and the support may consist of generalizations or fragmentary lists. Limited or inappropriate word choice may obscure meaning. Frequent and blatant errors may occur in the basic conventions of sentence structure, mechanics, usage, and punctuation, and commonly used words may be misspelled. |
| **Unscorable** | The paper is unscorable because<br><br>• the response is not related to what the prompt requested the student to do,<br>• the response is simply a rewording of the prompt,<br>• the response is a copy of a published work,<br>• the student refused to write,<br>• the response is illegible,<br>• the response is written in a foreign language,<br>• the response is incomprehensible (words are arranged in such a way that no meaning is conveyed),<br>• the response contains an insufficient amount of writing to determine if the student was attempting to address the prompt, or<br>• the writing folder is blank. |

# FCAT Writing Informal Rubric

*This is an informal rubric that you may find easier to use. Place checks next to the items as they apply to the essay you are evaluating. In this way you should be able to get a score for the essay.*

| Score | Focus | Organization | Support | Conventions |
|---|---|---|---|---|
| 6 | _____ Focused on topic, insightful, purposeful | _____ Logically organized, effective use of transitions, smooth flow | _____ Relevant, specific, substantial, committed to subject, may include creative writing | _____ Few, if any, errors, mature language, fresh expressions, varied sentence structure |
| 5 | _____ Focused on topic | _____ Logically organized, effective use of transitions | _____ Ample use of specific examples and details | _____ Few errors, mature language, varied sentence structure |
| 4 | _____ Focused on topic, few—if any—loosely related ideas | _____ Organized, some use of transitions | _____ Support is consistently developed but may not be specific | _____ Some errors in grammar, adequate word choice, variety in sentence structure |
| 3 | _____ Focused on topic, but contains loosely related ideas | _____ Some organization but may not be logical | _____ Uneven development of support | _____ Some errors in grammar, adequate word choice, some variety in sentence structure |
| 2 | _____ Addresses topic but may lose focus | _____ Includes beginning, middle, and end but may be brief | _____ Nonspecific support, erratic, ideas may be repeated | _____ Errors in basic grammar, common words spelled correctly, word choice is limited, predictable, vague |
| 1 | _____ Addresses topic but includes ideas that are only loosely related, may also include ideas not related to topic | _____ Weak organization, may be incomplete | _____ Little to no development of support, may only be fragmented lists or general information | _____ Limited or inappropriate word choice, many and obvious mistakes in grammar, common words misspelled |
| 0 | _____ Writing is not related to prompt or not enough writing to tell | | | _____ Illegible, in a foreign language, or incomprehensible |

# Index